"If you want to understand the threat from Communist China, read this book. It is the most insightful study of the sinister nature of the Chinese Communist Party and its ideology by scholars outside of China I have ever seen. Perhaps most importantly, if you want to know who Xi Jinping really is, how he thinks, why he behaves as he does, and the malicious plans he has for China and the world, as well as how the U.S. and the free world can stop him, this book is an essential read."

Cai Xia, *former Professor at the Central Party School of the Chinese Communist Party*

"*Understanding the China Threat* by Lianchao Han and Bradley Thayer is the most important book that I have ever read about the existential threat from the People's Republic of China (PRC). These two experts present a clear and compelling assessment of the Chinese Communist Party's ideological threat that remains unchanged since Mao, whose goal is to replace the United States as the world hegemon and rule by totalitarian force. This book is a clarion call for America and as someone who has devoted a lifetime to fighting the ideology of communism, I strongly encourage you to read this book and share widely, especially with our younger generations who have little knowledge or understanding of the threat of communism, especially Chinese communism. As the authors note, the threat is grave, but America can overcome our weak position and defeat the evils of the PRC by a return to our founding principles."

James E. Fanell, *CAPT USN (Retired), former Director of Intelligence and Information Operations U.S. Pacific Fleet*

"Lianchao Han and Bradley A. Thayer have written an exceptional book documenting why China is the global threat to U.S. interests today and for decades to come. Han and Thayer demonstrate why China's unparalleled expansion of their conventional and nuclear arsenals, employment of economic and ideological warfare, and penetration of Western societies are the deliberate result of the Chinese Communist Party's bid for domination. Their recommendations concerning the U.S. and allied response to the China threat should be heeded by U.S. national security decision-makers."

Admiral Cecil Haney, *United States Navy (Retired), former Commander, United States Strategic Command*

"On three occasions, the United States has faced an existential threat: from Great Britain in the Revolution, from the expansionist Nazi Germany, and from the nuclear arms of the Soviet Union. But this new threat, from China, is quite unlike anything America has faced before: it is ideological, commercial, diplomatic, and military and on an unprecedented scale. This brilliant book is chilling, but it also offers hope. It charts the brutal politics of Xi Jinping's emerging new world order, but shows precisely how the US can survive the onslaught, and win."

Dr. Rob Johnson, *Director of the Changing Character of War Centre, University of Oxford*

"*Understanding the China Threat* is the single most important and useful guide to the central threat facing the United States. Han and Thayer offer a sober and clear-eyed assessment of what the rise of China means for the future of this country. This is real-world intelligence that will be mission-critical for policymakers, citizens and CEOs for years to come."

Brian T. Kennedy, *Chairman of the Committee on the Present Danger: China and President, The American Strategy Group*

"In their latest work, Han and Thayer slay the canard that ideas don't matter—that unlike the Soviet challenge, Beijing doesn't mean to export a world-changing ideology. As the American and Chinese economies were purblindly intertwined, America itself came to question its birthright of freedom, perhaps uncoincidentally. *Understanding the China Threat* is a just-in-time dispatch on the 'People's Republic' and its baleful captain of the ship, Xi Jinping."

Curt Mills, *Analyst at Thiel Macro hedge fund and Contributing Editor of* The American Conservative

"For anyone seeking to understand the grave threat posed by China, this book is both authoritative and insightful. Lianchao Han and Bradley Thayer are realistic about the China threat and the West would do well to heed the warning that is found in the pages of this critically important volume."

Dr. Katrina Swett, *President of the Lantos Foundation and former Chair of the U.S. Commission on International Religious Freedom*

"Tracing the origins of Xi Jinping's totalitarian state to the foundations of ideological indoctrination, terror, and adulation of a god-like Emperor figure, laid by Mao in 1942–45 in the too-rarely mentioned 'rectification campaign,' a large-scale purge of those whose loyalty to Mao was suspect—conducted while the Americans and the Chinese nationalists were busy fighting the Japanese—the authors show how those foundations make today's People's Republic such a great menace to Americans and the world. Yet those foundations also create the regime's great vulnerabilities.

Written in a style that is both scholarly and also highly accessible, this book should be helpful for the growing audience of lay readers who have come to be skeptical of rosy myths about Communist China, probably the most dangerous adversary we have faced in the last two hundred years."

Ambassador Paul Wolfowitz, *a Senior Fellow at the American Enterprise Institute, and Distinguished Visiting Fellow at the Hoover Institution, is a former President of the World Bank, Ambassador to Indonesia, Assistant Secretary of State for East Asia and the Pacific, and U.S. Deputy Secretary of Defense*

UNDERSTANDING THE CHINA THREAT

This book examines the contours of the Sino-American confrontation and its future trajectories. It delineates the two major causes of the friction in Sino-American relations—change in the balance of power in China's favor and the conflicting ideologies of the two states—and emphasizes why it is imperative for the U.S. to hold on to its ideological principles. It demonstrates the ultimate and irreconcilable gap in the visions the two competitors have for international politics and consequently why conflict—certainly cold, and very possibly hot—is inevitable. The authors also suggest measures which the U.S. can adopt to sustain its leadership and deter China's ideology and vision for the future of global politics.

A significant contribution to the study of Sino-American relations, the volume will be of interest to scholars and researchers of international relations, foreign policy, and U.S. and Chinese politics. It will be of great interest to think tanks, public policy professionals, and the interested general reader.

Lianchao Han, Ph.D., Vice President, Citizen Power Initiatives for China.

Bradley A. Thayer, Ph.D., Director of Research, Citizen Power Initiatives for China.

UNDERSTANDING THE CHINA THREAT

Lianchao Han and Bradley A. Thayer

Routledge
Taylor & Francis Group

LONDON AND NEW YORK

Cover image: Chinese President Xi Addresses the Opening Session of
the U.S.-China Strategic Dialogue in Beijing. Image from Wikimedia
Commons. Provided by the U.S. Department of State. Public Domain.

First published 2023
by Routledge
4 Park Square, Milton Park, Abingdon, Oxon OX14 4RN

and by Routledge
605 Third Avenue, New York, NY 10158

Routledge is an imprint of the Taylor & Francis Group, an informa business

British Library Cataloguing-in-Publication Data
A catalogue record for this book is available from the British Library

Library of Congress Cataloging-in-Publication Data
Names: Han, Lianchao, author. | Thayer, Bradley A., author.
Title: Understanding the China threat / Lianchao Han and
Bradley A. Thayer.
Description: Abingdon, Oxon ; New York, NY : Routledge, 2022. |
Includes bibliographical references and index. |
Identifiers: LCCN 2022021470 (print) | LCCN 2022021471 (ebook) |
ISBN 9781032110837 (hardback) | ISBN 9781032255071 (paperback) |
ISBN 9781003283614 (ebook)
Subjects: LCSH: United States--Foreign relations--China. | China--
Foreign relations--United States. | United States--Foreign relations--
21st century. | China--Foreign relations--21st century.
Classification: LCC E183.8.C5 H1855 2022 (print) | LCC E183.8.C5
(ebook) | DDC 327.73051--dc23/eng/20220608
LC record available at https://lccn.loc.gov/2022021470
LC ebook record available at https://lccn.loc.gov/2022021471

ISBN: 978-1-032-11083-7 (hbk)
ISBN: 978-1-032-25507-1 (pbk)
ISBN: 978-1-003-28361-4 (ebk)

DOI: 10.4324/9781003283614

Typeset in Bembo
by Deanta Global Publishing Services, Chennai, India

For my mother, a disillusioned Chinese Communist who inspired me to oppose any form of totalitarianism.
Lianchao Han

For Eike
Bradley A. Thayer

CONTENTS

ACKNOWLEDGMENTS

Many individuals helped us in the course of writing this book, and we would like to take this opportunity to acknowledge their support. Over the years, we have had the opportunity to present our arguments in different fora and have had many exchanges with practitioners and academics who have helped us hone our arguments.

We would like to thank Dr. Rob Johnson, Director of the Changing Character of War (CCW) Centre, Pembroke College, University of Oxford, for the opportunity to present our argument and for the exceptional questions and comments we received. We are equally indebted to Thomas Heyen-Dube of the CCW Working Group, Nuffield College, University of Oxford, for allowing us to give a seminar on our arguments and for the comments and critique provided. Later, we had the opportunity to return to the University of Oxford for a UK Ministry of Defence–CCW conference on the China threat, and we are grateful once again to Dr. Johnson and Elizabeth Robson of CCW for their invitation to participate and assistance to make the conference a great success.

We have worked with Sandra Tolliver for years, and once again she has provided her exceptional editing abilities to this study. At Routledge, we are grateful to our editor Aakash Chakrabarty and his editorial team, especially Anvitaa Bajaj. They have aided us every step of the way from inception to publication, and we appreciate their unflagging support through the difficulties presented by the Covid-19 pandemic. We also thank the anonymous reviewers for their comments and strong interest and encouragement for this book. Lastly, we thank our friends and family for enduring our absence while we devoted time to this study.

1

INTRODUCTION

This book explains why China is a threat to the United States; second, why China and the U.S. are engaged in a new cold war and might quite possibly fight a hot war; and third, although China sought the confrontation, why the United States must win this struggle.[1] Directly put, China is the single most formidable peer-competitive threat the United States has ever faced. It alone has the potential to replace the United States as the world's hegemon, an ambition the Soviets once possessed but could not achieve because of their myriad weaknesses, particularly in the economic realm. We foresee a future in which China may have the ability to force Washington to cede its regional and global interests to Beijing's desires. China's willingness to use coercion, threats of force, and actual use of force to advance its interests provide a window into that future, as does its territorial expansion and militarization of the South China Sea. Accordingly, whether the United States can maintain its position as the preeminent force for free and open societies is the defining element of international politics in the 21st century, and the most immediate U.S. national security policy interest.

1.1 The Three Main Arguments

An understanding of the China threat entails comprehending the origin and rise of Communist China and its ideology, and thus why China is motivated for conflict with the United States.[2] These issues are significant and multifaceted. Acknowledging the complexity of major events in international politics, the great British diplomatic historian A.J.P. Taylor compared its study to police investigating a road accident.[3] The police first investigate the driver. Was the driver drunk or high? If yes, they have their culprit. If the answer is no, they turn to examining the car. Were the brakes bad? Did a tire blow? If the car is in good condition, they then turn to the environment. Was it raining, icy, or foggy?

DOI: 10.4324/9781003283614-1

Did the road have dangerous curves? Even the best driver, in the safest car made, probably will crash if he hits black ice, encounters fog, or a whiteout on a hairpin turn. Taylor's analogy is very helpful as we explore the China threat.

We make three major arguments to explain the causes of the China threat. The first is that China is a one-party dictatorship based on communist ideology. This makes it uniquely dangerous, as is demonstrated by its past democidal actions against its own people and its current genocidal behavior. For Taylor, this is the faulty and dilapidated car causing the accident. The Chinese Communist Party's (CCP) ideology is a form of communism that makes it an evil empire in the true and accurate sense that President Ronald Reagan meant when, in 1983, he famously described the Soviet Union as one. Reagan used the term to describe a wicked form of government that oppressed its own people as well as those that fell within its grasp. It reserved for itself the right to violate every human right, to aggress, to lie, steal, and deceive in the name of its odious objectives. The CCP is just as evil as the Soviet Union. Like the Soviet Union, the CCP's ideology is anchored upon unending violence and tyrannical control directed against its own people as well as others, and its imperial aspirations. Like the Soviet Union, the CCP reserves for itself the right to abuse the human rights of the Chinese people and even the world's population not only through the Covid-19 pandemic but through the CCP's nefarious intentions for all peoples.

The CCP's ideology has resulted in what we term the "Xi Doctrine," that is, Chinese leader Xi Jinping's plan to preserve his rule in China and to supplant the U.S. in international politics. Domestically, his objectives are to ensure the CCP's perpetual rule by crushing any dissent with his enormous internal security apparatus. This is even more formidable than any previous police state the world has witnessed, and involves high-tech surveillance, mega prisons, and concentration camps. Xi seeks to rejuvenate the nation through his rhetoric of a "Chinese Dream" to restore China's past imperial glory, but also to mobilize the population and prepare it for sacrifices that will be necessary as China's confrontation with the United States intensifies. Xi will ensure that no one within the CCP or military, and no other major figure such as Chinese billionaire Jack Ma—who disappeared from public life before resurfacing in 2021, having been duly chastised—will be able to challenge his leadership.

In the international realm, Xi's objectives are to use economic, ideological, diplomatic, and military means to expand China's might and supplant the United States as the world's dominant power. The economic means include the Belt and Road Initiative (BRI), Asian Infrastructure Investment Bank (AIIB), and other forms of investment and infrastructure creation. The ideological means are just as broad as the economic, centered on such noble messages as creating the "shared destiny of mankind" and spreading the new ruling model of socialism with Chinese characteristics, as well as Confucius Institutes around the world. For states of the Global South, China advances the "China model" for growth and modernization, which combines repressive political rule with the CCP's party-dominated economic system—all supported by China and requiring its goodwill to sustain. The ideological tools serve as a mask to conceal Chinese control. The diplomatic mechanisms are largely traditional avenues for expanding power, e.g., creating bases in Djibouti and Pakistan, and likely in Cambodia, the United Arab Emirates, and Equatorial Guinea, as a start to what ultimately will become a global network of intelligence military bases, and a tributary system. Finally, the military instrument, via the People's Republic of China's (PRC) conventional and nuclear growth, will cement China's gains and further its ambitions.

Given China's expansion, U.S. leaders and the American people must understand the PRC's ideology—in essence, "why is China a threat." This, in turn, requires explaining "why China fights," or the motivation of the CCP—comprehending what Xi and his clique want and why they are willing to fight the U.S. The Chinese seek confrontation in order to achieve their conception of victory—the realization of the Xi Doctrine; the fulfillment of the CCP's ideological goals; and China's replacement of the United States as the dominant power in international politics. China will fight because the United States is the single major impediment to its strategic objectives. The U.S. model of political liberalism and capitalism remains the most significant threat to the regime's existence and its justification for perpetual one-party rule. Beijing expects that the "China model," anchored on Xi's rule, the CCP-dominated economic system, and repressive politics, will replace the U.S. model as the global economic-cum-political template for development.

With the U.S. removed, there would be no single power, or constellation of powers such as Australia, Japan, and India, that could prevent Beijing from achieving its aims. Xi has advanced these objectives boldly and transparently in his conception of a hegemonic China by 2049—if not far sooner. The United States obstructs the realization of China's ambitions and thus is the focus of China's enmity.[4]

Equally, the U.S. and the American people must grasp their ideological motivation, or "why the U.S. fights"—that is, having been forced into this confrontation, why it must struggle to maintain its ideological principles of freedom and to preserve its dominant position in the face of the China threat. U.S. leaders seek to maintain this position because that is best for U.S. security, the security of America's allies, and the promotion of an ideology that ensures freedom and democratic government, open societies, and free markets as the dominant values of international politics. The United States fights for the international order it created after World War II and expanded after the Cold War. This liberal international order has been the foundation of stability since the end of the Cold War but is coming under enormous strain with China's successful rise and determined desire to replace it.

The two ideological conceptions of victory, or "why each fights," demonstrate the ultimate and irreconcilable gap in the visions the two competitors have for international politics, and consequently why conflict is likely. As we will demonstrate, the cold war with the PRC is well underway. The Sino-American "car crash" could be caused by only one factor—the driver, the car, or the environment—but we argue that because the driver is bad, as is the car, and the road conditions and weather are dangerous, a horrific car accident is probable.

The second argument involves the relative balance of power changing in China's favor at the expense of the U.S. Thus, Taylor would explain this as the road conditions and weather causing the car crash. The PRC is becoming wealthier in absolute terms—but also in relative terms, compared with the United States. Part of that wealth is siphoned off to further the PRC's military growth in conventional, cyber, and nuclear weapons. A slice goes to support China's investments and infrastructure-building in other countries. Thus, the relative change in the balance of power and China's willingness to use its increased power to challenge the U.S. is a major threat to Washington's position in the world.

The fact that China has become so powerful now—with the direct, essential, and strategically foolish help from the West, assistance that lamentably continues—means that it can implement and achieve its ideological goals. The implication of this increased power and capabilities is that it will change the present liberal international order and terminate the leadership of the U.S. in global politics. The lives of Americans and people around the world will be impoverished, shortened, and their souls deadened by a CCP victory. This is the logic of the CCP ideological ambitions and is the essence of what makes it an existential threat to the U.S. and the free world.

The third major argument of our study is that this is a confrontation the U.S. must win. The world is at a pivot point. Were China to successfully supplant the United States, totalitarian and authoritarian governments and exploitative economics would become the world's dominant form. Human rights abuses would accelerate, because there would be no superpower with the interest and ability to stop them. The greatest voice in the world would be a supremacist superpower led by a dangerous figure, Xi Jinping, and his clique, who act for their benefit above the good of China, and for the good of China before the rest of the world. The world would look very different, perhaps for a long time.

The U.S. must fight to maintain its position in international politics in order to maintain an open political and economic system. The Chinese are fond of boasting that the CCP lifted more than 745 million people out of poverty. In fact, it is the Western economic system that has done so. It is responsible for lifting those 745 million—plus countless millions more in Africa, South and Southeast Asia, the Persian Gulf states, including Saudi Arabia, Central and South America, and Europe after World War II and the Cold War. The liberal order created by the United States did this, and the U.S. should not be reluctant to call attention to its accomplishments. Washington must comprehend the fundamental advantages it possesses, including its open ideology and economic system, and its many allies and supporters around the world.

1.2 The Significance of the Book

This study makes five major contributions. Despite the importance of the necessity of understanding the China threat, policymakers in the United States and the West still do not fully grasp the nature and scope of the threat. Accordingly, the first reason this book is significant is because it explains the CCP's ideology to grasp the true nature of the China threat. The Chinese worldview is heavily informed by its ideology as each generation of CCP leadership advances. In turn, this determines the Party's and Chinese government's nature, organizing principles, political and socioeconomic structure and culture, and ultimate goals—what drives the CCP's actions. We explain that the CCP's ideology is essentially Leninist dictatorial ideology, which employed what we term the *Lumpen peasantry*, essentially ruffians as their shock troops, amalgamated with traditional Chinese characteristics of imperial aspirations (帝王思想) and the worship of imperial rule deeply rooted in Han-centric Chinese culture. These elements are both the wicked engine and the computer that, respectively, powers and controls the CCP car. Western scholars, policymakers, and the general public too frequently underestimate the ideological element of China's worldview and actions. They ignore its inherent totalitarianism and wrongly perceive it as benign and benevolent and non-communist ideology. In sum, they hope that changing the driver or installing new brakes will keep the CCP car from being a hazard on the highway. In fact, this is wishful thinking. The car's engine and the computer are destined to drive it toward disaster for the Chinese people and the world. From Mao Zedong's "catch up with the British and surpass the Americans," Deng Xiaoping's "realization of four modernizations," Jiang Zemin's "three represents," Hu Jintao's "scientific development," to Xi's "Chinese Dream," all should be considered representative of a consistent grand strategy.

The CCP's fundamental objective remains fiercely ideological and unchanged: to defeat capitalism and realize communism, which is the Marxist-Leninist path of irreversible social development, or more precisely to achieve socialist imperialism. According to its narrative, only the CCP can bear this historical responsibility. As a direct consequence, its absolute leadership and perpetual power are necessary. This ideology underpins China's rise and offers the world an alternative model of development and politics. Today, Xi's government is cleverly combining the revitalization of communist ideology with China's national rejuvenation to generate greater popular support through a nationalist-cum-ideological appeal than otherwise would exist via solely an ideological one.

The rise of the PRC brings with it a supremacist worldview that wants to buy off the states that it can, and to pick a fight with those it cannot. For decades, China was careful not to do so. But now, as its power increases, it challenges the United States and its allies with a strong desire to change the status quo and, ultimately, the liberal principles upon which that status quo rests. These actions make intense security competition and conflict with the United States and its major allies in the Asia-Pacific increasingly probable. Especially worrying are China's radically different and highly deceptive ideology, its determination to make it prevail, and its worldwide propaganda network to advance it. This includes the dangerous worldview that informs China's domestic and foreign policies—dangerous in particular for minority groups that directly or indirectly challenge Han supremacy, notably the Kazakh, Kyrgyz, Hui, and Uyghur Muslims in Xinjiang. In essence, the CCP's strategic goal to seek hegemony is deeply rooted in its worldview.

Second, we explain why China is a real and growing threat to the U.S. and to the free world, why it seeks a confrontation with the U.S., and why a cold or hot war between the two countries is likely. Our argument is contrary to the frequent claims that China is a benign and benevolent rising power; or its ambitions are limited primarily to combating internal problems and concerns; that China does not pose a significant threat to U.S. interests; or that China's only interested in becoming a regional power.[5] The logic of the balance of power is as close as we get to a law in international politics, and this logic dictates that the emerging powerful state to demand changing the status quo in its favor, triggering confrontation. The Cold War is over, as is the post-Cold War period of international politics in which the significant asymmetry in power favoring the United States permitted it to act without the possibility of the arrest of its power. Today we are at the dawn of a period defined by the rise of China's power, the expansion of its interests and demands, and the profound consequences these changes will have for all states. This power shift is the result of the PRC's rapid economic growth—which, ironically, it has achieved through the aid of the United States' decades-long engagement policy that opened its vast markets to China. With new wealth, technologies, and talent, China has modernized its military to the point where it is now capable of challenging the United States. In sum, the world is in a transformative period, not unlike previous eras of international change and unrest, such as after the Napoleonic Wars, World War I, or World War II. The balance of power is necessary but not sufficient to explain the conflict.

Third, if China supplants the United States, the rest of the world will have to adapt to China's ideology and the norms, principles, and values that Xi advances. If this happens, all of the stakeholders in the present international liberal order are likely to find it more difficult to advance fundamental Western concepts of free trade, individual liberty and human rights, and the importance of developing cultures of anti-discrimination in support of the rights of women and minorities. In many cases, the opposite of what the West values will become the new rules of international politics. Most Western elites have yet to consider fully what will be lost if China becomes the world's dominant state and just how different the world will be.

China's past and current actions provide empirical evidence of how Beijing will treat other international actors when China becomes more powerful. We reveal what immense and unprecedented human tragedies this dangerous car with its fanatic drivers have caused to its own passengers, pedestrians, and other cars, as well as what catastrophes the CCP is creating now and in the future since the Xi clique sees itself as the center of the universe. All other people are inferior, with varying degrees of inferiority. Such a neo-imperialist perspective is not an attractive model for winning allies and influence, and it also underscores why those who have a vested interest in the present order must consider the profound negative implications of China's dominance and labor to prevent it.

Fourth, the United States must adopt certain measures to win the struggle. We focus on the ideological dimension of this struggle because it is the greatest strength of the United States but, regrettably, U.S. decision-makers frequently neglect it. As a free and open society, the United States is a better ally for states in Africa, Asia, and Latin America than is China, which frequently abuses the people and resources of its erstwhile allies. In contrast to China, the United States is transparent with its friends in decision-making; it possesses a dynamic and inclusive society and has a history of protecting the interests of its allies. Free and open political principles make the United States a more valuable and dependable ally and a better leader for global politics. Its vision is far more inclusive and equitable for the world's small states and its great powers.

Fifth, we provide a framework for understanding the complexity of the China threat. International politics is informed by many peoples, countries, histories, religions, ideologies—just to start a list of the elements that make it intricate. When we study any major event in international politics—for example, Sino-American confrontation, the origins of World War II, or the start of the Iraq War—we use three tools, termed "levels of analysis," to gain insights.[6] Each of these levels may be thought of as a lens, bringing into focus and capturing insights into an event that the other levels miss. Most often, no single level of analysis captures everything; international politics is just too complicated. For major events, such as the causes of the Cold War, using multiple levels of analysis is necessary. To understand why the Cold War started, you have to understand Joseph Stalin and Harry Truman, but you also need to grasp the differences between the totalitarian Soviet Union and the democratic United States. And you also need to know why each of the two biggest states perceived the other as a threat.

The first level of analysis is the individual. If we study the cause of World War II in Europe through this lens, we examine why individual leaders cause war. This might be because of their psychology, beliefs, or ambitions. Viewed through the individual lens, the cause of World War II in Europe was Adolf Hitler's psychology, beliefs, and ambition. The Cold War started because Joseph Stalin wanted it. In essence, bad leaders cause war. For our study, employing Taylor's analogy, we argue bad drivers cause war. The car's driver—Xi Jinping—is one who accepts great risk. He is like a 16-year-old behind the wheel, willing to take risks he should not take out of machismo, anger, or ignorance. He has been fortunate so far, but the rest of us are held hostage to his luck. Our analysis about the future of the Sino-American relationship is pessimistic. We expect trouble, and a lot of it. There are multiple reasons for this, thus the causes of the conflict are overdetermined. The fact that Xi is in charge of China makes it far worse and war more probable than if a more cautious and better statesman, such as former Chinese leader Deng Xiaoping, were in charge.

The second level of analysis studies attributes of the state, whether the country is democratic or totalitarian, or an economic system, if the state is capitalist or communist. There are many attributes of states that cause war in addition to ideology and the economic system, such as religion or history. Considering World War II, we would argue that its cause in the Asia-Pacific was the militarism of the Japanese government, which led it to wage war against China and then against the United States, the British Empire, and their allies. The Cold War started because of the actions of the Soviet Union. Thus, bad states cause war. In the argot of our book, bad cars do.

The third level is the international system—specifically, anarchy or the absence of government in the international system. In international politics, there is no government above the level of states, no world government that can force states to behave. This means that a state can behave badly and get away with it—invading another state, for example. This is in contrast to hierarchy, where there is government, as in domestic politics. Because there is government within states, it is far less likely to get away with behaving badly. Laws, police, and a judicial system with lawyers, prosecutors, juries, and judges all work to ensure that a criminal is caught, tried, and punished for his crime. Under the anarchy of the international system, states can get away with committing crimes because there are no prosecutors, juries, or judges to stop them—especially great powers—from doing what they want. China is building and militarizing islands in the Philippines's territory in the South China Sea. The Philippines took China to the Permanent Court of Arbitration, which ruled in favor of the Philippines in 2016, but China has ignored the ruling. That is an unfortunate example of the unjust environment of international politics, and it is hard luck for the Philippines.

Using the third level of analysis, we explain the cause of war—for example, the Cold War—through the environment (or condition) of international politics. The Cold War was the result of an environmental factor: the two greatest powers usually see each other as their principal threat. This is because each has the power to hurt the other significantly; the United States could have destroyed the Soviet Union in the Cold War, and the Soviets could have the U.S. Thus, superpowers always are rivals. It is an environmental fact of life in the competitive realm of international politics—just as Coke will always compete with Pepsi and Amazon with Alibaba. It has little to do with Stalin's or Truman's psychology, or the totalitarian politics of the USSR or the democratic politics of the U.S. It has everything to do with the distribution of power in international politics.

Therefore, from the perspective of the third level of analysis, the Sino-American confrontation, hot or cold, happens because of a specific environment in international politics, just as the physical environment causes you to wear a sweater when it is cold. In sum, a bad environment can contribute to war. To recall Taylor's analogy, the international environment is like a twisting and turning road that is icy and snowy, on which China and the U.S. are driving at night.

Thus, we argue that two fundamental factors explain the source of the Sino-American conflict: China's ideology and the growth of Chinese power, which has forced the U.S. to respond to the threat Beijing poses. Both sources of the confrontation are deep and suggest that it will be long-lasting. Therefore, it is probable that China is and will continue to be the major threat to the U.S. in the 21st century.

We emphasize, first, the cause of the struggle is inherently ideological. Here we are making a second-level analysis argument: There is something wrong with the CCP's car. Ideology illuminates what the victor will gain and the defeated power will lose. It inspires leaders and populations. In this case, it provides an understanding of the intensity of China's passion—its hatred for the U.S. for hindering its return to its rightful position, and its determination to defeat its most powerful foe. The United States needs a concomitant level of strategic focus and passion.

Second, the Sino-American struggle is material—economic and military power matter, particularly the shifting balance of relative power from the U.S. to China. Here we are making a third-level analysis argument: The cars may crash because of the environmental conditions—the future of the Sino-American relationship is on a dangerous road at night. Again, this shift in material power feeds ambition in China and fear in Washington.[7] China is getting much stronger economically, and thus militarily and diplomatically. It has become a source of technological advancement. Its universities do not lead the world yet, but scholarship from Chinese academics is now the peer of their Western colleagues.

That growing strength is driven by China's ambition, which fuels it. Given its strong nationalistic and ethnocentric beliefs, China as a rising hegemon would challenge any dominant state. A state can have ambition but not enough power to act on it. Presumably, the Vatican has the ambition to make everyone a Catholic but it does not have the power to do so; for that reason, the United States does not consider the Holy See to be a threat. Not so with the PRC. China has the ambition, and now has the power. The heart of our argument is that China is a threat because of its intent and capabilities.

The world must perceive China for the existential threat it is. For more than a generation, the U.S. has not understood the nature and scope of the China threat. The U.S. was deceived after the Tiananmen Square Massacre in 1989 and decided to continue supporting China's economic development. China was also able to take advantage of Western countries' openness, the accommodating environment—the excellent road conditions and weather—created through the decades-long engagement policy and strategic cooperation during the War on Terror and the focus of the U.S. on the invasion of Iraq and its aftermath, to steal critical technologies from the free world. These events offered China periods of strategic opportunity to gain in strength, and especially relative power in relation to the U.S. When the West was hit by the 2008 financial crisis, China's leadership made its strategic judgment that the U.S. was in decline and China was rising. China's perception was that it was the time for China to move into the world center to lead with its rule. China's open challenge to the existing world order clearly makes severe security competition almost inevitable between the two most powerful states because the U.S. must defend its interests, including sustaining the present international liberal order.

1.3 Overview of the Book

Our argument commences in Chapter 2. We argue that the China threat is significant by beginning our examination of the CCP's ideology through the analysis of the CCP's history and origin of its extreme violence and aggression. We explained that the CCP was founded by the Soviets and dominated by the Chinese *Lumpen peasantry*, which combines Marxist-Leninist violent class struggle and revolution theory with Chinese ruffianism and the Chinese imperial psyche that postulates the victor becomes king, the defeated an outlaw. In essence, the CCP car is a Soviet knockoff. Its ideology and ruffian tradition make it the largest and most dangerous cultish organization, as does its long-term strategic goal to destroy the present liberal international order and create a new communist utopia. To understand why this is the most dangerous car, we examined the origins of the CCP's violent revolution before and after it seized state power, how it is driven by Marxist-Leninist ideology, and the catastrophic consequences of the CCP's unprecedented mass killings.

We analyze Mao Zedong's ideology, his use of peasant ruffians and his treachery enabled him to launch the violent peasant movement in 1927, the subsequent armed insurrection, the establishment of his cultish dictator status, and the seizure of complete power within the Party during the Yan'an Rectification Movement to achieve his imperial aspiration. In the chapter, we explore his ambition to lead the communist world, surpass the UK and, ultimately, the U.S. We also explain why Maoism, or "Mao Zedong Thought," is essential to understand the CCP's threat because it set the dangerous course followed by all generations of CCP leaders. The CCP's rule in China is defined by terror, lies, and deception. It has not changed, even after China opened up to the outside world and introduced some mechanism of market economy. Maoism ensures that China's rise will not be peaceful, and the Sino-American conflict is inevitable.

The second issue we address in Chapter 2 is the CCP's poisonous fruit—or the noxious gases of the CCP's car, if you will. We demonstrate that China's repressive and violent ruling model was exported to developing countries. In turn, it caused suffering inflicted on their own people by communist regimes such as North Korea and the Khmer Rouge. We also identify CCP aggression against China's neighbors during the Cold War as the result of the regime's ideology and approach to global politics. This included support for worldwide revolution; struggle with the Soviet Union over leadership of the Eastern Bloc and international communist movement; a history of hegemonic expansion; the territorial expansion including the conquest of Tibet and the East Turkestan Republic (Xinjiang); war against the United Nations and South Korea during the Korean War; aggression against India and Vietnam; and the conflict over Taiwan. Through these, we show that China's foreign policy was always a continuation of its domestic policy.

The third subject of the chapter focuses on the Leninist and Maoist concept of "socialist imperialism" (社会帝国主义) or "communist imperialism" in the communist world's discourse, which we believe is the true nature of the CCP's ideology. This is socialism in rhetoric but domination—imperial control—over China's population and other states in world politics. Understanding socialist imperialism permits us to place Maoism, and thus the CCP's current ideology of "Xi Jinping Thought," in the larger context of communist thought: their intellectual debt and dependence is on Leninism. This allows us to explain China's past and current behavior, predict its future course of action, and thus illuminate the nature of its threat.

In Chapter 3, we present evidence to show that the China threat is not just real, but growing at an alarming speed. This is because the current driver of the car, Xi Jinping, is the world's most dangerous man. First, we examine the factors that influenced Xi as a young man, including his "Red DNA," his Red Guard fanaticism, his opportunistic deceit, and how the hardship of the CCP's internal power struggle he encountered hardened his heart and affirmed his conviction to be the victor. These feed his ambition and animus toward elements in the CCP and allow us to explain the impact of major international events upon him, such as the fall of the Soviet Union. Second, we examine Xi's neo-Maoist ideology. Xi needs to revive Maoism fully in order to justify his own dictatorship, to increase his legitimacy as true and authentic heir of Mao and savior of the Party, and to prevent the Chinese people from questioning the CCP's one-party rule. Xi's aim is to achieve Mao's cult leader status, and Mao's ultimate goal of creating one leader, one party, one ideology, and one culture in China. Internationally, just as Mao desired, Xi seeks to create an alternative order of socialism with Chinese characteristics to replace liberal democracy, and become the leader that saves the troubled world in the process by showing the correct and luminous path for mankind. Third, we advanced the "Xi Doctrine." The consequence of this doctrine is that China will fight the United States because it is the single major impediment to China's strategic objectives. With the U.S. removed, there is no single power, or alliance of powers that could stop China from achieving its strategic goals. Xi has transparently and boldly advanced those aims in his conception of a hegemonic China by 2049—the final, grand strategic objective of the Xi Doctrine. In fact, Xi seeks to realize these ambitions as early as possible if he can secure 10–15 more years of his rule to exploit the strategic opportunity China has to catch up with the U.S. The United States is the main barrier to the realization of China's ambitions and its ideological opponent, and so it is the focus of China's enmity. The U.S. will remain the focus of the CCP's enmity until it is defeated by the CCP. Fundamentally, Xi has intensified the cold war with the U.S. and is actively preparing for a hot war against the U.S.

The final goal of Chapter 3 is to present the implications of Xi's leadership and the Xi Doctrine. We considered five. First, the "Chinese Dream" is a cover for socialist imperialism—the Dream is simply a neologism for the CCP's domination and restoration of China's past imperial glory. Second, Xi's expansion is intended to create a new order for international politics. Third, the People's Liberation Army (PLA) is preparing for war and the West should anticipate that conflict may come in this decade. Fourth, the CCP's digital dictatorship allows the regime to efficiently police the Chinese people. Fifth, the CCP's infiltration of Western societies, media, and universities is ubiquitous through the United Front Work Department and related means, for intelligence collection and for influence.

Chapter 4 explains how the shift in the relative balance of power makes China the primary threat to the U.S. and the free world. Think of this relative change as the road condition. The weather is no longer bright and sunny for the U.S., but is now freezing rain and sleet, mixed with snow, with whiteout conditions expected later. At the same time, the road has changed from straightaway to mountainous, with hairpin curves. The Sino-American struggle is material—economic and military power are important, particularly the shifting balance of relative power from the U.S. to China. This shift feeds ambition in Beijing and fear in Washington. Given the CCP's ambitions and the population's strongly nationalistic and ethnocentric beliefs, China as a rising hegemon would challenge any dominant state. Indeed, a far weaker China confronted both the U.S. and Soviet Union during the Cold War. For the first time, China is the challenger to the dominant state. This is something new in the history of empires, and the example of China shows you can be on top, lose it all, and return to greatness, even dominance. In historical context, this is a remarkably impressive feat—unmatched by any empire in history.

Chapter 5 captures the necessary U.S. response in facing this clear and present danger from China. We illuminate what the U.S. must accomplish to meet the challenge from Xi and the CCP. The U.S. must fight for its position as the dominant state in the face of China's challenge. U.S. leadership seeks to maintain this position because that is best for, first, U.S. security; second, the security of its allies; and third, the promotion of its ideology to ensure that freedom and democratic government, open societies, and free markets are the dominant values of international politics. The U.S. seeks to maintain the status quo, its position in global politics, and the order it has known and that both the U.S. leadership and population expect to continue. That expectation was conceived and conditioned in the calm geopolitical seas of the 1990s and 2000s.

That time is past. As China has risen, the U.S. must now battle to maintain its place in the world and the dominance of its military, economy, ideology, and technological leadership. Indeed, the U.S. is forced to fight to defend its position, allies, and values. But this cannot be wholly a defensive war. The United States must actively confront China in each realm and put China on the back foot in order to ensure that the U.S. and its allies triumph in each and every aspect of the competition. While the military and economic components are essential, ideology is equally critical because it motivates the U.S. response to China with a comprehension, energy, and vigor that material forces cannot—as the U.S. Navy contends, "Ships don't fight, men do." People fight to defend their country and ideology. Machines, equipment, economies, and technology do not. Accordingly, U.S. ideology is the spine that supports U.S. power. Ideology can unite and inspire the American people, as well as America's sympathizers around the world, and it explains why the world should resist China's ideology and vision for the future of global politics.

We suggest eight measures the United States should adopt to sustain its leadership. The United States must, first, see China for what it is: the enemy. China is a hostile, revolutionary state intent on replacing the U.S. as the world's dominant power. Second, ideology matters, and U.S. leadership must place greater emphasis on ideology as a central component of why the U.S. should confront the CCP and why the U.S. must win. China is winning the world's hearts and minds, and the U.S. must recognize that China's ideological campaign is a U.S. national security threat and elevate its response. Third, the U.S. must employ trade as a weapon to cut off China's lifeline for becoming a superpower. Fourth, the U.S. should launch an international movement to aid China's Muslims and other religious minorities. Fifth, the U.S. must call international attention to China's arms race and unwillingness to advance an arms control agenda. This is a strong indication that China is not interested in strategic stability. The world should require that China curb its nuclear and conventional armaments because it is the right policy to prevent an arms race. To address China's dangerous military expansion, the U.S. must strengthen its military capabilities to check its bid for domination. Sixth, the U.S. must strengthen its deterrent posture in the Indo-Pacific, including expanding its conventional and nuclear presence in the region, in conjunction with allies, and extend deterrence to Taiwan. Seventh, the U.S. must defend its technology leadership position and prevent China from dominating the commanding heights of advanced technology. Eighth, the U.S. should promote a free and open internet to defeat China's Great Firewall and close the global digital divide to strengthen the liberal world order.

Lastly, Chapter 6 presents the four major conclusions of our study. First, the United States can and must win. War with China, cold or hot, provides the United States with the ability to explain the ultimate reason for the struggle: freedom is legitimate and superior to repressive rule, but freedom must be defended. The ideology of the U.S. unifies the American people and like-minded people around the world and explains why China should be resisted. Ideology, once again, explains "why we fight." The United States must contrast its dynamic, innovative, free, and open society—one that can correct its flaws—with the increasingly wealthy but ethnocentric, racist, and closed Chinese society. That stark recognition essentially captures the profound differences between the two societies.

Second, the role of ideology is essential. U.S. ideology can serve to undermine the legitimacy of authoritarian rule in the minds of the Chinese. It also elucidates why the U.S. must win the Sino-American conflict. Our focus is on ideology because it provides the United States with key advantages in the Sino-American conflict. The West went through a civil rights movement to create a culture of anti-racism in its societies. In China, the idea of a civil rights movement that would aid the condition of women and minorities, and so undermine the Party's supremacy, is unthinkable. As a free and open society, the U.S. is a better ally for states in Africa, Asia, and Latin America than is China, whose alliances and partnerships are often characterized by abuses. The United States, however, is transparent with its allies and has a history of protecting their interests and treating them as equal partners. Free and open political principles make the U.S. a valuable, dependable ally.

The CCP—particularly, under Deng—has been clever, even artful, in its deception. It has pretended to be a benign rising power, and its penetration of U.S. and Western elites and economic ecosystems has created complacency toward accurately recognizing the China threat. There is historical precedent for this. The U.S. was slow to recognize the threats of Hitler's Germany and Stalin's Soviet Union. The past is prologue, and so it is essential for national security that U.S. policymakers and the public recognize the true threat that China poses.

Third, the U.S. must possess the confidence that it can win the struggle with China. To achieve victory, senior national security decision-makers must be convinced that the United States can maintain its international dominance with no hostile peer competitor challenging the position. This might appear self-evident but it is not. When we examine the history of America's grand strategy, there have been many times when the United States seemed weak or in decline—unable to cope with the British threat in the 18th and 19th centuries; the Soviet threat or the rise of Japan in the 20th century; or with China today. Equally, at these times, there were senior U.S. officials and experts in accord with this declinist sentiment. U.S. policymakers may not have such confidence because they overestimate the opponent's strength or exaggerate its weakness. U.S. decision-makers must have confidence in victory over a peer rival.

Fourth, to win, the United States not only must have the confidence that it can do so but also must target the CCP's weaknesses. In such a war, the greatest ally of the U.S. is the Chinese people, who will join in the fight if Washington can capitalize upon Beijing's weaknesses, starting with the fact that the CCP is an illegitimate regime. Political legitimacy requires explicit or implicit consent from the population. The CCP's ideology rejects such consent; it is dangerously incoherent, and only diehard Party members believe the neo-Maoism of Xi Jinping. The U.S. should not accept the regime's legitimacy and should consider the CCP to be the equivalent of South Africa's apartheid regime, with a goal of isolating Beijing as the world did Pretoria.

The second major weakness is China's enforced digital isolation, which permits the CCP to sustain its grip on power and prevent the strengthening of a civil society that could become an existential threat to its rule. In our view, the internet is the CCP's most critical vulnerability that may ensure America's victory in the struggle. The CCP's recognition of its weakness is evident. Like all tyrannical regimes, the CCP relies on deception, lies, and misinformation to firmly control the free flow of information. This permits the CCP to conceal and obfuscate its atrocities and gross human rights abuses and thus maintain its grip on power. For years, the internet made it more difficult for the regime to hide the truth.

Finally, perhaps the most effective way to exploit China's weakness is for the West to close the digital divide and promote the free flow of information. As China's strength increases, Xi's digital dictatorial ambition expands. He has intensified China's global public opinion and psychological warfare campaigns against democracies. The CCP is concentrating its forces in both of these forms of warfare to what the Party terms "Gong Xin," meaning literally "to storm the hearts." The CCP believes that whoever rules information rules people's minds and hearts. Whoever rules people's minds and hearts will dominate global opinion and narratives. In this war, psychological supremacy is the key. However, the inherent contradictions of Xi's ideology and the regime's rule by terror and deception ensure that the political system is vulnerable and unsustainable. To defeat China's new world order of socialism with Chinese characteristics, we must strengthen our liberal world order globally. The free flow of information, the key advantage of the liberal order, is both a sword and shield for the West, and must be employed to defend the free world and defeat the CCP.

Notes

1 We note that China's animus is direct not just at the United States but to liberal, democratic states more broadly. Unless otherwise indicated by context, we will use the U.S. as a shorthand for all liberal, democratic states.

2 Few books in the field of international relations have addressed related questions. The most important of these is Michael Pillsbury's *The Hundred-Year Marathon: China's Secret Strategy to Replace America as the Global Superpower* (New York: Holt, 2014). In contrast to Pillsbury, the focus of our work is on the ideological motivations of the Sino-American conflict from both sides. Graham Allison's *Destined for War: Can America and China Escape Thucydides's Trap?* (New York: Houghton Mifflin Harcourt, 2017) centers on the distribution of power, leaving out ideological motivations for conflict, which we address. Similarly, John Mearsheimer's *The Tragedy of Great Power Politics* (New York: Norton, 2001, updated 2014) focuses on the inevitability of a Sino-American conflict. He contends that China seeks regional hegemony out of necessity because of the pressures of an anarchic international system. Like Allison, Mearsheimer fails to examine the important role of Chinese ideology in driving the conflict. An excellent study is Rush Doshi's *The Long Game: China's Grand Strategy to Displace American Order* (New York: Oxford University Press, 2021). Yet Doshi does not recognize the dangers of Xi Jinping and his clique's belief in communism and their determination to sustain it in the People's Republic of China (PRC) and impose it upon the world; second, his policy recommendations are defensive. Finally, an exceptional study from the U.S. perspective is Elbridge A. Colby's *The Strategy of Denial: American Defense in an Age of Great Power Conflict* (New Haven, CT: Yale University Press, 2021).

3 A.J.P. Taylor, *The Origins of the Second World War* (London: Hamish Hamilton, 1961), pp. 135–136.

4 Our study fully expects a confrontation between the PRC and the United States. Of course, we recognize that the relationship might be irenic. Two key works that suggest the relationship will be peaceful are Henry Kissinger's On *China* (New York: Penguin, 2012); and Hugh White's *The China Choice* (New York: Oxford, 2012). Our study critiques both for underestimating the causes of a confrontation and its necessity to ensure the continuation of America's values and principles for governing international politics.

5 Richard Hanania, "There Is No Thucydides Trap Between the U.S. and China," *RealClearDefense*, June 8, 2020. Available at: <https://www.realcleardefense.com/articles/2020/06/08/there_is_no_thucydides_trap_between_the_us_and_china_115359.html?mc_cid=c2be98be31>. Accessed January 22, 2022.

6 Classic description of levels of analysis and their benefits and limitations are J. David Singer, "The Level-of-Analysis Problem in International Relations," *World Politics* 14, no. 1 (October 1961): 77–92; and Kenneth N. Waltz, *Man, the State, and War: A Theoretical Analysis* (New York: Columbia University Press, 1959).

7 This argument is well captured in Allison's *Destined for War*. Also see Zbigniew Brzeziński, "Can China Avoid the Thucydides Trap," *New Perspectives Quarterly* 31, no. 2 (2014): 31–33; and John M. Friend and Bradley A. Thayer, "China's Use of Multilateral Institutions and the U.S. Response: The Need for American Primacy 2.0," in Kai He and Huiyun Feng, eds., *China's Challenges and International Order Transition: Beyond the "Thucydides's Trap"* (Ann Arbor, MI: University of Michigan Press, 2020), pp. 259–279.

2

THE IDEOLOGY OF THE CHINESE COMMUNIST PARTY

Its Innate Aggression Will Cause Conflict with the United States

This chapter begins our explanation of why China is a threat to the United States and the free world. In it, we analyze why the China threat is real and why China seeks confrontation with the United States. It does so because of the CCP creed. Its Marxist–Leninist ideology, combined with Mao Zedong's employment of ruffians as shock troops to do his bidding—the *Lumpen peasantry*—and traditional Chinese imperial aspirations, drives the Party-state to perpetuate its rule in China and seek global dominance through the creation of a China-centered world order. China's hegemonic ambition is anchored in the belief in the superiority of communism and the inevitable death of capitalism and its imperialism. The Party's ideology and leadership allow us to understand the Party's determination to maintain control and what would propel it to go to war. The CCP perceives the U.S. as the major obstacle to achieving its goals.

This chapter has two objectives. First, it analyzes the origins of the CCP and its four generations of leadership prior to Xi Jinping—Mao Zedong, Deng Xiaoping, Jiang Zemin, and Hu Jintao—to show how the CCP grew to become the largest cultish organization in the world, and why it is the most dangerous threat to the U.S. and the free world. We argue that the CCP's ideology drives the Party-state to seek to maintain control of China through the most repressive rule of terror and deception and to achieve global hegemony through spreading communist world revolutions, as it did in the past, and today through exporting the model of socialism with Chinese characteristics. This is part of the CCP's contending-for-hegemony (争霸) imperialistic tradition. Its communist ideology compels a grand strategy of dominance: It must control the people of China and the political, ideological, and economic ordering of global politics and cannot accept challenges to its rule, domestically or internationally. We examine China's hegemonic ambitions, its history of expansion, and explain the CCP ideology and its evolution from Mao to Xi.

DOI: 10.4324/9781003283614-2

Second, we apply this argument to the empirical record of unprecedented violence toward the Chinese people and belligerence in international politics. The CCP's repressive, expansionist nature poses the most significant danger to liberal democracy that these polities have faced since World War II. In fact, the CCP's ideology—wedded to China's power and the infiltration of Western businesses, finance, government, media, and academic and scientific establishments—ensures that liberal democracies will confront the greatest oppositional power in their histories. This is because China's strength already surpasses German, Italian, Japanese, or Soviet power.

Although states are increasingly aware of the grave threat posed by Communist China, many still fail to grasp the scope, magnitude, severity, and urgency because the true belligerent nature of China's ideology is occluded, misunderstood, or dismissed as insincere. There is a profoundly mistaken belief that the Chinese are not really communists and that they do not take their ideology seriously. Some hold the impression that communism ended with the demise of the Soviet Union.

However, Xi led his Politburo Standing Committee (PSC) members to renew their Party oath in 2017 and 2021, vowing to fight for Communism the rest of their lives. Even absent awareness of China's threat, the world is heading down the path of an ultimate conflict triggered unilaterally by Communist China in its process of becoming the dominant power and creating a China-centered world order. This will end open societies and rules-based international order as we know it. The defining feature of this struggle is that it is a life-and-death war between two political systems, two ideologies, and two ways of life because the CCP has made it so. To grasp the China threat and expose its deceptions and violent nature, we need to dissect Communist China's past leadership, ideology, strategic goals, and tactics employed.

2.1 Communist China Is a Defective Car Operated by a Dangerous Driver

Understanding how China rules domestically will enable us to see how it would rule the world if it achieves its goal. To continue using the car crash analogy, this accident will happen because of the bad car. As "the car," China has profound structural flaws in its design, myriad mechanical defects, and software bugs, all of which make it inherently dangerous to its 1.4 billion passengers and other cars on the international highway. China is controlled by a totalitarian regime modeled on Marxist–Leninist–Maoist dictatorship, so the car's design is far from modern. It is a Soviet knockoff designed to hazard pedestrians and other motorists, disrupt traffic, and damage the road all at the same time. Not only is the CCP a threat, but the car's driver, Xi Jinping, is too. As we will explore in Chapter 3, he is a reckless driver with complete disregard for human life and seeks to set the rules for all.

In recent years, the CCP has mobilized its entire Party-state power to market its bad car and driver. While this takes several forms, the CCP propagandized the so-called "Zhongguo Zhi zhi" (中国之治), meaning literally the "Rule of China" (中国之治), also termed the "Governance of China," "China Model," or

"China Solution," claiming that they are the best in the world because China has found the secrets of making the greatest "car." The CCP's Fourth Plenum of the 19th National Congress summarizes the Rule of China as a political system of "socialism with Chinese characteristics." Because of the CCP's firm leadership and state ownership, the Party has created "two grand miracles"—rapid economic development and long-term social stability. As the Party stated, "After more than 70 years of exploration and development, China has formed a system that works, works well and is efficient."[1] In Chinese, the term "Rule of China" has a strong imperial connotation; Chinese emperors and their official scholars often used such a term to describe their brilliant reigns. The desire of the CCP to link its rule to China's glorious past is obscene.

How the CCP rules is often captured by Mao's characterization of the Party's three "magic weapons." In 1939, Mao Zedong argued that the CCP's rule was based on the United Front, Leninism, and the People's Liberation Army (PLA).[2] Mao advanced this argument in his writing, "Introducing *The Communist*."[3] He argued: "The united front, armed struggle and Party building are the three fundamental questions for our Party in the Chinese revolution."[4] As a result of the CCP's struggles since its founding in 1921, "we are now able to handle the questions of the united front, of armed struggle, and of Party building in the correct way. It also means that our 18 years of experience" since its founding "have taught us that the united front, armed struggle and Party building are the CCP's three 'magic weapons,' its three principal magic weapons for defeating the enemy in the Chinese revolution."[5]

We amend Mao's argument and submit the CCP's control is anchored on four magic weapons—namely, employing the Chinese communists' own phrases, "the barrel of a gun" (枪杆子), "the handle of a saber" (刀把子), "the holder of a pen" (笔杆子), and "the purse strings" (钱袋子). The "barrel of a gun" refers to the PLA, "the handle of saber" to the police and jails, "the holder of a pen" to the propaganda apparatus, and "the purse strings" to economic resources.

The CCP, past and present, uses these weapons alternatively or in combination to create a Red Terror through violence and repression. For those who are obedient, want to join it, or can be lured to its cause, it provides security, economic benefits, and camaraderie. Those who oppose the CCP's rule or its leaders or policy are eliminated physically or "vanished" in jails or labor camps, or cut off from the means of their livelihoods, while its enormous propaganda apparatus creates and repeats lies to indoctrinate its people. Since the Rule of China will be extended to the world, these "magic weapons" will continue to be employed.

2.1.1 Marxist–Leninist–Stalinist Ideology and the Importance of Mao's *Lumpen Peasantry*

The violence, treachery, and deception in the Rule of China come from Marxist–Leninist–Stalinist violent revolution theory and practice. It is also rooted in China's 2,000-year tradition of wars, brutality, and repression of peasant uprisings to maintain the throne. This culture of violence became much more prevalent in the CCP because its base is similar to the *Lumpenproletariat*, defined by Karl Marx as the dregs of society and an underclass devoid of class consciousness.[6] For Marx, this group could not be part of the proletariat revolution. But Bolshevik leader Vladimir Lenin thought otherwise. As early as May 1923, the Communist International had conveyed Lenin's instructions to the CCP: "Only by drawing the peasants, the majority of the Chinese population, i.e., the small peasants, into the movement will the Chinese revolution be victorious," and that "the central question of all Chinese policy is the peasant question."[7]

However, mobilizing Chinese peasants to rebel was not easy because most of them were content with their situation. Unlike feudal Europe, in rural China the status between landlords and peasants frequently changed. If a poor peasant worked hard and was thrifty, he could rise to become a landlord. The tension between rich and poor peasants was low, even if the gap in wealth was large. Most of them lived peaceful lives in accordance with what they thought was the natural order of things, and it was not easy for them to break generations of village harmony and rise in rebellion.

In contrast to the principles of Maoism and the CCP's hagiography, the Party's support did not come from the peasantry but from the rural *Lumpenproletariat*— the dregs of the peasantry, the riffraff, and loafers. They should be considered a *Lumpen peasantry*, because they were rural, and, as discussed, this is the term we use to describe them. The *Lumpen peasantry* existed in the long history of China. They were a marginalized group that held no regular jobs, had no roots, and roamed between cities and the countryside. Some of them begged for a living; some were bandits and gangsters. They had no sense of belonging to the countryside and no sense of responsibility, so they dared to rob and kill and were regarded by the country people as hooligans who disturbed the peace. During turbulent times, they often played a critical role in dynasty change or regime changes.

According to Wang Xuetai, a scholar of Chinese culture, they were cast aside by society and became anti-social, wanting the world to fall into great chaos with the hope of gaining benefits. They were aggressive and violent because they had nothing to lose. The group was uncivilized and uneducated, and displayed naked cruelty and barbarism without constraint or governance by moral principles.[8] This group absolutely worshiped martial force, violence, and power, which reflected the Chinese imperial mentality and aspirations that are deeply rooted in Chinese culture. It embraced the belief that a commoner can become an emperor or king, favoring the concept of the victor becoming an emperor and the defeated an outlaw. From the Dazexiang Uprising (209 BC) led by Chen Sheng and Wu Gang against the Qin dynasty (221–206 BC) to Li Zicheng's rebellion (AD 1644) to overthrow the Ming dynasty (1368–1644), there were hundreds or thousands of such bloody popular revolts led by the Chinese *Lumpen peasantry* against authorities. This is a critical force that has caused the rise and fall of empires for over 2,000 years in China.

In the 1920s, the Soviet Union was the established leader of the communist world. Recognizing that revolutionary progress was not advancing swiftly enough, in 1926, Soviet leader Joseph Stalin asked the Kuomintang (KMT) and the CCP to work together as the former's army launched the Northern Expedition (1926–1928) against warlords. Both parties agreed to carry out rural land reform by demanding that landlords reduce rent and interest payments but did not use violence to confiscate their land. However, by late 1926, Stalin was displeased with the moderate land reform policy and instructed the CCP to intensify the class struggle to further it.

To accelerate change, Mikhail Markovich Gruzenberg, known by the alias Borodin, who was Stalin's representative to Sun Yat-sen and the Kuomintang, and the *de facto* leader of the CCP at the time, followed Stalin's orders. Borodin urged both parties to take action and directed them to use the *Lumpen peasantry* as agitators. Borodin said, "The peasant movement in both Hunan and Hubei provinces is too quiet, and the peasants are not willing to rise up, so we should use the rural thugs and riffraff to mobilize the masses," because they dared to fight and kill.[9] In one of his speeches, Borodin said: "The riffraff are the bravest, the most determined and the most decisive."[10] He made it clear that to mobilize the peasantry, it was necessary to use the ruffians as the "vanguard of the revolution."[11]

Borodin's instruction triggered violence in southern China. In Hunan, where Mao grew up, riots by the *Lumpen peasantry* were common. Mao had strong imperial aspirations. In a conversation with Edgar Snow, he admitted that as a young man, he worshiped emperors such as Qin Shi Huang and Han Wu Di. This was perhaps what drove Mao to get involved with the CCP. Mao was the official appointed by Kuomintang and the CCP to lead the peasants' movement. He fully implemented the instruction from Stalin and the Seventh Enlarged Conference of the Communist International (Comintern), making the solution of the rural land issue the center of the Chinese Revolution. Mao used Borodin's tactic of using thugs, gangsters, and ruffians to incite the peasants' movement in 1926 and 1927. They employed violence against landowners, and took their land and redistributed it among themselves under a political slogan, "Down with the local tyrants and evil gentry, and all power to the peasant associations."[12] This echoed the Soviet slogan of a decade earlier: "All power to the Soviets" or workers' councils—in essence, all power to working-class representatives. Mao urged the use of violence to seize power:

> A rural revolution is a revolution by which the peasantry overthrows the power of the feudal landlord class. Without using the greatest force, the peasants cannot possibly overthrow the deep-rooted authority of the landlords, which has lasted for thousands of years. The rural areas need a mighty revolutionary upsurge, for it alone can rouse the people in their millions to become a powerful force.[13]

As a result, the movement caused many killings, great disruption of society, and loss of property, and set the stage for far greater destruction in the decades to come.

Mao later published a report about his investigation of the peasant movement in Hunan, which detailed the excessive violence that was the catalyst of the change. He summarized nine ways to strike against landlords and particularly praised the method of "putting a tall hat to parade from village to village."[14] This cone-shaped pointed hat, made of paper, was meant to humiliate the wearer. This likely was Borodin's idea because such a hat was foreign in China but regularly used in Medieval Europe. Mao summarized the movement by identifying what was revolutionary about it. In short, all those the gentry had despised, those they had trodden into the dirt, people with no place in society, people with no right to speak, had audaciously lifted their heads and taken power into their hands. They now ran the township peasant associations, which they turned into something fierce and formidable.

In reality, the rural areas of Hunan and other southern provinces fell into great chaos. The social framework collapsed, violence was rampant, and terror was widespread. The peasants' associations often set arbitrary and random criteria for who should be considered "local tyrants and evil gentry." Some believed that any landowners were local tyrants and all gentry were evil. Some places classified all those who owned more than eight acres of land as local tyrants, and all those who wore long robes as wicked gentry. The families of many officers of the Kuomintang army in the Northern Expedition became the victims of violence, which was the main reason for the subsequent split and vendetta between the Kuomintang and the CCP.[15]

Like previous leaders of Chinese peasant uprisings, Mao believed it was necessary to form an army and establish a base of operations. Mao worshiped power and held that military power is the ultimate form of power. He did not hide his imperial aspirations and announced them through his conversations and writings. In one of the poems, Mao implied that he was greater than the great emperors before him. At the same time, he also claimed that he was the revolutionary king of the mountains—the leader of outlaws. In September 1927, he launched the Autumn Harvest Uprising, one of the CCP's earliest armed uprisings against Kuomintang authorities. Although his insurrection and the Hunan Soviet government failed within a few months, Mao was convinced that his strategy could work. He continued to the Jinggang Mountains on the border between Hunan and Jiangxi provinces, to establish a base with his remaining peasant army. Many of the *Lumpen peasantry* joined Mao's army in September 1927. After the uprising failed, many who participated in this violent rural revolution later joined Mao's guerrilla warfare.

Thus, it was not the working class or the peasantry but the *Lumpen peasantry* who formed the core of the CCP's early leadership and the base of the Red Army. This is the origin of the innate violent behavior of the CCP. Its 100-year history is almost always dominated by radical leftist members who originated with the *Lumpen peasantry* rural revolution. In a real sense, we should consider the CCP to be a giant cult or violent gang. Its members always are on the communist political "left," and it is much safer to side with violent radicals and leftist extremists than with moderates (the "right"). These early fanatics of the CPP believed in Mao's counsel that

a revolution is not a dinner party, or writing an essay, or painting a picture, or doing embroidery; it cannot be so refined, so leisurely and gentle, so temperate, kind, courteous, restrained and magnanimous. A revolution is an insurrection, an act of violence by which one class overthrows another.[16]

In the wake of the failed Autumn Harvest Uprising, Mao wrote his *Report on an Investigation of the Peasant Movement in Hunan*, which has become one of the CCP's seminal documents. Every CCP member today is required to study this report.[17] Clearly, the party wants to instill its violent essence, its "political DNA," into new members. In fact, the CCP's external "wolf-warrior" style and internal repression and control can be traced back to the *Lumpen peasantry* movement initiated by Mao. His movement was anti-social, anti-human, and anti-intellectual, violent and barbaric, without principles or moral boundaries. Party members lived in a world of conspiracy; they enjoyed creating enemies for political gains and sought to maximize the interests of their clique. This is the origin of the CCP's culture of violence to this day.

The peasant movement led to the CCP's armed rebellion, which triggered a series of tragic events that pushed the Party further into violence. After his failed armed uprising, Mao's troops were reduced to fewer than a thousand men. He realized that he must follow Lenin's model of unified leadership over the military, Party, and government to succeed. He started by establishing absolute control over the military by installing Party officials into its ranks. On September 29, 1927, Mao reorganized his forces and set up Party organizations in the military. Each company had a Party branch; each battalion and regiment, a Party committee. Party representatives, similar to Soviet political commissars, were assigned to all military units at and above the company level. The Party representatives served as Party chiefs of the units. Even squads and platoons had Party groups. Soldiers were recruited to join the Party. This was the beginning of the long-lasting CCP practice of "the Party commanding the gun."

When the CCP drew its lessons from the collapse of the Soviet Union, a key factor it perceived was Soviet leader Mikhail Gorbachev's weakening of the military through his reforms and the loss of ideological certainty regarding the infallibility of the Communist Party. The danger of institutionalizing the CCP's absolute control over the military is that it makes the military a private army of the paramount Party leader.

Mao also realized the importance of territory for his Red Army. He tricked the bandits occupying the Jinggang Mountains into becoming his sworn brothers and integrated them into the Red Army. Within a couple of years, Mao had increased his troops and enlarged his territory. He essentially controlled the Jiangxi Soviet base, achieving this through extreme cruelty and brutality. According to Hong Kong journalist Cai Yongmei, Mao's Jiangxi Soviet base was organized as a violent totalitarian society with the Red Army at its core, and all power belonged to the Soviet government at all levels down to the villages.[18] In addition to the powerful CCP secret service, the State Protection Bureau, and the Workers' and Peasants' Procuratorate, there were other dictatorial groups such as the Communist Youth League, the Red Guards, the Young Pioneers, the

Poor Peasants League, the Workers Unions, and the Women Delegations, all of whom created a Red Terror and exercised tight control over Soviet areas.

To expand its territory, the CCP forced the peasants to join the Red Army through a powerful political campaign; even teenagers and old men were compelled to join. To break the Kuomintang's military sieges, the Red Army adopted the "burn and kill" scorched-earth policy: Village after village was burned, and tens of thousands of people lost their homes. The Red Army behaved worse than bandits, committing atrocities such as mass killings, kidnappings for ransom, pillaging, and lootings.[19]

Mao and his *Lumpen peasantry* were cruel to enemies and comrades alike. Mao was able to control the Jiangxi Soviet base, but, since he was only a regional leader and not the top CCP leader, his authority was sometimes questioned. In 1930, a policy difference erupted between Mao and the South-Western Jiangxi CCP leadership. Mao wanted to confiscate all land in the area, but the local leaders suggested following the central committee's instruction to confiscate only bad landlords' land. The local leaders also disagreed with Mao's reorganization plan and asked it to be approved by higher authorities. Mao felt this challenged his authority, so he made up an excuse to purge those who disagreed with him, labeling them as 'anti-Bolshevik elements and launching a terror campaign against the so-called "Anti-Bolshevik League." Soon a wave of terror swept through the Jiangxi Soviet base. Many Red Army officers and soldiers who came from the landowning class or were educated became targets, and torture was used to obtain confessions, which implicated more people, thus creating a vicious cycle.[20] The crackdown on the Anti-Bolshevik League within the CCP is another event that reveals the CCP's violent culture.

No exact number of victims who died in the purge is known today—it lasted throughout the Long March (1934–1935)—but according to General Xiao Ke's memoir, the death toll for the whole incident exceeded 100,000. In addition, from 1931 to 1935, the population of the 15 counties in the Jiangxi Soviet area fell by more than 500,000, and a similar percentage drop happened at the neighboring Fujian Soviet base. The total population of the Central Soviet area fell by more than 700,000, accounting for 20 percent of the population. Today, the CCP acknowledges the Anti-Bolshevik League campaign was an error and that those killed or tortured were innocent. In 1983, Jiangxi posthumously recognized the 238,844 people killed in purges as revolutionary martyrs.[21]

2.1.2 Mao Zedong Thought and the Yan'an Rectification Movement

In the Long March, the CCP Red Army fled to the Northwest to escape pressure from the KMT's army. Mao fled to Shanxi under the excuse of marching to the battlefield of anti-Japanese invasion. In reality, Mao and his army avoided battle, recuperating and getting stronger while watching the Kuomintang's army sustain high casualties.

After his failed peasant uprising of 1927, Mao spent ten years establishing his leadership. He realized the power of "barrels of the gun" and founded the CCP's own military, established a base, and survived the deadly encirclement of the Kuomintang. He had gained more power and authority than any previous leader in the CCP's short history. At the beginning of the Long March in January 1935, Mao was added to the CCP core leadership as a PSC member, assisting Zhou Enlai in military decisions. At the end of 1936, he became chairman of the revolutionary military committee, essentially controlling the Red Army. But Mao was not the Party chief. Although he formed an alliance with Zhang Wentian, a Soviet-trained CCP general secretary, Mao could not control the whole CCP.

As Confucius said, if "there will be no right title, words will not be proper" (名不正言不順).[22] That is why some scholars contend that lacking authority to shape the Party's ideology and theory bothered Mao the most.[23] A majority of CCP members "blindly" worshiped Stalin and the Soviet Union. CCP comrades who studied in the Soviet Union and were proficient in Marxism–Leninism held power over the interpretation of Marxist-Leninist ideology within the Party, while Mao—the peasant revolution leader—did not. According to Jin Guantao, an expert on the CCP, Mao once said with great emotion: "If you don't form an 'ism,' even if you become the leader, you may be overthrown while you are still alive."[24] Thus, "Maoism" should be thought of as his effort to ensure his position as the CCP's leader.

In November 1937, Stalin and Georgi Dimitrov, head of the Comintern, sent Wang Ming, former CCP chief, back to Yan'an to ensure that Mao could work with Chiang Kai-shek in the newly formed United Front against a Japanese invasion. But Mao had his own plan. He wanted to deceive Chiang to believe he would cooperate, though his real goal was to use the opportunity to rapidly take territory behind the battle lines and enlarge the CCP forces without fighting the Japanese. As head of the Chinese *Lumpen peasantry* revolution, Mao had a deep hatred of intellectuals, especially those educated in the West or the Soviet Union. He framed them as the Party's "dogmatic" elements. He once denounced Soviet-trained comrades as "fools who are worse than pigs" and scolded that knowledge and dogma are "even more useless than shit."[25] He never liked Wang Ming, whom he mockingly called the "imperial envoy."[26]

Upon his return, Wang quickly established his authority in the Party as Stalin's envoy and held power to interpret the CCP's ideology. After Wang arrived in Yan'an, more people attended his speeches and fewer were interested in what Mao had to say. Mao saw that Wang directly threatened his authority and his plan to seize power from Chiang Kai-shek. At the same time, more than 40,000 students came to Yan'an with the hope of fighting Japanese invaders, but Mao's refusal to engage in real fights made them question his passiveness. These young students also found Wang's ideas more appealing.[27]

Through trickery, Mao was able to put Wang in his place during the Sixth Plenum held in September 1938. Mao sent two confidants to Moscow to lobby for support, and they obtained Dimitrov's oral instruction that Mao should head the CCP.[28] Zhang Wentian, then CCP chief, was a weak leader, and Mao took advantage of him by using soft and harsh tactics, including playing matchmaker to find a wife for Zhang. As a result, Zhang handed the power to Mao without any formal process. Mao was an expert in feudal court trickery and power struggles to achieve absolute control of the CCP. He carefully planned a campaign to cement his authority over not only the military and Party, but also its ideology. Against that background, Mao launched the Yan'an Rectification Movement.

Historian Gao Hua has documented and analyzed this incredible incident.[29] Gao concludes that the Yan'an Rectification Movement was the first political campaign Mao launched, which profoundly influenced China's course in the 20th century. In this campaign, Mao employed measures such as ideological transformation, political clearance of cadres, and a purge of counterrevolutionaries to remove the remaining influence of the May Fourth Movement's liberal and democratic ideology, as well as de-Russification to move the CCP toward total "Maoization," or the triumph of Mao Zedong Thought.

Mao launched the Yan'an Rectification Movement to consolidate his power by instilling his ideology and building his cult personality. Yan'an was the CCP's headquarters after the Long March. Preparation for the movement began in 1938, and it ran on full scale from 1942 to 1945. During World War II, Mao and the CCP's Red Army were not focused on fighting Japanese invaders but instead were occupied by internal power struggles. Within a year of the 1937 Japanese invasion, the Kuomintang and CCP agreed to cooperate again to oppose the Japanese. In 1938, the Eighth Route Army, renamed Red Army, was enlarged from 30,000 to 300,000 troops and, by 1945, it grew to 900,000, largely financed by the Soviet Union and the CCP's opium trade.

The significance of the Yan'an Rectification Movement to the CCP cannot be overestimated. The study of the Yan'an Rectification will help us to better understand the CCP's political actions, ideology, and inner workings. In fact, without understanding the Yan'an Rectification Movement, one cannot truly understand the CCP's nature and mentality—why there are concentration camps in Xinjiang, the wolf-warrior diplomacy, the CCP's propaganda, or any other developments in the evolution of the Party and Communist China. This is because the Yan'an Rectification Movement is both an encyclopedia and a "how to" manual of the CCP's political operations. Significantly, Xi Jinping repeatedly has emphasized the importance of the Yan'an Rectification Movement. He has used similar tactics to consolidate his power and wage ideological warfare to manipulate and control people's minds in China and around the world.

We argue that the Yan'an Rectification Movement was a massive conversion that turned the CCP from a violent *Lumpen peasantry* organization into a violent, cult-like organization through coercive and repressive methods and techniques of brainwashing and indoctrination. In essence, it made Mao the equal of Stalin. The CCP gave Mao "The Leader" status and whipped the Party into cultic conformity. It provided Mao with absolute power over the military, Party, government, and ideology. All Party members and cadres became Mao's tamed subjects. After the Yan'an Rectification Movement, the CCP possessed the characteristics of a cult: A leader with a unique and messianic mission, who held absolute authority over Party members.

Mao Zedong Thought was put into the CCP Constitution, elevating it to the highest authority and making it the CCP's guiding principle. It is the duty of every CCP member to study, understand, propagandize, and follow Mao Zedong Thought in his or her work.[30] Liu Shaoqi, who was Mao's deputy but later was killed by Mao during the Cultural Revolution, lauded Mao at the time: "Our Comrade Mao Zedong, not only the greatest revolutionary and statesman that China has ever known, but also the greatest theoretician and scientist that China has ever known, not only dared to lead the whole Party and the whole people in an earth-turning battle, but also had the highest theoretical literacy and the greatest theoretical courage."[31] With such praises, Mao completed his effort to secure his divinity. In the process, the Party formed a set of effective practices for political campaigns or mind-control and manipulation, which CCP leaders have used since then.

Mao also used Marxism–Leninism–Stalinism in the indoctrination campaign to build his personality cult. After examining the former Soviet secret archives, historians Alexander Pantsov and Steven Levine concluded that Mao was a loyal follower of Stalin.[32] Only after Stalin's death did Mao dare to deviate from the Soviet model with a more radical policy. In fact, Pantsov and Levine demonstrate that Stalin and the Comintern had been helping Mao consolidate power and build a personal cult within the CCP.[33] Mao's legitimacy came from the Soviet Union, as did his funding. Pantsov and Levine documented the CCP's dependence on Moscow for funding from 1921 through the early 1950s.[34] All Mao wanted at the time was to become "China's Stalin," as Hu Qiaomu who worked closely with Mao recalls.[35]

Pantsov and Levine's research reveals a critical trait of Stalin and Mao, or Communist Party leaders like them—that is, deception. According to Pantsov and Levine, the doctrine of Mao's new democracy, which is considered a key component of Mao Zedong Thought, actually came from Stalin. It was Stalin who made Mao accept the New Democracy Doctrine in the late 1930s and did not allow Mao to abandon it until Stalin's death in 1953. For geopolitical reasons, Stalin wanted to change tactics. He talked with Wang Ming and Kang Sheng in November 1937 before they returned to China, revealing to them his intention to deceive not only Chiang Kai-shek and the Chinese *bourgeoisie*, but also the Western *bourgeoisie*, fooling them into believing that the communist parties of all countries had abandoned violent revolutions against them. Stalin said the real purpose of the concept of a people's democracy was introduced to deceive the enemy.[36] Mao later wrote his book, *On New Democracy*, which the Yan'an Rectification Movement Committee announced as the most important fundamental theoretical work on Maoism and directed all cadres to study carefully and repeatedly. Before seizing power, Mao and the CCP promised they would pursue democracy, oppose one-party dictatorship, hold universal elections, and ensure inalienable civil rights, which tricked many Chinese people into believing and supporting them. In 1945, Huang Yanpei, a democratic party leader, asked Mao how he would avoid falling into the historical periodic pattern of the rise and fall of dynasties. Mao answered that the CCP had found a new way—democracy—to do just that.[37]

In his book, Gao details the process of the Yan'an Rectification and tells what happened between February 1942 and April 1945, the three years of an intensified campaign, until the CCP's Seventh Congress in 1945. According to Gao, the campaign went through three stages: First, rectification of incorrect styles of work; second, investigation of cadres; and third, the purge of counterrevolutionaries.[38]

Mao started the political campaign with some issues that appeared to be less serious—the Party's style of study; style in the Party's internal and external relations; and style of writing. But behind these styles, Mao directed the Party to fight against subjectivism and factionalism. These steps were intended to make CCP members obedient and loyal to Mao. He framed Wang Ming and others as "dogmatic" and said they did not know how to apply Marxism–Leninism to the Chinese situation, and that Wang and his supporters who studied in the Soviet Union had formed a faction within the Party in violation of Party discipline. Mao formed a three-person committee to lead the Party's study, appointing himself as the head and Liu Shaoqi and Kang Sheng as his deputies, and used the group to replace the Politburo.

Mao ordered all cadres to stop daily work and focus mainly on studying the indoctrination materials he prepared for the rectification. He also came up with many strict and thorough rules about how to conduct study sessions. In addition to a top-down organizational system in charge of the forced indoctrination, specific requirements included how many hours one must devote to study (two hours daily), how to divide people into groups, how they should take and keep study notes, and how to give regular tests and examinations. Mao insisted that taking notes was a requirement and the Party's iron discipline must be carried out. Mao said that only by taking notes could one think about and understand Marxism—though it was clear he meant Maoism.

Participants were instructed to constantly reflect on oneself, based on the study—so-called "self-criticism," which became a defining characteristic of Maoism. Mao required that during reading and discussion, cadres must reflect on their own work and thoughts, and on their entire life, to see if these were inconsistent with Mao's ideology—like confessing one's sins to obtain forgiveness from the Party. This self-examination or self-criticism had to be done in accordance with the conduct criteria set up in Mao's booklets. Everyone was required to be honest about their backgrounds, conduct, behaviors, and even their innermost thoughts, without reservation, and then to disclose them publicly.

In parallel, Mao demanded that people criticize each other, based on their self-reflection, to help purify their minds and correct any conduct inconsistent with

Mao's ideology. This was often done in so-called "self-criticizing and criticizing meetings," in which one person would confess his or her sins or shortcomings and the other participants would criticize or denounce him or her by pointing out what was missed or concealed to further expose the person.

At the campaign's initiation, Mao used a strategy called "lead the snake out of the hole," in which people were urged to freely give their views, comments, opinions, and complaints about the Party and its leaders. The study committee encouraged cadres to use big character posters to criticize Party leaders' working styles. Some people, such as Wang Shiwei, began to question and criticize the privileges and special treatment of high-ranking officials, particularly the hierarchy of the CCP's special supply system for its top echelon, which held down educated cadres and favored those with peasant backgrounds. This practice actually institutionalized the tradition of the peasant rebellion principle of "reward for merit," and makes today's CCP system the most strictly hierarchical in the world, with special status and treatment provided by one's rank. Wang also attacked the CCP's hiding behind the battle lines. He argued:

> Patriotic youths from the Kuomintang-ruled areas came to Yan'an with anti-Japanese enthusiasm but found that the ball in the CCP's Central Auditorium of Yan'an was held all night long, a scene of singing and dancing to extol the good times.[39]

Mao was furious and decided to use Wang Shiwei to usher in the second stage of the Rectification Movement—the great denunciation stage, in which those who criticized the Party and its leaders were denounced repeatedly. The CCP investigated cadres, establishing a dossier system to track everyone that the CCP continues to use today. During this second stage of rectification, Mao issued his notorious "Talks at the Yan'an Forum on Literature and Art," in which he demanded:

> Literature and art fit well into the whole revolutionary machine as a component part; they operate as powerful weapons for uniting and educating the people and for attacking and destroying the enemy, and they help the people fight the enemy with one heart and one mind.[40]

He insisted that CCP literature artists and writers must have a correct class stand, which was always the Party's. People with the correct stand should not sneer at the Party's shortcomings.[41] Since then, using art and literature to recruit members to the CCP's cause and brainwashing them has become a key component of the Party's ideological warfare. Any writing criticizing CCP's policies or its leaders is always considered to be counterrevolutionary. In 2014, Xi Jinping repeated Mao's view about art and literature. Xi believes these must be used to serve the "great rejuvenation" of the Chinese nation.[42] After many meetings denouncing him, Wang Shiwei was branded as a Trotskyist and a traitor and was expelled from the Party in October 1942. He was later decapitated, by order of CCP top leaders, and his body was thrown in a dry well.[43]

Mao used the Wang Shiwei incident to create an environment of terror to obtain forced fidelity from all cadres. He instructed the Party to pay attention to clearing up elements such as Wang Shiwei, and claimed there were hidden enemies everywhere in Yan'an. Mao fabricated that more than half of the intellectuals among cadres of the Central Committee, the Military Commission and the Border Region were "bad guys," such as the Trotskyists, the Kuomintang, and Japanese spies. On November 21 and 23, Mao attended a CCP senior cadre meeting, denouncing "some counterrevolutionary spies and Trotskyists using Party members as a cover" to carry out anti-Party activities.[44] He said the Rectification Movement should solve the problem of clarifying not only the proletarian and non-proletarian (half-hearted individuals), but also the revolutionary and counterrevolutionary (two-hearted individuals), and he demanded that "attention should be paid to the anti-spy struggle."[45] The meeting attendees decided to implement a re-registration of Party members and assigned a quota to purge traitors and spies, which accounted for 10 percent of Party members.[46]

This led to the second stage of the Rectification Movement—cadre review and investigation and interrogation, aimed at rooting out Wang Ming's supporters, under the cover of anti-factionalism within the Party, and imposing forced fidelity to Mao. The interrogation included self-examination and mass evaluation, and then the Party organization made a final assessment. It required Party members to give a fresh account of everything they had done without reservation. But it soon became violent. The movement targeted those who offered their comments about the Party or Party leaders in answering Mao's call. Struggle sessions—a form of public humiliation and torture that had been used during the Hunan peasants' movement against landowners—were held against people with "erroneous thoughts." In addition, struggle sessions were held to settle scores with Wang Ming, Zhou Enlai and other leaders who took "erroneous" lines in the past that diverged from those of Mao.[47]

Mao urged the use of torture to coerce confessions. According to the recollection of Chen Yuanfang, the United Front Work Minister of Jingbian County at that time, forced confessions were extracted through mental and physical torture, which were used alternately or together. Mental torture included seemingly endless interrogation of a suspect and the employment of all kinds of pressure, threats, and tricks, such as offers of better treatment and good food, and retainment of Party membership if he confessed. Physical torture included days and weeks of interrogations, sleep deprivation, making a suspect sit on the rack, or electrification or hot iron branding, and faked executions.

The hysterical confession rally was another way to extract confession. During these rallies, one by one, individuals were pushed to the stage. Their comrades denounced and humiliated them. As rally participants shouted deafening slogans, victims would admit that they were agents of the KMT or the Japanese. Those who refused to "confess" were tied up and dragged away to prison or a torture chamber. These confession rallies caused people to "panic to the extreme," Mao said. His confidant Ren Bishi said, "Confession rallies are an extremely serious war of nerves, in a sense more powerful for some people than any torture."[48]

The forced confessions resulted in several fake spy networks in Yan'an, which led to thousands of arrests and arbitrary killings. Some committed suicide to avoid torture, including the wife of Ke Qingshi, a CCP senior leader. According to CCP historical sources, by the end of December 1943, intellectuals in Yan'an numbered over 40,000; the book *Hu Qiaomu Remembers Mao Zedong* reveals that "within one year, from 1943 to 1944, 15,000 agents were cleared out of tiny Yan'an alone."[49] Mao's secretary, Li Rui, later found out from a KMT official's diary that the KMT had no informants in Yan'an, which made him realize that all were Mao's fabrication.[50]

As the Yan'an Rectification Movement reached its peak, Mao made his move to secure control of the CCP. On March 20, 1943, he assumed the position of Chairman of the Politburo and set up the Secretariat, which consisted of Liu Shaoqi, Ren Bishi, and Mao as chairman. Thus Mao granted himself the power to have the final say on issues discussed in the CCP, and made all CCP bases report to him personally. By the end of the Rectification, Mao controlled the Party, its ideology, military, and government.

The Rectification Movement produced practices or tactics for the CCP's political campaigns, including a forced thought-transformation system—study sessions, note taking, and examination. Self-criticism and public criticism ended all privacy; people exposed each other for non-Party conduct and remarks. Everyone's past was archived. The Party imposed political clearance, denounced people, and forced them to undergo confession rallies and torture.

According to Mao's former aide, Li Rui, Mao's "Anti-Little Broadcaster" (小广播) campaign effectively turned people into instruments of the Party. As a true totalitarian ruler, Mao wanted to know from where people got their information and who spread unofficial news—in other words, who said what to whom about him and the Party. So, he ordered each person to fill out the "little broadcaster" form regularly. The form was the equivalent of filing a report about any bad things said or heard about the Party and its leaders. If one failed to report and was reported by others, the person became a target for "rescue," which meant arrest, denouncement, or worse treatment. In the end, no one dared to think or speak freely.[51]

The control of information and of the press were key results that came out of the Rectification Movement. The CCP has termed this as control of the "holder of the pen." Mao and his propaganda chief Hu Qiaomu first cut off information flow from the outside world and then ensured that the Party commanded the press. Any printed words were to reflect Mao's views, essentially changing the news reporting function to that of being a manipulative tool of the Party. The Party's press and publications were to fabricate facts if the revolution required this. The propaganda department and supreme leader determined what should be reported, how soon it should be reported, and from which angle it should be reported. Media became a weapon to manipulate public opinion and combat the enemy. Like food and other privileges, news was released in accordance with an individual's rank under the CCP's hierarchy. Certain ranks could read pre-designated news. After the Rectification Movement, all the newspapers in the Yan'an area, except *Jiefang Daily*, essentially stopped publishing.[52]

Mao's tactics are exactly how tyrants for centuries have brainwashed followers and recruits—by creating terror and an environment of fear; applying peer pressure to overcome someone's doubt; creating a system of rewards and punishments; inducing a sense of powerlessness and dependency; isolating victims from the outside world; controlling information; exploiting people's weaknesses and need for community; and eliciting confessions by exploiting fear and guilt. All of these tactics were intended to create and maintain Mao's god-like image and absolute control. Mao clearly displayed dark personality disorders, and in subsequent political campaigns, he and other leaders employed these practices and tactics to achieve the Party's goals.

In our view, the driving force for Mao's fanaticism in the Yan'an Rectification is his imperial mentality and aspirations. Mao was a student of how Chinese emperors controlled people throughout Chinese history, as well as of Stalin's dictatorship. He believed as a would-be Chinese ruler, like previous emperors, he represented the supreme power and all must obey him absolutely. Through the Rectification, Mao became a *de facto* emperor, replacing divine imperial power from Heaven with self-claimed divine power authorized by the people. In Yan'an, he even tried to draw up a plan for his imperial court, according to veteran writer Ding Ling.[53] As Sun Yat-sen pointed out, the Chinese desire to be an emperor is the root cause of endless chaos in the country, the tragedy of comrades killing comrades, and the whole country's trapping in protracted wars against each other for years.[54] Before his death, Mao's political campaigns were to defend or expand his *de facto* absolute imperial power. So were his successors' campaigns, with varying degrees of success. In essence, the CCP's absolute leadership replaced the absolute power of Chinese monarchies. Thus, through the looking glass of imperial aspirations we can gain insight into China's politics in the past, as well as today.

2.1.3 Mao in Power: Land Reform and the Campaign against Counterrevolutionaries

After the CCP seized state power, Mao launched land reform campaigns, in which land forcibly taken from landowners was redistributed among peasants. Many tactics forged in the Hunan Peasant Movement, the Purge of the Anti-Bolshevik League, and the Yan'an Rectification Movement once again were employed. These included using the *Lumpen peasantry* to agitate peasants and involve them in rallies to denounce the Party's enemies and in violence, including torture and killings. According to the CCP's official account, beginning in the winter of 1950 and ending in 1953, the land reform confiscated and expropriated some 115 million acres and distributed them among 300 million peasants, freeing the peasants from paying 30 million tons of grain in rent to landowners.[55] Not only land but all other assets, properties, and household items were plundered.

Mao and the CCP could have carried out the land reform peacefully, such as through legislation and state policy. But characteristically, Mao insisted upon using violence. He first sent CCP teams to China's rural areas and divided peasants into different classes. Those who were labeled as landlords became targets for violence. "Dou Dizhu" (斗地主) means striking landlords literally, though some have translated it as "fight the landlords," which is not accurate because this was a state-launched, state-backed, one-sided infliction of mental and physical torture, pitting one group of people against the other. There was no way for landlords to fight back. Scholars believe that more than four million landowners were beaten to death, executed, or committed suicide.[56] As with the Yan'an Rectification Movement, the CCP ordered a quota for how many class enemies its organizations needed to uproot in the land reform, which was 10 percent of the total peasant population. Based on this quota, more than 30 million people were to be branded as "class enemies" and subdued. Later, the quota was modified to 3 percent, still producing at least nine million.[57]

In 1956, Liu Shaoqi, vice chairman of the CCP, explained why violent methods were required to carry out the land reform: To force the peasants into gaining the correct class consciousness by completely defeating the landlord class and isolating the rich peasant class politically. As a result, the peasants would closely follow the CCP.[58] Ironically, within a couple of years, the CCP took back the redistributed land from the peasants and formed people's communes for agriculture production. Even today Chinese peasants rent their land from the Party-state.

China's land reform was the largest property and asset redistribution in history. It also was the largest identification of people by class for political purposes, akin to the Third Reich's order for all Jews to wear the yellow Star of David as a badge of identification and isolation. China's landlord class and rich peasant class were considered to be enemies of the people and so must be watched closely and forced to reform through labor. Branding affected every aspect of the victim and his children for generations, thrusting them into the lowest caste of society. The Party-state officially sanctioned violence against these people, including extralegal killings.

Along with land reform, Mao launched the "Campaign to Suppress Counterrevolutionaries." Official rhetoric said this campaign would eliminate residual KMT opposition and suppress its supporters, but Mao took advantage of the outbreak of the Korean War to implement his mass killing program and create terror among the people so that no one dared to think about challenging the CCP's rule. Mao told Public Security Minister Luo Ruiqing, "Don't waste this opportunity. I'm afraid this is the only time to suppress counterrevolutionaries, and there will be no more. This is a once-in-a-lifetime opportunity. You must make good use of this capital."[59] Liu Shaoqi made similar remarks. The Korean War drew the world's attention away, and covered up China's domestic atrocities.

In 1951, Mao ordered all regions to carry out mass executions, particularly in big cities. He admonished city leaders for not carrying out killings severely and on a large scale, instructing them to do so without delay. Mao also gave arbitrary targets for killing. In a telegram, he told Shanghai Party officials that "it will be necessary to execute one or two thousand people in order to solve the problem this year."[60] Mao also told the head of the CCP South China Bureau in Guangdong Province, "You have already killed more than 3,700, which is good. Kill another 3,000 or 4,000. ... We can kill 8,000 or 9,000 people this year as a target."[61] Mao later set a quota to kill one-thousandth of the total population.

However, the final number of killings exceeded the original quota. According to Chinese government data from 1954, there were 2.62 million counterrevolutionaries arrested, of whom 712,000 were executed; 1.29 million were sentenced or sent to labor camps; 1.2 million were put under surveillance. Yin Shusheng, a former high-ranking public security official, has pointed out that data only reflected the numbers from the first stage of a three-stage campaign, which actually lasted for more than three years.[62] Therefore, the true number of people executed was probably much higher. Some estimates put the number of executions at one million to two million, or more.[63] Mao himself later said in the Lushan meeting that the CCP killed one million people during the campaign—and he claimed it was necessary because their deaths prevented a rightists' "rebellion," which was his classic mendacity.[64]

Importantly, most scholars miss the key point of this campaign by accepting the CCP's framing of it as counterrevolutionary rather than an effort by Mao to consolidate his power. A closer examination reveals that this slaughter happened in peacetime, and the so-called "counterrevolutionaries" were mostly employees or servicemen of the previous government, who surrendered because the CCP promised to forgive and forget their past conduct. Then the CCP broke its promise, rounded up and killed more than a half-million people in four months. The mass executions exceeded those of the civil war between the KMT and CCP.[65] Professor Guo Tingyu of the Free University of Berlin noted that about 3 million people who served in the Nationalist Army were executed, as were about 1.4 million KMT members who remained in mainland China.[66] In Sichuan, under Deng Xiaoping's leadership, the CCP killed all former KMT personnel above the position of head bailiff.[67]

The key is not just how many people were killed, but also why the CCP carried out this atrocity. We submit that the causes were a combination of the CCP's ideas of class struggle and ambition, which required the employment of *Lumpen peasantry* violence and cruelty. Like all totalitarian regimes, through mass killing, the Party can eliminate perceived potential enemies and, more importantly, create terror so that no one dares to oppose its dictatorship. CCP leaders' speeches reveal their intention. In 1950, Liu Shaoqi told police officials that "all counterrevolutionaries can be killed cleanly."[68] In 1951, Mao instructed,

"In many places, they are too fearful to kill counterrevolutionaries openly and with great fanfare. This situation must be changed immediately."[69] As a result, public trials and executions were held everywhere, with sentences handed down and executions carried out on the spot.

Scholar Hu Ping offers a more profound explanation of these gross human rights abuses. He contends:

> No ruler could have gone that far down the road of political persecution if only out of hatred, if only to preserve power, if only because of its ferocious and evil nature. It was the communist ideology that not only rationalized hatred, rationalized the selfish desire to maintain one's own power, and rationalized a vicious and evil nature, but also gave them a veneer of unparalleled sanctity. This is what creates unprecedented evil.[70]

After the land reform and the Campaign to Suppress Counterrevolutionaries, China's population lived in fear. As the CCP continued its political campaigns, the fear deepened. At the same time, favors, privileges and economic benefits were granted to CCP followers, and more promises were made to induce loyalty. All of this created Stockholm syndrome on a massive scale. Most Chinese developed positive feelings toward the CCP and willingly joined its cause.

One important lesson that we must learn from Mao's mass killings is that the CCP cannot be trusted. It may sincerely negotiate and make a promise, but whether it will keep the promise really depends on its political needs. If the CCP achieves the goal for which it made a promise, it will not hesitate to break the promise. China always insists that it means what it says, but in reality, that is never the case. Deception is deeply rooted in the Chinese ruling class and in Lenin's teachings. CCP leaders always appear dignified in form, but insincere in substance. This deception is often justified as "the unity of principle and flexibility"—as long as it serves the Party's fundamental interests.

The CCP's treachery and deception also can be demonstrated by its use of political campaigns to plunder the private sector after seizing state power in 1949. A founding goal of the CCP stipulated that the Party would "eliminate the private ownership of capitalists and confiscate the means of production, such as machinery, land, plants and semi-finished products, into social public ownership."[71] Before PLA insurgents were about to take over China in 1948, the CCP formed a strategy to achieve this goal by using public-private partnerships and buyouts to transition to socialist public ownership. But, at the same time, CCP representatives were dispatched to talk to capitalists and owners of private enterprises in major cities to encourage them not to flee China, promising that the Party would protect private ownership of national industry and commerce. Many believed the promise and stayed.[72]

But as soon as it seized state power, the CCP began to tighten its control of private enterprises, which then dominated China's industry and commerce. For example, in 1950, Chen Yun accelerated state control over the private sector in

Shanghai by placing all raw materials, capital, and sales channels under government control. In particular, Chen stepped up the collection of taxes and forced private business owners to buy public debts. Meanwhile, owners of private enterprises were to continue to pay workers' wages and were not allowed to close their factories. All cash of public enterprises was deposited in state banks, and loans to private banks and private enterprises were not allowed, which caused great hardship for the private sector, which lost the ability to run businesses.[73]

To survive the CCP's ruthlessness, there were some rent-seeking activities from Chinese capitalists, but on a limited scale. Mao used corruption as a pretext to launch the "Three-Antis Campaign" in 1951. The original motive, according to Chinese scholar Xu Lei, was the CCP's financial difficulties caused by the Korean War. Financial difficulties led to increased production and thrift, which evolved into anti-corruption, anti-waste, and anti-bureaucracy.[74] Although the campaign targeted the CCP's "corrupt cadres" who became too close with China's private business owners, it actually was aimed at collecting evidence of how private entrepreneurs corrupted their cadres and undermined the socialist economic order.

In 1952, Mao instructed the CCP that the main contradiction was between the working class and the national capitalists, and said the capitalists must be treated as a hostile class.[75] The "Five-Antis Movement" was ignited to demonize and persecute private business owners and industrialists on charges of bribery, tax evasion, theft of state property and economic information, and cheating on government contracts. Again, it employed methods of the Yan'an Rectification, to report and denounce one another, with confessions and rallies, public humiliation, and torture. Owners of private enterprises became a despised group. In just four months, 876 business owners in Shanghai jumped from buildings to their deaths. Some have estimated that in Shanghai alone, more than 10,000 capitalists died as the result of the campaign. Among them were China's indigenous industrialists such as Liu Hongsheng, then known as the "King of Coal," who had worked hard to build his business. Chen Yi, then mayor of Shanghai, even made fun of the wave of suicides by jokingly asking, "How many paratroopers have landed today?" in reference to those who jumped to their deaths.[76]

The extensive campaign affected a majority of China's capitalists and owners of private enterprises. According to statistics from more than 450,000 private industrial and commercial companies in nine major cities, including Beijing, Tianjin, and Shanghai, 76 percent of the total number were guilty of differing degrees of the "five crimes." All offenders were to pay "fines" for their crimes. In the end, the CCP plundered over 30 trillion yuan (old currency) from owners of private enterprises, equal to more than half of China's Korean War spending.[77] Chinese government data, published by the Party History Research Office of the CCP Central Committee and four other departments, show that more than 323,100 people were arrested, more than 20,000 were sentenced to death, and more than 280 committed suicide or "disappeared" during the Three-Antis and Five-Antis campaigns.[78] This is definitely an underestimated number, since there were many more industrialists and businessmen who were forced to commit suicide in Shanghai.

The campaign delivered a fatal blow to China's private sector. The CCP Soviet-style planned economy drove it out in its First Five-Year Plan, which began in 1953. Private enterprises and private capital were not allowed to participate in economic construction activities. Then the CCP adopted a policy of eliminating private ownership by using, restricting, and transforming capitalist industry and commerce, and gradually replacing private ownership with state ownership. Mao instructed his cadres that Marxists have no hearts, and they must make capitalism and small-scale private production extinct.[79] Mao came up with a scheme called "four horses to share the rich pastoral," to redistribute the earnings of private enterprises, dividing them among the state, enterprise provident fund, employee benefits and bonuses, and private shareholders. The private enterprise owners' dividend was reduced to 20.5 percent. These owners lived in fear after the Five-Antis Movement and "voluntarily" accepted Mao's plan.

The CCP began to forcibly add "public shares" to private enterprises and sent cadres to run and manage enterprises as state representatives. Mao still felt that the progress of taking over the private sector was too slow, and he demanded its acceleration. Soon the CCP devised a buy-out program with a fixed rate of interest, paying 5 percent interest to private shareholders for a certain period of time. The valuation and number of shares were determined by the Party-state; private owners had no say. In 1966, the CCP stopped paying interest and essentially completed nationalizing private enterprises. In the end, the Party-state robbed 810,000 business owners of their properties.[80] For example, the Kweichow Moutai Distillery was formerly known as the Ronghe Brewing House, the Chengyi Brewing House, and the Hengxing Brewing House. In 1952, Wang Binggan, the fourth-generation owner of Ronghe, was shot for allegedly possessing firearms and his company was confiscated and compensated with only 500 yuan, the supposed value of his fixed assets. The CCP took away the other two brewing houses for 15,000 yuan and 25,000 yuan, respectively, which were radical prices for such valuable assets. The three private enterprises were merged to form the state-run Kweichow Moutai Company.[81] Today the company valuation has reached $500 billion; it is one of the world's most valuable consumer-goods companies.[82]

Thus, CCP treachery enabled it to plunder private assets once again. Private enterprises disappeared within seven years of the CCP's seizure of state power. Another good example of how the CCP employed treachery and deception to trap its victims through mass political campaigns is the "Anti-Rightist Movement." In 1956–1957, Mao and the CCP invited all citizens, particularly China's intellectuals, to freely and openly air their views about the regime during the so-called "Hundred Flowers Campaign." When some reluctantly expressed themselves and criticized the CCP's governance, Mao framed them as madly attacking the CCP in order to overthrow the regime. A crackdown on Chinese intellectuals followed. Many were labeled as rightists; they were purged and sent to labor camps. The CCP acknowledges that 552,973 people were wrongly classified as rightists nationwide. When China opened up to the world and began to reform in 1978, it "corrected" 552,877 people from their rightist classification; only 96 people were not corrected. Even today, the CCP insists the campaign is necessary, but it is absurd for the CCP to use 96 rightists to justify the purge of more than a half-million people. In fact, declassified documents reveal the actual number of those classified as rightists was much higher—more than 4.6 million, with 3.2 million rightists and 1.4 million center-rightists. All of them were punished one way or another; 4,117 people were killed during the campaign, and many vanished in prisons or gulags.[83]

Scholars differ about why Mao initiated this purge, but what is unambiguous is that Chinese intellectuals had no intention of overthrowing the CCP. Framing intellectual rightists as attacking the CCP is Mao's conspiracy. At the beginning of the campaign, when Mao called on people to openly criticize the CCP, no one really came out to do so. Only after the CCP repeatedly harassed and lured them into what Mao termed this "overt scheme" did intellectuals and citizens begin to come forward. The CCP once again broke a promise not to retaliate against its critics, using their views to purge the dissent. In his study of the rightists' views, historian Naranarayan Das concludes that they were neither against socialism nor the CCP leadership, but merely pointed out that the Communist Party had deviated from its proclaimed ideals and goals.[84]

We argue that Mao perceived that his absolute authority was weakened after the Eighth National Congress of the CCP—the first session of which was held in 1956—in which Mao Zedong Thought was no longer mentioned in all official documents, including the CCP Constitution. This represented a major setback for Mao, even though it was his idea under pressure from the Soviets. Hu Qiaomu later explained that the Soviet Communist Party refused to recognize Mao Zedong Thought. The phrase was never mentioned by the Soviet press, and when it appeared in CCP documents, the Soviets would delete it. Because China needed aid from the Soviet Union, and kept unity with the Soviet Communist Party, Mao agreed to drop Mao Zedong Thought.[85]

But he clearly was not happy. Li Zhisui, Mao's physician, recalled that the resolutions of the Eighth CCP National Congress angered Mao, and he wanted to launch an attack on the Liu Shaoqi-controlled Party organization. Mao announced at the Second Plenum in November 1956 that a Party-wide rectification would begin in 1957.[86]

2.1.4 Mao and the Great Leap Forward, the Great Famine, and Cultural Revolution

Throughout his life, Mao was obsessed with power and absolute control, likely a clear display of obsessive-compulsive disorder (OCD), anxiety disorders, or personality disorders. He saw himself as China's Stalin and was keen on establishing his own cult of personality, which he achieved with the Yan'an Rectification

Movement. Mao's cult became a prominent feature of CCP culture until his death in 1976. Like Stalin, he enjoyed being worshiped as an all-powerful, all-knowing god-like leader. When Stalin died in 1953, Mao became paranoid about his own mortality, despite the fact that everywhere he went people greeted him with a wave of imperial chanting for a "10,000-year-long life." He offered to withdraw to the second line, meaning no daily management of Party-state affairs, but soon he felt that his absolute power was weakened. Liu Shaoqi controlled the Party organization, which concerned Mao.

Mao again employed the Rectification tactics to ensure his control. He explained at the beginning of the Great Proletarian Cultural Revolution (1966–1976) in October 1966 that the first-line and second-line division arrangement made after Stalin's death had created many "independent kingdoms."[87] No doubt, this was Mao's primary motive, rather than rooting out revisionists in the Party, or counter-attacking the rightists' attempt to overthrow the CCP rule.[88] Mao often used the "one stone, many birds" approach. As the leader of the *Lumpen peasantry*, Mao despised and distrusted intellectuals and used them as scapegoats to fit his style. But the key was to keep his cult of personality and absolute power intact.

The Anti-Rightists Campaign put Mao back in the driver's seat, which greatly enlarged his cult of personality and directly led to the two greatest disasters in the PRC's history—the Great Leap Forward (1958–1962) and the Cultural Revolution. The origins of the Great Leap Forward are found in Mao's second trip to the Soviet Union. In November 1957, during the Moscow Conference, Mao proposed the strategic concept of "surpassing Britain and catching up with the United States" within 15 years.[89] To achieve this, he launched the Great Leap Forward campaign. He wanted China to move with the speed of "one day is equal to 20 years." He started the all-population steel-making movement to double China's iron and steel production in 1957; everything else was to yield to this priority.

By the end of 1958, 100 million people were involved in steel production, accounting for two-fifths of the country's working population at the time. Millions of backyard furnaces were built across the country. Trees were chopped down, iron was scraped from everywhere, and skilled and strong workers were moved to steel making. Local cadres were fearful of the Anti-Rightist Campaign and competed to fulfill or over-fulfill quotas and fake production numbers. Little of the steel made was actually usable, and the environment was badly damaged in the process—crops rotted in fields, contributing to the Great Chinese Famine from 1959 to 1961.[90]

To boost agricultural production through public ownership and large-scale organization, Mao took the land back from Chinese peasants by forcing them to form people's communes, similar to Soviet collective farms. Previously allowed household plots used to supplement food supplies were banned under these communes. The CCP central government controlled agricultural production and set high production quotas for local leaders to fulfill.

Again, local officials, fearful of being labeled as rightists, often chose to over-fulfill quotas and report faked grain production. They competed with each other in a so-called "Sputnik launch" to see who could achieve the highest crop yield. It was so named because the Soviets put the first artificial satellite, Sputnik, into orbit at the time, which was considered the highest achievement for all socialist countries. "Rice Sputnik," "wheat Sputnik," and many other "Sputniks" were launched. The highest mu (Chinese acre, six mu = one acre) yield of wheat was 4,293 kg in Qinghai, and the highest mu yield of rice was 65,217.5 kg in Guangxi, over 100 times more than normal crop yields.[91] It was done by removing shoots of grain from various fields and carefully transplanting them. This absurd exaggeration was widely spread at the encouragement of Mao and the CCP's propaganda apparatus, resulting in what later was called the "illusion of superabundance" (浮夸风). Mao concluded that the Soviet theory of "Soviet rule plus electrification" meant that communism was outdated and that, with the Chinese invention of the People's Commune experiment, China probably would enter communism earlier than the Soviet Union. China would surpass Britain and catch up with the United States in just three to five years.[92] The CCP even issued a document informing its members that China had entered the communist society, but to avoid being jealous of other socialist countries, it must keep it confidential.

To race into a communist society, the communes set up 3.4 million "communal kitchens" where everyone was to eat instead of at home. Food was prepared for free, without limitation. The government ordered laborers and assets of production teams for its use without compensation. Over-reported grain production and fake high crop yields meant that the government greatly increased grain expropriation and purchase under the "state monopoly of the purchase and marketing of grain." Mao needed the increased revenue from agricultural products to support his military industrial expansion. There were floods and droughts as well. All these unfortunate events triggered the deadliest famine in China, perhaps the greatest man-made disaster in history.

The government expropriated and requisitioned "surplus" grain, based on artificially inflated grain production numbers. Communal kitchens took the peasants' grain away, along with their kitchen ware. Soon these kitchens had no food to provide, and the peasants had no grain at home. The great famine began.

The death toll was staggering. The CCP never published an official number. *The Seventy Years of the Communist Party of China*, edited by Hu Sheng, mentioned for the first time that "the total population of the country in 1960 was 10 million less than that of the previous year."[93] The 1995 China Disaster Report, published by China Statistics Press and compiled by the National Bureau of Statistics and the Ministry of Civil Affairs, indicated that China's unnatural death rate in 1960 was around ten million. In 2011, an official publication of the *History of the Chinese Communist Party* again claimed that, because the birth rate substantially decreased and the death rate significantly increased, official statistics showed the country's population in 1960 was ten million fewer people than in the previous year.[94] The data are only for one year, but the famine lasted for three years, and the statistics failed to mention how many died of starvation.

The research of Yang Jisheng, a former *Xinhua News Agency* reporter, concluded that between 1958 and 1962, 36 million people died of starvation in China.[95] Historian Frank Dikötter's study showed as many as 45 million people died as a result of the famine.[96] Li Chengrui, former director of China's National Bureau of Statistics, estimated the death toll at about 22 million.[97] The true number may be never known, but a massive number of deaths caused by deliberate deprivation of food is an indisputable historical fact, a crime against humanity. The tragedy in Xinyang district can demonstrate this point. The first people's commune was set up with great enthusiasm there. In 1959, the grain production was 50 percent lower than in 1958, only 1 billion kilograms (kg), but it was falsely reported as 3.6 billion kg. As a result, the government requisitioned 18 percent more grain than in the previous year. Much of the requisitioned grain was taken through violence carried out by CCP cadres and their militia, who arrested more than 10,000 people. An estimated 700 people died in prison or detention. The peasants were left with only 50 kg of grain for the whole year, enough for roughly three months. The CCP later admitted that 500,000 people died "unnaturally" in Xinyang, but the actual number was much higher. China's then-Vice Premier Li Xiannian and Tao Zhu, the first secretary of the Central and Southern Bureau of the Communist Party, went to Xinyang on November 12, 1960, to investigate what happened. Five months later, Tao said, "I think we should stop counting the number of deaths; it is already more than 1 million."[98] At the time, state grain warehouses and depots in the region were full of grain requisitioned from surrounding areas, but the government refused to provide relief for the starving population. Cannibalism occurred.[99] By any standard, this was mass murder, not a well-meaning mistake. Mao and other CCP leaders knew that their policies caused and sustained the famine.

Afterward, Mao again withdrew from day-to-day Party leadership. But he never admitted his crimes and blamed rightists for opposing his policies. Mao soon perceived that his absolute authority was diminished, and increasingly he felt left out. He became a figurehead, which triggered his suspicion and discontent with Liu Shaoqi, the successor he had designated. He began several political campaigns to strengthen his authority and cult of personality.

The Great Cultural Revolution was the most significant of these campaigns, and it led to another major disaster in the country. Mao's confidant, Hu Qiaomu, said that when the Soviet Communist Party criticized Stalin at its Twentieth Congress, this deeply irritated Mao.

> In order to prevent China's Khrushchev, big and small, from rising up later and whipping his corpse, Mao decided to preempt and root out those who opposed his personal worship, those who "had rebellious bones in the back of their heads," those who had opposed him before, those who had not behaved obediently enough, and even those who he thought

their achievements overshadowed his, and those who didn't look right, and all of them, regardless of their positions, must be treated as "sleeping Khrushchev" and he was prepared to eliminate them in stages and batches. ... During the Cultural Revolution, his cult of personality rose to its peak.[100]

Mao once again employed the tactics he used in Yan'an. On May 16, 1966, he ordered the Cultural Revolution to begin, to purge bourgeois representatives who had infiltrated the CCP and society in an attempt to restore capitalism. Mao wanted to prevent the "sleeping Khrushchev" from seizing his power. He formed the Central Cultural Revolution Group (CCRG) and appointed his wife, Jiang Qing, to control it. In August 1966, Mao removed Liu Shaoqi as his successor, replacing him with Marshal Lin Biao as he reshuffled the CCP leadership. Mao told young people that revolution is no crime, that to rebel is justified, and he called upon them to bombard the *bourgeoisie* headquarters. Soon students from colleges, high schools, and even elementary schools organized themselves as Mao's Red Guards.

At Mao's and the CCRG's encouragement, the Red Guards first targeted their teachers and principals by holding denouncing rallies. They tortured their victims. Since the young people were indoctrinated by the CCP's violent ideology, they moved rapidly. Within a few weeks, the Red Guards had killed 1,772 schoolteachers in Beijing alone.[101] Beijing city later re-estimated 10,275 were killed during the terror of the Red August. The violence quickly spread throughout society. Any non-communist element became a target—former landlords, employees of KMT governments, rightists, religious believers, intellectuals, capitalist roaders who were CCP officials were framed as pulling the revolution in a capitalist direction. Then they turned on each other. Mao sent his army to crack down on factions he disliked. Liu Shaoqi died in the persecution, and in 1971, Lin Biao was killed in a plane crash while fleeing to the Soviet Union. Many more innocent people were killed, committed suicide, or were sent to prisons and labor camps.

As with other incidents, the exact death toll is unknown. Widely cited numbers include Marshal Ye Jianying's estimate that 100 million were persecuted and 20 million killed. The research of Su Yang at the University of California showed at least 750,000 to 1.5 million people were killed in rural China—the same number of people were disabled through torture—and at least 36 million people experienced varying degrees of political persecution. The CCP History Research Office estimated more than 4.2 million people were imprisoned, more than 1.7 million people died unnaturally, over 135,000 people were executed as counterrevolutionaries, about 237,000 people died in factional fights, and more than 7 million were injured and disabled.[102] Jin Zhong, a Hong Kong reporter, interviewed a CCP insider and obtained official data showing that 3.42 million were killed, 0.55 million were missing, and 113 million people were persecuted.[103]

2.1.5 After Mao: Deng Xiaoping, Jiang Zemin, and Hu Jintao

The Cultural Revolution ended in 1976 when Mao died. Through an internal power struggle, Deng Xiaoping got the upper hand and became the CCP's paramount leader. He endorsed opening up China and reforming its economic policy. Many in the West got the wrong impression that Deng had ended the practice of Mao-style political campaigns. In fact, he did not. As China opened up, Western ideas and lifestyles also were introduced. As early as 1980, Deng warned about "bourgeois liberalization" and directed the CCP to oppose Western ideas and stop the tendency to worship capitalism and advocacy for bourgeois liberalization.[104]

In 1983, Deng launched a political campaign to "remove spiritual pollution." In October that year, he alerted the Party that it was still necessary to criticize "leftist" views on ideology, but the top priority on the ideological front was correcting rightist views and ending liberal tendencies.[105] In 1986, students in at least 11 cities took to the streets to protest against government corruption and demand democracy. Like Mao, Deng ousted his deputy Hu Yaobang and launched an anti-bourgeois liberalization campaign to get rid of Western liberalism. Because many within the Party were still fearful of the Cultural Revolution, they resisted a widespread purge. New Party chief Zhao Ziyang managed to end the campaign by expelling a few leading dissidents from the Party.

However, a violent campaign against bourgeois liberalization happened under the cover of law. In 1983, the CCP initiated the "Strike Hard Campaign" against so-called criminals who had disrupted public order and social stability, but the campaign included those who enjoyed a Western style of life. Deng claimed that this special period called for special measures and he ordered a strike on "criminal offenders," to punish them harshly and quickly. The campaign lasted for three years, resulting in many arrests, imprisonments, and executions.[106]

The campaign employed the tactics used during Mao's era to create terror. There was a quota for killings, which the CCP hid behind the law. For example, the CCP quickly amended its criminal law to add over a dozen crimes punishable by death, including hooliganism. In 1984, Amnesty International estimated that tens of thousands of arrests and several thousand executions took place in the first three months of the campaign.[107] Chinese government data show that in the first stage of the campaign, over 1 million people were detained and arrested, and 24,000 people were executed. The entire campaign ended with a total of 1.8 million arrested, 1.7 million sentenced, and 321,000 labor-reformed.[108] Some scholars believe that as many as 960,000 were executed. Many people were wrongly killed or imprisoned for minor offenses or for having a Western lifestyle.

Jiang Zemin initiated the second "Strike Hard" campaign in 1996 to prepare for Hong Kong's return and the CCP's 15th National Congress. More than 420,000 people were convicted of various crimes; more than 300,000 were sentenced and 260,000 received prison terms of five years or more, life imprisonment, or the death penalty.[109] Subsequently, he launched a third campaign, which claimed to close more than 5 million so-called "criminal" cases. In 2010, the CCP launched the fourth such campaign under Hu Jintao. In 2014, Xi Jinping also launched a "Strike Hard" campaign against Xinjiang Uyghurs under the name of anti-separation, anti-terrorism, and religious extremism, resulting in mass arrests, imprisonments, and executions.

The CCP copied the political campaign method of the Soviet Communist Party but added cruel Chinese characteristics to it. In the 100 years since its founding, the CCP has carried out more than 100 political campaigns to create fear and indoctrinate people to form a giant cult. The key is to use class struggle and force people to inflict mental and physical pain or death against each other to secure conformity and achieve the leader's goal.

For the CCP, violence is inherent. Deng himself was a victim of Mao's political campaigns, but he ordered the purge of many others. It was the same for Liu Shaoqi. It is reported that Deng's last words were "no more political campaigns," but when he was China's paramount leader, Deng not only carried out at least five nationwide political campaigns but also ordered the PLA to massacre hundreds or even thousands of pro-democracy protesters in 1989. Deng's notorious remark that "200 deaths will bring 20 years of stability for development" reflects the CCP's violent nature, no matter how hard it tries to hide.[110] The CCP never examines itself thoroughly to find what is wrong internally; it always blames foreign hostile forces for its problems. After the Tiananmen Massacre, Deng accused the U.S. of prompting the pro-democracy protests. His subsequent anti-peaceful evolution campaign lasted for years.[111] Yet, in perhaps Deng's most significant act, in the wake of the Tiananmen Square Massacre, Deng stressed on economic reform and development while continuing to crack down the dissent and clean up Western influence. In doing so, he was able to minimize the West's reaction and prevent the West from acting to overthrow the CCP and advance the cause of Chinese democracy. That act of cunning statesmanship kept the CCP in power and laid the foundation for China's tremendous growth in power to the point where it is now a rival to the U.S. That China could be a peer of the U.S. would have been unthinkable in 1989 and reveals Deng's unscrupulous strategic genius.

Jiang Zemin, the third-generation CCP leader, initiated an anti-religion campaign during this tenure at the suggestion of Chen Yun, another veteran CCP leader, after the collapse of the Soviet Union and Eastern Bloc countries. Chen believed that uncontrolled regions brought about the downfall. Jiang first repressed Tibetan Buddhism, Uyghur Islamism, and Christianity, and then launched a brutal assault on Falun Gong, a Chinese spiritual movement. Falun Gong is an offshoot of *qigong* (气功) exercise, a traditional breathing meditation for self-cultivation and healing. At the beginning, the Chinese government helped to promote Falun Gong and many CCP cadres participated as a health care measure. It had more than 70 million practitioners in the 1990s, even though founder Li Hongzhi's teaching was considered controversial. Jiang's anti-religion campaign gradually expanded to *qigong* groups, which increased the tension between the CCP and Falun Gong. In April 1999, an article criticizing

Falun Gong as being superstitious and harmful for youths triggered more than 10,000 sit-in demonstrations on sidewalks outside Zhongnanhai, the compound of the CCP leadership. Jiang decided to crack down on the group because he perceived the large size of organized religious groups as a security risk to the regime. As a result, millions of Falun Gong practitioners were rounded up, sent to thought-transformation camps, imprisoned, tortured, or killed. According to the World Organization to Investigate the Persecution of Falun Gong, the CCP killed about one million people and harvested many victims' organs for profit.[112] The persecution is one of the worst campaigns that mobilized the whole Party and society, and it has been ongoing for 22 years.

Hu Jintao, a fourth-generation CCP leader, told the Party that it no longer should *zheteng* (折腾), meaning that it should avoid self-inflicted mistakes brought on by political campaigns and movements. But he also launched five political campaigns to ensure CCP ideology remained and continued Jiang's anti-religion and Deng's anti-peaceful evolution campaigns. During his tenure, Hu also persecuted Falun Gong and intensified the CCP's suppression of dissent under the name of maintaining societal stability and building a harmonious society.

In 2008, peaceful demonstrations broke out in Tibet to commemorate the Tibetan 1959 uprising. Chinese security forces used force on the peaceful protesters, and the clashes resulted in over a hundred dead. Thousands disappeared.[113] In 2009, an inter-ethnic clash took place between the Han Chinese and the Uyghurs in Urumqi, the capital of Xinjiang, which resulted in violence. The government used armed police to crack down on Uyghurs, and the official death toll was 197 people.[114] The actual number likely was much higher. Thousands were arrested, imprisoned, or "disappeared," and some were executed. After the incident, Hu launched a Strike Hard Campaign and escalated the suppression of Uyghurs under anti-terrorism and religious extremism rules, which led to systemic repression of Xinjiang Muslims.

Xi Jinping, the fifth CCP leader, has fully inherited Mao's treachery, including his political campaign methods. Since assuming power in 2012, Xi has conducted over a dozen nationwide campaigns, which we examine in the next chapter. Xi's violent approach drives him to be aggressive and brutal in dealing with perceived regime security risks. Like Mao, Xi displays dark personality traits and he copies Mao's cultic practices to gain absolute control of China and its people. A good example is the mass detention of two million Muslims in Xinjiang internment camps or thought-transformation centers in an attempt to eliminate religion or any alternative ideology. In addition, Xi has carried out forced sterilizations, rapes, torture, forced labor, and other gross human rights abuses in the region. The U.S. government and a few other democracies have rightly determined that Xi's ordered atrocities in Xinjiang constitute genocide. In fact, this is not the first time the CCP has committed genocide against ethnic groups, which we discuss in the next section.

Another often ignored CCP mass murder is its birth control policy, which also has all the necessary elements of genocide. Mao mimicked the Soviet Union, urging people to have more children, but in the early 1970s he changed his mind and wanted to restrict births. Deng followed Mao's policy and implemented China's infamous one-child policy. Both Jiang and Hu intensified the enforcement of Deng's policy, stipulating that the regime must approve when citizens can marry and have a child. Unlike Mao's naked violence, the post-Mao CCP often passes laws to cover its atrocities. The Party-state's constitution says that birth control is the duty of Chinese citizens. In practice, forced IUDs, sterilizations, abortions, induced births, substantial fines, and other abuses frequently take place. In some cases, CCP birth control officials carry out late-term abortions—as late as nine months. Even if the baby is alive when aborted, medical personnel will use various methods to kill him or her, because the parents do not have a government-issued birth permit. China has acknowledged that, as of 2019, it has killed 400 million babies through its birth control enforcement.[115] This mass murder not only has damaged the health and lives of many people, but also inflicted deep psychological injuries, with tragic effects on Chinese families and society.

Evidence shows that the CCP is a politicidal, genocidal, or democidal regime, as political scientist and scholar of mass killings R.J. Rummel described it.[116] In absolute figures, the CCP is a bigger mass murderer than Hitler or Stalin—in fact, the worst in all of history. The CCP's domestic politics of violence, inhumanity, and ambition for perpetual and absolute control ensures that any China-centered world order is the greatest danger to the free world. The rhetoric of peace-loving, common prosperity, and a shared future is "all mouth and no trousers," as the Chinese say. The CCP's history of foreign policy and practice can predict what it will do if it becomes the dominant world superpower. In the following section, we examine China's past behaviors in international affairs to argue that the CCP's external agenda is an extension of the internal.

2.2 Communist China's Hegemonic Expansion Is Innate Because of Its Ideology

Maoist ideology and the nature of the CCP mean that it must continue to push for proletarian revolution worldwide. The great historic mission of the CCP "liberating all mankind" cannot be accomplished without continuing the revolution elsewhere in the world. Thus, its hegemonic expansion is innate. The leaders may change, but the essence of the Party remains the same—and is built into Communist China's DNA. Xi's latest nationwide political campaign to return to the CCP's founding principles and original mission, and his global initiatives demonstrate the point. We consider six issues that document the CCP's historical expansion.

2.2.1 Communist China's Support of World Revolution

The CCP's support of revolutions, principally in the Third World during the Cold War, is the first issue. In 2009, when Xi was vice president of China, he spoke at the Chinese Embassy in Mexico City to the staff and some Chinese Mexican elites, claiming,

> In the midst of international financial turmoil, China was still able to solve the problem of feeding its 1.3 billion people, and that was already our greatest contribution to humankind, but some foreigners with full bellies and nothing better to do engage in finger-pointing at us.

He went on: "First, China does not export revolution; second, it does not export famine and poverty; and third, it does not mess around with you. So, what else is there to say?"[117]

But Xi clearly was duplicitous. China does exactly those things. In the 1960s and 1970s, China trained Mexican Communist guerrilla fighters aiming to launch a revolutionary war in the country and appointed Xiong Xiaohui, a spymaster, to be its first ambassador to lead the effort. The CCP's open support of communist revolutions in the world lasted until the early 1980s. Now China does not openly advocate for revolution, and even has promised not to export the China model, but it still claims that the model points the world in the right direction and that the world should build upon a China-centered new order of "community of common destiny for mankind." Xi uses multiple approaches, such as the BRI, to replace Mao's armed struggle, but the aim remains essentially the same: World dominance. Because of its deceptive nature, Xi's subtle approach may be more dangerous than Mao's. An analysis of the CCP's past support of world revolutions can shed light on Xi's scheme for world dominance.

The CCP was founded and financed by the Soviet Union and directed under Stalin through the Comintern, or Third Communist International. The CCP's first constitution made it clear that it must carry out an armed revolution and act in solidarity with the Comintern. The Comintern's goal was to "struggle by all available means, including armed force, for the overthrow of the international *bourgeoisie* and the creation of an international Soviet republic as a transition stage to the complete abolition of the state."[118] This is based on what Marx and Lenin believed in—world revolution. However, in practice, Lenin advocated for taking the initiative to create favorable conditions for revolutions rather than passively waiting for strategic opportunities to arrive. In other words, Lenin promoted exporting revolution globally under so-called "proletarian internationalism," which holds that all communist revolutions are a single, global communist revolution. After one country wins communist victory, it has a duty to spread revolutions around and help struggling comrades in other parts of the world until they all win victory over capitalism, imperialism, and the *bourgeoisie*. Exporting revolution is a communist's obligation.

In 1960, the CCP passed a resolution at its Ninth Plenum stipulating that supporting the struggle of oppressed nations and peoples against imperialism is its internationalist duty. In August 1965, China published a long article by

Mao's designated successor, Lin Biao, titled "Long Live the Victory of the People's War," in which he stated: "Socialist countries should rightly consider it their communist duty to support the revolutionary struggles of the people in Asia, Africa, and Latin America."[119] Such ideological thinking is still stuck with Chinese communists.

On the eve of the CCP's seizure of state power, Mao dispatched his deputy, Liu Shaoqi, secretly to visit Moscow. During the visit, Stalin directed the CCP to take on more obligation in the international revolutionary movement, saying there should be a division of labor between the CPSU and CCP—that is, China would focus on supporting revolutions in colonial and semi-colonial countries and the East, and the Soviet Union would concentrate on the West.[120]

The CCP took Stalin's instruction as an imperial decree. A month after the PRC was established, China held an international workers' union conference, in which Liu Shaoqi urged delegates from other countries to follow the "China path"—the United Front, Communist Party's leadership, and armed struggle— and launch revolutions. Liu asserted this model worked for the colonies and semi-colonies, and the key was to build revolutionary armies. Mao later explained: "It didn't matter, either the Soviet Path or the Chinese Path; isn't the October Revolution all about to fight? What path? Fight is the path."[121]

According to He Fang, a senior CCP official working closely with Zhang Wentian, a former top CCP leader and foreign minister, Mao believed the world was about to reach the peak of proletariat revolutions. Mao famously remarked: Either the war triggers revolutions or the revolutions stop the war. Mao therefore made the CCP's foreign policy focus one of launching the world revolution and waging revolutionary wars in Asia, Africa, and Latin America. The CCP at that time believed that imperialist power and control in these regions were the weakest, and proletariat revolution was likely to succeed. China would first take Southeast Asia, then Asia, and use the region as the revolution center and spread revolution across the world.

He Fang recalls that in the 1950s, China participated in a fund in Bucharest to support the world revolution. The Soviet Union gave the most money to the fund, followed by China. The Communist Party in countries that have not seized state power and have no income depends on this fund's financial aid to carry out activities.

During the Cultural Revolution, Mao instructed the Party that all of China's work must focus on waging an early war, war at a grander scale, and a nuclear war. Mao further instructed the CCP:

> We in China have become not only the political center of the world revolution, but we must also become the military and technology center for the world revolution, to give them weapons. Now we can give them weapons openly; that is, inscribed Chinese weapons (except for some special areas); that is, to openly support, to become the arsenal of the world revolution.[122]

Marshal Lin Biao, on behalf of Mao and the CCP, made three critical points in 1965: First, world revolutionary conditions have matured. Second, Asia–Africa–Latin America should be the regions where the communists launch the revolution and use these "rural areas" to encircle the Western world. Third, it was entirely natural for China to export revolution.[123]

Thus, the CCP had been "exporting revolutions" at a great cost. In addition to training guerrillas, supplying weapons, and sending combatants to subvert legitimate governments, it also provided financial support to incite revolutions and insurgencies. Most of these activities were secretive. In 1973, the CCP's support of the world revolution cost about 7 percent of state spending. From 1950 to the end of 1964, China's foreign aid amounted to RMB 10.8 billion, equivalent to 27 million workers' entire year's wages. The CCP even let the Chinese people tighten their belts and die of starvation in order to export revolution. According to declassified documents of the Chinese Foreign Ministry, during China's Great Famine, the CCP shipped tons of grain to support the world revolution. For example, 10,000 tons of rice went to Guinea, 15,000 tons of wheat went to Albania, and China provided 2.36 billion yuan to support foreign insurgents. The money could buy enough grain to save millions of lives.[124]

In the 1950s, China trained revolutionary leaders in about 18 African countries, provided financial support, and supplied arms to them, and sent them back to their countries to launch revolutions.[125] But Communist China's focus was Southeast Asia. It incited and launched armed insurgencies in Malaysia, Vietnam, Laos, Cambodia, Indonesia, Thailand, Burma, Singapore, and the Philippines. The CCP not only supported them materially, with money and weapons, but also provided military advisers, radio stations, and other equipment. The CCP trained and armed mass killers such as Kim Il-sung, Ho Chi Minh and Pol Pot, and so contributed to the loss of millions of innocent lives.

For example, in the 1950s, the CCP attempted to launch a revolution in Cambodia and its embassy in Phnom Penh to direct Cambodian communists even though it kept friendly relations with the Sihanouk government. In 1952 and 1957, Pol Pot made two secret trips to China for training and study of Mao Zedong's military strategy. In November 1965, Pol Pot went to Beijing for a third time to search for "the truth of the revolution." During his three-month training in Beijing, CCP leaders such as Chen Boda, Kang Sheng, and others taught Pol Pot violent ideology and methods such as cleansing the class ranks.[126]

The CCP provided ideology, arms, and money to support the Khmer Rouge. In 1970 alone, China provided weapons that could arm a 30,000-man army.[127] With China's help, the Khmer Rouge quickly grew from a few hundred men to an 80,000-man army. It seized state power in April 1975. Immediately, it began to drive more than two million people in Phnom Penh to rural areas, and killed tens of thousands of innocent people in the process. Mao praised Pol Pot during his visit in June 1975. Mao told Pol Pot that the Khmer Rouge had figured out a better way than China to carry out a revolution. Mao said it would not be possible for China to do what the Khmer Rouge did to move the entire population out of Phnom Penh within a few days. Mao told him: "We approve of what you do. Much of your experience is better than ours. China is not qualified to criticize you. ... You are basically correct."[128] In 1975, China gave $2 billion in interest-free loans and $40 million in "gifts" to support the Khmer Rouge's genocidal rule.[129] However, within three years, eight months, the Khmer Rouge had purged its own comrades in the name of cleansing the ranks nine times, and, in the course of its disastrous misrule, slaughtered 1.5–3 million people. According to Chinese government data published in the International Statistical Yearbook 1995, Cambodia's population plummeted by a third during the Khmer Rouge's time in power.[130]

Malaysia is another example of China's exporting communist revolution. The predecessor of the Malaysian Communist Party (MCP) was the overseas branch of the CCP, established in the 1920s, and most of its members were of Chinese origin. Thus, the Party was always under CCP command and the CCP appointed its leadership. According to Chin Peng's memoir, when the MCP was about to give up its armed struggle to become a legitimate party by entering into negotiations with the authorities in 1955, Mao told Chin Peng and other MCP leaders that "the word 'surrender' cannot be found in the communist diction-ary," and warned that if they surrendered to the enemy, they could never hold their heads up in front of others. The MCP returned to the jungle to continue its armed revolution in 1957. In 1961, Deng Xiaoping demanded that the MCP not give up its military struggle, and as the revolutionary climax was about to sweep across Southeast Asia, the MCP was to make good use of this moment and step up its military struggle. Both Mao and Deng promised to provide whatever aid the MCP needed. The revolution went on, resulting in over 10,000 deaths. Chin Peng later apologized for killing innocent people.

Mao urged the leaders of the Communist Party of Laos, Burma, and Vietnam to recruit ethnic minorities in China to fight, because they were very capable fighters.[131] Mao also demanded that the Laotian Communist Party send troops into Thailand to spread revolution. In Southeast Asia, most of China's aid went to Vietnam and Cambodia. As soon as Ho Chi Minh took power, China provided weapons, ammunition, other military equipment, and medical supplies. The CCP trained Vietnamese troops in China and sent a military advisory team to Vietnam. For more than three years thereafter, China provided Vietnam with military supplies and assisted the Central Committee of the Viet Cong in organizing important campaign operations. Mao often personally reviewed battle deployments and gave instructions on battle plans.

The CCP wanted to spread the war to Laos and Cambodia to help "liberate" both countries, and the advisory team went to Laos to assist with operational command. From 1962 to 1966, China provided Vietnam with 270,000 guns, more than 540 artillery pieces, more than 200 million rounds of bullets, more than 900,000 rounds of artillery shells, more than 700 tons of explosives, 200,000 sets of uniforms, more than 4 million meters of cloth, and mosquito nets, rub-ber shoes, side dishes, and communication equipment. China entered Vietnam with 23 detachments of more than 320,000 people, including air defense combat troops, railway troops, national defense engineering construction troops, and road construction troops.[132] This armed revolution, incited and supported by Communist China, ended as a disaster. Rummel's mid-range estimate places total deaths in the Vietnam War at 2.4 million from 1954 to 1975.[133]

Communist leaders in China believed that with so many Chinese in Southeast Asia, they could export communism and change the political orientation of Southeast Asia. China's push for a communist revolution in Indonesia also ended with tragedy and mass murder of the Chinese. In the international communist camp at the time, the Indonesian Communist Party was a pro-China, anti-Soviet faction. In the first half of the 1960s, the Indonesian Communist Party used Indonesian leader Sukarno's pro-communist stance to establish a united front to gain strength and momentum. But Mao was dissatisfied with the delay in carrying out armed struggle. So, in 1965, when right-wing military forces suppressed the Indonesian Communist Party with hundreds of thousands of Party members and killed left-wing activists, Mao was happy, saying this was a good thing because the Indonesian Party had to go into the jungles to fight, which it did. Internally, he made it clear: "Don't think that the Indonesian revolution has gone bad," according to Yang Kuisong of Peking University.[134]

Despite the setback, China became even more aggressive in supporting the Communist Party in Thailand, Malaya, Burma, and other countries to establish armed forces and revolutionary bases during the Cultural Revolution. In Burma, most communists were Chinese. As early as 1951, China trained a group of more than 80 people from Burma for guerrilla warfare. Even though the Chinese communist government had reached an agreement with the Burmese government, promising that the CCP would not support the Burmese Communist Party, during the Cultural Revolution, Mao sent a large group of Burmese Communist Party members back to the country to launch an armed revolution and encouraged these communist leaders to come to China to recruit soldiers. The CCP also sent more than 200 active-duty soldiers to join the Burmese communist army, and built a radio station in China to broadcast propaganda to Burma. More than 10,000 Red Guards rushed to Burma to join the revolutionary war.[135] This caused chaos and the loss of innocent lives. Even today, guerrilla warfare continues in the country.

Still fighting Mao's revolutionary war is the Communist Party of India (Maoist), which uses tactics such as "encircling the cities from the rural areas," seizing state power with arms, and eventually realizing socialism and communism. To achieve its goal, the Communist Party of India (Maoist) continuously launches attacks. According to Indian media reports, it has caused more than 6,000 violent incidents, resulting in the deaths of at least 3,000 people.[136]

In Latin America, the CCP helped to set up organizations in Brazil, Peru, Bolivia, Colombia, Chile, Venezuela, and Ecuador during the Cultural Revolution, including two insurgent groups: The "Ejército Popular de Liberación" in Colombia and the Maoist guerrilla group in Bolivia. Venezuelan communists also engage in armed and violent activities. Peru's "Shining Path" was led by Abimael Guzmán, who went to China in the 1960s to receive training in guerrilla warfare under the CCP International Liaison Department. His group carried out numerous terrorist attacks, including assassinations, bombings, beheadings, and deaths by stoning or by placing victims in boiling water. It massacred many peasants who were perceived as being against the communist struggle.[137] The Truth and Reconciliation Commission later estimated that Shining Path was responsible for the death or disappearance of 31,331 people.[138]

According to China's official account, of 48 countries that established or semi-established diplomatic relations with the CCP in the year or so before and after 1967, nearly 30 had diplomatic disputes with the CCP because of its export of the communist revolution. Where China exported revolution, disaster followed. China also distributed 4.6 million copies of Mao's work in 25 languages to 148 countries and regions around the world. The *Xinhua News Agency* commented that this propaganda campaign would make Mao Zedong Thought deeply rooted in the hearts of the people, arousing the masses of working people around the world and triggering a widespread world revolution to win the victory of communism. Today, Xi Jinping has followed Mao's playbook. About 20 million copies of Xi's two-volume tome, *Xi Jinping: The Governance of China*, have been distributed to 160 countries, exporting the communist revolution under the guise of the China model.

2.2.2 China's Initial Fight for World Leadership against the Soviet Union

On the eve of the CCP's seizure of state power, Mao sent Liu Shaoqi to Moscow. Stalin directed Mao to be responsible for revolutions in colonial and semi-colonial countries, and the Soviet Union would be responsible for the revolution in the West and developed countries. CCP insider He Fang says that Mao respected and feared Stalin, and he took Stalin's orders seriously, but Mao also had the ambition to become the leader of the communist world, so he was extremely zealous in inciting armed revolutions in Asia. When Nikita Khrushchev assumed power shortly after Stalin's death, Mao believed that he should lead the communist world, not Khrushchev. Khrushchev's speech at the CPSU 20th Congress and the Hungarian Uprising of 1956 further convinced Mao that Khrushchev was politically immature and inexperienced in handling international affairs. Mao reasoned that he should replace Khrushchev as leader of the communist world.

This idea got support from the Italian Communist Party leader and some Asian communist leaders. But Khrushchev treated Mao as an important partner of the communist world. When he visited China in 1954, Khrushchev gave Mao a gift of China's national emblem made of gold, weighing a ton, which Mao scornfully called bribery. Khrushchev also signed seven agreements with the CCP, returned the Lushunkou Naval Base to China, provided a military loan of 520 million rubles, and extended help to establish 156 industrial aid projects.

Mao needed Khrushchev to give him nuclear technology, so his ambition was somewhat checked at this time.

However, Mao secretly continued his fight to lead the communist community and eventually triggered the split between China and the Soviet Union. After carefully examining official records of both countries, Shen Zhihua, a Chinese historian on Sino–Soviet relations, concluded that it was Mao's eagerness to become the world communist leader that caused the Sino–Soviet split.

Shen believes that not only did Mao want to accelerate China's economy to leapfrog over the United Kingdom and the United States, but from the beginning, he targeted the Soviet Union as his primary rival. As early as 1956, Mao said, "The Soviet Union and China are both socialist countries. Can we achieve more and quicker? Can we build socialism in a faster, better, and less expensive way?"[139] Mao also believed that China's 13 years of development equaled the Soviets' 40 years. Mao's campaign of catching up to the UK and surpassing the U.S. was really aimed at the Soviet Union. Khrushchev advocated for the policy of peaceful competition with capitalist countries and proposed to surpass the United States in 15 years. Mao felt that Khrushchev was ahead of him in this aspect. On the one hand, he echoed this idea by proposing that China surpass the UK in the same time frame. On the other hand, he wanted to be bolder than Khrushchev with economic development. Soon China announced the Great Leap Forward, centered around the slogan of "Surpassing the UK and catching up with the U.S." Mao specifically desired that China surpass the Soviet Union within five years in steel production. He believed China could achieve communism earlier than the Soviet Union, in fewer than 15 years, and China could be stronger than its Big Brother. Mao mocked the CPSU. As mentioned above, the CCP even issued a document to announce China had entered communism, but to avoid other countries' jealousy it would not openly announce it. More importantly, Mao insisted that Marxism's center had moved to Beijing.[140]

The communist world held a meeting in Moscow in November 1957. Mao attended, missing no opportunity to twist Khrushchev's tail; he conspired with his supporters and effectively stole the show. Mao made his famous speech about "the East wind prevailing over the West wind," saying that China would overtake the United Kingdom in 15 years and then surpass the United States. The "Moscow Declaration," issued at the end of the meeting, was the product of concessions and compromises between the Chinese and Soviet communist parties. It affirmed that the CCP was on equal footing with the Communist Party of the Soviet Union (CPSU). Mao and Khrushchev shared parallel leadership in the world communist movement.

To fight for leadership, Mao claimed that China's People's Communes and the Great Leap Forward offered a better and faster path to communism than the Soviet Union's devices. Khrushchev's proposal for a peaceful transition to socialism was a betrayal of Marxism and Leninism, Mao said, and he labeled Khrushchev as the ringleader of revisionism. Khrushchev refused to endorse Mao's Great Leap Forward and People's Commune movements, maintaining that doing so would betray the

International Workers' Movement. In July 1959, *Pravda* published Khrushchev's review of mistakes that the Soviet Union made in the 1920s, including the establishment of communes in rural Russia. This angered Mao further, since he was in the middle of an internal power struggle that included denouncing Marshall Peng Dehuai at the Lushan Conference. As a consequence, Mao launched a Sino-Soviet Union ideological debate that lasted until the demise of the Soviet Union.

Mao challenged the CPSU's leadership position in the world communist movement. He accused the CPSU of failing to treat the CCP on equal footing, unilaterally generating the agenda for the communist movement, and interfering in the internal affairs of other parties. He demanded dual leadership. But when Khrushchev agreed to this, Mao hypocritically refused to accept the proposal.

In Khrushchev's memoir, he repeatedly mentioned the topic of Mao seeking the leadership of the world communist movement. In 1960, Khrushchev told Peng Zhen, a CCP leader, that China wanted to dominate the leadership of the international communist movement.[141] He said to other Soviet leaders that whenever he saw Mao, he saw Stalin, as if they were cut from the same cloth.[142]

During the Cultural Revolution, Mao and the CCP no longer hid their world ambition. After China successfully tested its first nuclear device (atomic bomb) in 1964, and its thermonuclear device (hydrogen bomb) in 1967, Mao declared that China was the political center of the world revolution and the CCP propaganda apparatus announced that the world had entered a new era of Mao Zedong Thought. The CCP campaigned to impose Mao's personality cult as the greatest world leader to all peoples. Mao cared about nothing but power.

In March 1969, the Sino-Soviet tension escalated into an armed border conflict on Treasure Island (Damansky Island to the Soviets) in the Ussuri River, with smaller clashes in May along the Amur River, and in August at Lake Zhalanashkol. That year was a perilous one for Beijing and Moscow—an all-out war might have started. But Mao knew that China was much weaker and had no chance of winning. So, he declared that the Soviet Union was the biggest problem for China and began to woo the U.S. to offset the Soviet threat.

Deng called off Mao's world revolution after assuming power in 1978, in order to focus on China's modernization. He knew that China needed the West's help to achieve the CCP's goal, just as Mao sought Soviet aid to rapidly become an important world power. But it did not mean the CCP had relinquished its world ambition. When the Soviet Union and Eastern Bloc countries collapsed, a group of top CCP leaders came to Deng and suggested that China assume Moscow's leadership role to take responsibility for the communist world. Deng knew that China had no sufficient strength to do so and rejected the proposal, insisting that China should adopt the "*Taoguang Yanghui*" (韬光养晦) strategy— that is, "bide its time," an ancient trick used by rulers to fool their enemies by pretending to be weaker and without ambition, while secretly gathering strength to strike back when the opportunity arrives. Like Mao, Deng acted as the self-proclaimed leader of the Third World but avoided challenging the United States.

However, Deng blamed the U.S. for the 1989 pro-democracy protests in China, which nearly brought down the CCP regime, and he believed that the "black hands" behind this "counterrevolutionary riot" were hostile Western countries, particularly the United States. This misjudgment came from the CCP's political psyche of creating external enemies to consolidate power and shirk its responsibility. To counter this "peaceful evolution," Deng put forward his overall strategy for regime security: The "two hands approach," in which the regime's security depended on whether the CCP could retain the country's economic growth and ruthless repression of any dissent. Deng's foreign policy focused on these priorities.

Jiang faithfully followed Deng's policy, but Hu began to shift to striving to make achievements after the 2008 global financial crisis caused by the U.S. subprime mortgage crisis, which made the CCP believe that the U.S. was declining. China increased confrontation with the United States and demanded reforms in international norms. Chinese government scholars claim that

> as a rising superpower, China's political and economic success naturally has made its ideology become the dominant one for the world to follow. Only China can replace the United States to lead the world with the largest economy and most powerful military in the next few decades.

In other words, China must be in the driver seat and has its own rules to lead the world.[143]

Under this new strategic judgment, when he came to power in late 2012, Xi gradually began abandoning Deng's *Taoguang Yanghui*. Instead, he wanted to take action to make great achievements. That meant openly and directly challenging the U.S. global leadership position, which we discuss in the next chapter. The power-hungry CCP and its leaders have a history of fighting for the world leadership position, and if it was less explicit in the past, today this has become all too obvious.

2.2.3 China's Hegemonic Expansion before Xi

China will continue to conceal its global ambition to neutralize resistance. For example, in September 2019, Wang Yi, foreign minister and state councilor, delivered a speech at an event co-hosted by the National Committee on U.S.–China Relations and the U.S.–China Business Council on the sidelines of the annual United Nations General Assembly in New York. Wang told the audience that he rejected the views of those who believe Beijing is aiming to surpass the United States as a strategic power, saying that "seeking hegemony is not in our DNA."[144] He said China was a developing country,

> still far behind the United States. China has no intention of playing a form of 'Game of Thrones' on the world stage. For the foreseeable future, the United States is and will still be the strongest country in the world.[145]

Chinese state media followed the same line. A *Xinhua* 2018 editorial claimed that the cultural values that sustain Chinese civilization are those of peace, harmony, and commitment to the common good. The Chinese reject the pursuit of hegemony. Expansionism is not in the Chinese nation's blood, and thus never has been on its agenda.

However, during the Sino-American meeting in Anchorage in March 2021, U.S. Secretary of State Antony Blinken criticized China for threatening the rules-based order that maintains global stability through its misconduct in Xinjiang, Hong Kong, and Taiwan. Yang Jiechi, the CCP's Politburo for foreign affairs, tartly responded: "What China and the international community follow or uphold is the United Nations-centered international system and the international order underpinned by international law, not what is advocated by a small number of countries of the so-called rules-based international order."[146] This is typical Chinese behavior. On the surface, China pretends to be a law-abiding member of the international community. In reality, it often breaks and undermines international norms. For decades Beijing has ignored basic human rights and political rights affirmed by the UN.

Such rhetoric is nothing new. All of the CCP's paramount leaders have made similar remarks. "Never seeking hegemony" originated with Mao Zedong in the late 1960s and early 1970s, when he issued one of his highest directives: "Dig deep underground holes, accumulate grain widely, and do not seek hegemony in the world" (深挖洞、广积粮、不称霸). He paraphrased Zhu Sheng, a great strategist in the Ming dynasty 600 years ago, when Zhu advised Zhu Yuanzhang, the would-be emperor of the Ming dynasty, to raise high the city walls, collect more grain, but delay the declaration of hegemony. So the real meaning of Mao's "not seeking hegemony" was to bide his time while opposing the Kremlin's seeking hegemony in the communist world.[147] But according to Shen Zhihua, a few years prior to Mao's remarks, Mao visited Moscow in 1957 and made a shocking statement to international communist leaders about how to deal with U.S. imperialists. "Since we are so powerful, why negotiate with it?" Mao said.

> Let's simply wage a war to fight it over. If you do not hit your enemy, it will not fall. As a rule, where the broom does not reach, the dust will not vanish of itself. Nuclear war is no big deal. There are 2.7 billion people in the world; if half of them die in a nuclear war, the other half remains. China has 600 million people; if half of them die, we still have 300 million. I am not afraid of anyone.[148]

Zhou Enlai managed to put Mao's deception into the Shanghai communique during Richard Nixon's first visit in 1972, stating, "China will never be a superpower and it opposes hegemony and power politics of any kind." Deng continued the strategy of delaying the declaration of hegemony when he came to power. The 1978 communique states that both countries agree "neither should seek hegemony in the Asia-Pacific region and each is opposed to efforts by any other country or group of countries to establish such hegemony."[149] It continues, "China will never be a superpower and it opposes hegemony and power politics of any kind."[150]

Similar language is used in the 1978 "Sino-Japanese Treaty of Peace and Friendship," in which the two parties declared that neither should seek hegemony in the Asia-Pacific region or any other regions, and that each opposed efforts by any other country or group of countries to establish such hegemony.[151] It was also in a speech Deng delivered at the UN in 1974, when he even went so far as to say:

> If one day China should change her color and turn into a superpower, if she, too, should play the tyrant in the world, and everywhere subject others to her bullying, aggression and exploitation, the people of the world should identify her as social-imperialism, expose it, oppose it, and work together with the Chinese people to overthrow it.[152]

Following Deng, Jiang made the promise that China would never seek hegemony in a speech at Cambridge University in 1999. Hu Jintao, Jiang's successor, not only repeated the rhetoric but added that China would "never engage in expansion" in a keynote speech at China's Boao Forum for Asia Annual Conference in 2008.

Xi Jinping, on numerous occasions, has stated that China will never pursue hegemony and that "the broad Pacific Ocean is vast enough to embrace both China and the United States." In 2018, during a speech to mark 40 years of market reforms, Xi said that China would not seek hegemony nor develop "at the expense of other countries' interests."

This is typical CCP deception, an ancient strategy from Sunzi, or Sun Tzu, who, in the *Art of War*, points out that deception is the first principle in warfare. He says:

> All warfare is based on deception (兵者，诡道也). Hence, when we are able to attack, we must seem unable; when using our forces, we must appear inactive; when we are near, we must make the enemy believe we are far away; when far away, we must make him believe we are near.[153]

Deception is a core principle of Chinese strategic culture. *The Art of War* is a must read for all students of China. When CCP leaders promised not to seek hegemony, they were dissembling. Their promise is nothing but a tactic of "deceiving the sky to cross the ocean" and to fool other world powers that China is by no means a threat so that they will relax their vigilance. When the U.S. let down its guard, China gained the time to match, and then surpass, other great powers to dominate the world.

CCP leaders' words never match their deeds. They say one thing but do the opposite. When Mao promised not to seek hegemony, he was actually inciting and exporting revolution to the world. To win the communist victory, he pushed for a war to "strike early, strike on a grand scale, and strike with nuclear weapons," which was the basis for China's grand strategy in the 1960s and 1970s.[154] From Mao to Xi, CCP leaders have not changed their objective of world hegemony.

2.2.4 Occupation of Tibet and Annexation of the East Turkestan Republic

How China occupied Tibet can demonstrate its objective of dominance. Tibet's historical territory would make it the world's tenth-largest nation. When the CCP defeated the KMT in 1949, Mao coerced the Tibetans to sign the "Seventeen-Point Agreement on Measures for the Peaceful Liberation of Tibet." The agreement promised Tibetans that they could maintain their religious and political system, their way of life, and no social reforms would be carried out without the consent of the Tibetan government. This became the first model of "one country, two systems" that China later applied to Hong Kong and Taiwan. But the CCP soon launched land reform and other reforms in 1956, aiming to fundamentally change Tibet's political, economic, and social structure. In 1958, the CCP initiated yet another campaign, the "Democratic Reform of Religious System." The People's Commune and Great Leap Forward movements resulted in a large-scale famine that aggravated ethnic conflicts in Tibet, causing armed resistance. The CCP responded with genocide, killing or jailing almost all adult males in some Tibetan areas, according to the former deputy police chief of Qinghai Province.[155]

The bloody massacre caused an influx of refugees into Lhasa in early 1959, and the PLA had begun preparations for military action. This imminent danger forced Tibet's leader, the Dalai Lama, to flee to India on March 17, 1959. The CCP's deception and broken promises triggered the Tibetan people's uprising that year, and the CCP responded with a bloodbath. Some scholars estimate that about 10 percent of the Tibetan population was killed, wounded, or imprisoned.[156]

Before 1949, the East Turkestan Republic, an independent state, was governed by Uyghurs and Kazakhs in northwest Xinjiang. In the late summer of 1949, the PLA coerced the KMT government's military to surrender, and then took over Xinjiang. It conspired with the Soviet Union by killing key leaders of East Turkestan and annexed it into the People's Republic of China. Led by Wang Zhen, the PLA crushed the remaining resistance in Xinjiang, continuing with the mass killing of Muslims in the region. Wang, who became known as the "Xinjiang Butcher," boasted that his slaughter ensured that not a single counterrevolutionary would appear in the next 50 years.

In 1950, the CCP launched a land reform campaign in Xinjiang. Wang sent Deng Liquan, another leftist fanatic, to Southern Xinjiang to confiscate a large amount of land owned by mosques and ranchers. Simultaneously, the Xinjiang government cracked down on Islam. It took over the religious schools and later banned all Madrasas and religious classes, as well as teaching children the recitation of scripture. Under the religious "reform campaign" from 1958 and 1960, the CCP abolished the "feudal privileges and exploitation system" in

Islam and banned clerics from performing religious functions. In 1962, the Great Famine and the CCP's repressive policies caused a Muslim uprising. The PLA killed many protesters and forced tens of thousands to flee to the Soviet Union.

During the Great Cultural Revolution, Mao's Red Guards circulated flyers with messages such as "Take action to destroy Islam now!" across China. The Red Guards destroyed many remaining mosques, and burned a great number of religious scriptures and Islamic items. Clerics were ridiculed and shamed in public. Many were sent to do hard labor, but some were beaten to death. Islamic culture and customs were considered to be one of the "Four Olds" and banned. China's official data show that immediately after the CCP occupation of Xinjiang in the early 1950s, Xinjiang had 29,500 mosques and 54,500 Islamic clergymen. By the end of the 1950s, there were 15,000 mosques and 14,000 clergymen. After the ten years of the Cultural Revolution, only 2,930 mosques remained.

After years of aggressive Chinese government policies and incentives to drive Han migration to Xinjiang, the Han Chinese population increased from 290,000, or 5 percent of the total population in 1949, to today's 10.9 million.[157] That is an increase of 38 times, or 42 percent of the total population, while the percentage of the Uyghur population dropped from 76 percent to 45 percent.[158]

2.2.5 The Korean War

While waging war against Tibetans and Uyghurs and other Muslims, Mao also tried to expand his power and influence by sending CCP members to Korea in 1950. Kim Il-sung was a member of the CCP dispatched by the CCP Manchuria committee to fight against the Japanese at the China–Korea border. Stalin and Mao supported Kim's military invasion operation to seize the Korean peninsula.

Before the Korean War, Mao gave Kim three PLA divisions and two regiments in 1949, with a total of 69,200 soldiers, constituting the main combat force of the Korean People's Army and accounting for 46.5 percent of Korean forces. Most of them were Chinese citizens of Korean origin living in China's Yanbian district. On June 25, 1950, Kim used the CCP-provided troops to execute his long-planned war of aggression against South Korea, capturing Seoul in three days and almost the entire Korean peninsula within a month and a half. Mao delivered another 100,000 ethnic Korean soldiers, equipped with Soviet weapons, to Kim in 1951. These troops included ethnic Koreans from northeastern China, North Koreans, and 50,000 Korean captives who were trained to become soldiers in China after the war began.[159]

When Kim was defeated, Mao decided to invade Korea. He and the CCP fooled the Chinese people by accusing the United States of being about to invade China and mobilizing millions of troops to invade Korea. He launched a campaign to "Resist U.S. aggression and aid Korea to protect our homes and defend our countries." The Korean War was Mao's attempt to be a leader of the world communist community and to gain Soviet help to modernize China,

Although often overlooked today, the Korean War was one of the most brutal wars in the 20th century, causing the deaths of five million people. More than half of these—about 10 percent of Korea's pre-war population—were civilians. Almost 40,000 Americans died in action in Korea, and more than 100,000 were wounded.

2.2.6 Sino-Indian and Sino-Vietnamese Border Wars

In 1962, China waged a border war with India. A disputed Himalayan border was the main pretext for the Sino-Indian War, but the real reason was that Mao desired to lead the communist world and Third World. As we have mentioned, Mao fought Khrushchev for leadership of the world revolution. But since India was then considered to be the leader of the Third World, and Prime Minister Jawaharlal Nehru's influence in the world was soaring, Mao wanted to fight to inflict a humiliating military defeat upon Nehru. This would create conditions for expanding China's influence in the Third World. Mao also wanted to divert attention on the disaster that he brought with the Great Leap Forward, and to punish India for allowing the Dalai Lama exile in the country. Mao's planning and deployment of war against India was a couple of years before the Sino-Indian War that took place in October 1962 during the Cuban Missile Crisis. In a sudden attack in two theaters, a large number of PLA forces overwhelmed Indian troops, causing several thousand casualties. Sino-Indian armed conflicts have continued throughout the years. In 2020, Xi ordered the largest border skirmish since 1962, killing more than 20 Indian soldiers. The skirmish clearly was aimed at challenging the U.S.–India alliance and inciting hyper-nationalism at home.

Concerning Vietnam, China eyed the South China Sea for years. Beijing took advantage of the U.S. withdrawal from Vietnam to launch the Battle of the Paracel Islands, seizing the disputed islands in 1974. China first sent its militias as fishermen to fish and process seafood and provoked the South Vietnamese Navy to drive them away. Then he dispatched the PLA Navy to defeat the Vietnamese. The U.S. response, led by Henry Kissinger, was weak, which emboldened China. It achieved *de facto* control over the Paracels—a critical first step for China's expansion in the South China Sea.

In 1979, when the China-supported Khmer Rouge was about to be evicted from power by Vietnamese forces, Deng claimed that Vietnam was a rogue country and China needed to teach it a lesson, an attempt to save the genocidal Pol Pot regime. He again used a border dispute as a pretext to launch a war. Additionally, by challenging Soviet-supported Vietnam, Deng wanted to ingratiate himself with the U.S. to gain trust and aid from Washington to modernize China. The Soviet Union had become the number one enemy of China, and Beijing's influence was declining in East Asia because of its push for armed revolutions in the region. To regain influence and compete with the Soviet Union for leadership of the communist world, China's military action came when the Soviets were busy preparing for war against Afghanistan and the U.S. was improving relations with

Beijing. The disastrous Cultural Revolution had caused people to lose faith in the CCP leadership and created a crisis of confidence in the CCP's rule over China. Deng saw the need to launch a war against the aggressors, in order to consolidate his power and reignite nationalism. Even though the Cultural Revolution greatly weakened the PLA's combat ability, Deng insisted on waging war.

On February 17, 1979, 300,000 Chinese troops amassed in Yunnan and Guangxi began a carpet bombardment of areas adjacent to China. The PLA fanned out about 20 kilometers into Vietnam and captured 11 border towns in under two days. According to unofficial statistics, the war left 26,000 Chinese dead and 37,000 wounded. An estimated 30,000 Vietnamese died, and 32,000 were wounded. More than 100,000 civilian casualties occurred. Chinese front-line commanders reportedly ordered troops to kill anyone who approached, which caused many civilian deaths. Yet the war ended with China's humiliating defeat at the hands of the Vietnamese military, who fought the PLA to a standstill.

In late 1987, under the pretext of building an observation post sponsored by the United Nations Educational, Scientific and Cultural Organization (UNESCO), China deployed troops to the Spratly Islands, where it did not occupy any reefs at the time. In 1988, China provoked Vietnam, causing a series of confrontations, and, in the end, initiated a sea skirmish that killed 64 Vietnamese sailors. China took six reefs in the Spratly Islands. According to the *Global Times* website, this battle pushed China's coastal line over 1,000 km southward. Now China has occupied 11 reefs and militarized them; these have become outposts for China's global expansion. China's leaders understand how to hide their aggression, and they are nibbling away at freedom of navigation and other countries' territorial waters, much like the way that a silkworm consumes mulberry leaves.[160]

2.2.7 Conflict over Taiwan

China has not accepted the country's division and so has never forsaken the use of force against Taiwan. The PLA has provoked many armed conflicts and applied other measures to subjugate Taiwan. One of the most dangerous was the Third Taiwan Strait Crisis, also called the 1995–1996 Taiwan Strait Crisis. The CCP's third-generation leader, Jiang Zemin, attempted to use Taiwanese President Lee Teng-hui's visit to the U.S. and Taiwan's elections as a pretext to forcefully take over Taiwan. He ordered the PLA to launch a large-scale exercise in the Taiwan Strait and to seize the island if Lee moved away from the "One China" policy. Only when the U.S. sent a carrier group to the Strait did China abandon its invasion plan. Jiang made four attempts to invade Taiwan through large-scale military exercises. In 2005, Jiang's successor, Hu Jintao, passed China's Anti-Secession Law, which authorizes China to use military force to take Taiwan if the One China policy changes. Today, Xi Jinping's provocations have become even more frequent and aggressive. For example, in September 2021, China's PLA sent 19 aircraft into Taiwan's "air defense identification zone," including several bombers that can carry nuclear weapons, intending to intimidate Taiwan.

This type of PLA Air Force (PLAAF) sortie has occurred numerous times under Xi. At an event marking the centenary of the Communist Party of China's founding in July 2021, Xi stated that "resolving the Taiwan issue and achieving the complete reunification of the motherland is a historic task to which the CPC is firmly committed." This means it is only a matter of time before China invades Taiwan. Chinese leaders have framed Taiwan's independence as the greatest and most realistic threat to the communist regime's security—the core of China's interests—but they forget that Taiwan has not been under China's control for more than 100 years. The Republic of China (RoC) has been an independent country for over 110 years, and the United Nations Charter affirms the right for people's self-determination. China's threat to Taiwan demonstrates its territorial expansion, particularly considering that the PLA is militarizing the first island chain of major archipelagos stretching from the coast of mainland East Asia into the South China Sea. Beijing is buying up small island states in the second strategic island chain, which extends from Japan to the Mariana Islands and Micronesia in the Pacific. Moreover, China continues the race to build the world's largest naval and submarine fleet and is about to take two-thirds of the world's 50 major ports. These activities are in preparation for China's ultimate showdown to assume world dominance.

2.3 The Heart of the CCP's Ideology from Mao to Xi: "Socialist Imperialism"—Imperial Domination with Socialist Rhetoric

This chapter has demonstrated that China's threats and dangers posed to the free world have stemmed from its cultist and violent Marxism–Leninism–Maoism ideology since the CCP's founding in 1921 and its expansion since the PRC's founding in 1949. Because of fanciful, hyperbolic words and phrases used by the CCP, revised with each generation of leadership, its substantial ideological content seems elusive. It evolves according to the practical needs of each leader's politics. However, no matter how many changes have occurred, the CCP's ideology has never departed from the core doctrines of Marxism–Leninism–Maoism. This remains: Uphold the dictatorship of the Communist Party and eliminate capitalism to achieve communist society through class struggle and world revolution.

The CCP claims that its ideology is an incontestable, irrefutable truth. Pretending its ideology is a science, Deng once said: "I firmly believe more and more people will come to Marxism, because it is a science."[161] The "Xi Jinping Thought on Socialism with Chinese Characteristics" is now also said to be "a science."[162] It also frames CCP ideology as a historical law—the law of progressive development—coming from the special powers and insights of its leaders. Thus, the ideology is considered divine and infallible; no one can challenge it. The CCP members and Chinese people must believe in and remain loyal to this ideology, and no competing ideologies are allowed. To give people false hope, it claims the communist utopia is a haven. As China expands globally, its ideology has spread across the world. If it becomes the dominant power, it will impose this cultish ideology on all peoples.

By nature, the CCP ideology is aggressive, belligerent, and violent. It relies on violence and terror to gain authority. This ideology openly declares that its ends can be attained only by the forcible overthrow of existing social conditions—in other words, by smashing the old world and creating a new one. Violence is the main means through which the CCP gains power.

The CCP's ideology propagates class struggle, pitting people against each other. In this struggle, according to Mao, "some classes have won the victory and other classes have been eradicated. This is history." Karl Marx and Friedrich Engels made class struggle the central facet of social evolution: "The history of all hitherto existing human society is the history of class struggles." Mao followed Marx's idea, claiming that all class struggles in the world are aimed at seizing and consolidating state power. This ideology leads to revolutions that "are violent acts through which one class overthrows another," the dictatorship of the proletariat that has resulted in the so-called "communist revolution," full of blood and violence. The Red Terror under communism has lasted for about a century, bringing disaster to dozens of countries and costing tens of millions of lives.

The CCP's ideology is destined to weaken and eliminate private ownership of land and assets and establish state ownership. Even though the CCP has modified this to allow some private economy, the dominant position of state economics and ownership cannot be undermined, as Xi insists, because it is the institutional guarantee to ensure the Party's rule over the country and the success of the socialist system. To ensure the CCP's development interest, it is bound to expand globally, seeking markets and jockeying for positions to acquire strategic materials.

Minister Wang Yi says, China has no hegemonic DNA.[163] He clearly forgot the education he received during his formative years. For decades, Chinese youths were taught to "Keep our motherland in heart, but eye the whole world in view," and that "We must realize that two-thirds of the world's people live in great misery, and we must go to liberate them. The great leader is not only the supreme leader of the Chinese people, but also the guiding light of the proletariat around the world, and the reddest sun for the world's people."[164] China's global ambition is determined by this cultish ideological DNA inserted by the CCP's creator and enhanced by subsequent leaders. The ideology drives Communist China to expand globally and seek world dominance. No matter how it frames this to cover its real intention, such as replacing communism with "a common destiny for mankind," the essence remains the same. This has become more evident as Xi has campaigned to export the Party-state's political system of "socialism with Chinese characteristics" as a "new choice" for the world.

Many Western politicians and scholars have attempted to pinpoint China's ideology and define the nature of the country's political system. More Western scholars believe that communists in China remain only in name, and some even suggest that the CCP should rename itself the "Chinese Confucian Party." Many use labels such as state capitalism, authoritarian capitalism, crony capitalism, bureaucratic capitalism, kleptocratic capitalism, state socialism, or totalitarianism to describe China's regime.

China's state media and its apologist scholars insist that China is a special type of socialist country—"socialism with Chinese characteristics." This is because, they argue, state authoritarianism has never been a guiding ideology in China's political reform, nor in its political practice. State authoritarianism is a closed system, and the rulers or ruling class rely on state power to govern for their self-interest, often limiting political participation and citizens' rights—but China is not like that, they argue. Not only has China achieved rapid economic development, but it also set up an open and equal democratic political system and created its own path to socialism. Therefore, to describe "socialism with Chinese characteristics" as state capitalism, they believe, is to demean or downplay the Chinese model by putting it into the pedigree of capitalism or state authoritarianism—and this denies China's socialist achievements and the superiority of the China model.[165]

Of course, China's arguments are not worth refuting because they are not based on fact or reality. Xi Jinping, in his most important, 3.5-hour speech delivered at the CCP's Nineteenth Congress, used "socialism" 73 times, the most frequently mentioned word, including the phrase "socialism with Chinese characteristics" 59 times. On November 11, 2021, the CCP passed the *Resolution of the Central Committee of the Communist Party of China on the Major Achievements and Historical Experience of the Party over the Past Century*, which makes clear that the CCP is "staying committed to communist ideals and socialist convictions."[166]

We argue that China's ideology today is not orthodox Marxism, even though it inherited Marx's core ideas concerning a proletarian dictatorship and cherry-picked other ideas to justify and ensure the CCP's perpetual rule. Instead, the nature of its polity is "socialist imperialism" (社会帝国主义) in the communist world's discourse. Maoism, and thus the CCP's current ideology, must be placed in the larger context of communist thought, and the roots of the idea are found in Lenin. He defined socialist imperialism as "socialist in words, imperialist in deeds."[167] In essence, the ideology is a veneer; the true nature of the CCP's rule, as with the Communist Party of the Soviet Union, is domination of its people through terror and lies, with strict control of the political and social structures, and external domination of international politics through expansion. The Soviets failed in both respects, although they managed to inflict horrific suffering on their population and the populations of their allies. Like the Soviets, the CCP has inflicted unimaginable horrors on the Chinese people. Unlike the Soviets, it remains to be determined whether the CCP will succeed in dominating global politics.

When China broke up with the Soviet Union in the early 1960s, the CCP used social imperialism to label the CPSU. In 1964, Mao responded to an open letter of the Central Committee of the CPSU, in which he attacked Soviet leader Khrushchev's phony communism and attacked the USSR as itself becoming an imperialist power while maintaining a socialist façade.[168] Mao later was accused of the same by Albanian communist dictator Enver Hoxha.

Two other terms that Mao used to attack the CPSU—"socialist fascism" (社会法西斯主义) and "socialist militarism" (社会军国主义)—also fit the reality of today's CCP. That is, the Party is defined by totalitarianism, the forcible suppression of opposition, state dominance of the economy, and the strong belief that China should develop, maintain, and use a strong military to expand its interests. China's ideology is based on Marxism–Leninism–Maoism mixed with Sino-centric imperialism and ultranationalism.

China long ago introduced a market mechanism to boost the economy of the Party-state by modifying its communist economic system, including replacing rigid central planning with profit-seeking state-owned enterprises, and allowing some private companies to coexist. But its economic liberalization is quite limited and Chinese leaders never intended to have the private sector dominate the country's economy. In fact, the state continues to monopolize key sectors, and state-owned enterprises make money for the Party. All land belongs to the Party-state. When buying an apartment, the owner gets only the right to use the apartment, not the land. Peasants do not own land.

China's private sector appears to be vigorous, but the CCP can easily make or break it. It uses the private sector to help create employment and generate revenue for the Party-state. But when private enterprises get bigger, China's government must curb them. It will never allow them to grow out of control. The CCP has advanced a policy of common prosperity to aim at redistribution of wealth by plundering successful private enterprises. All assets in China essentially belong to the Party-state.

In addition, the PLA is the Party's private military, loyal only to the paramount leader. Media outlets are under absolute Party control. The stability maintenance system or security apparatus crushes any dissent without mercy. China's political, economic, social, and ideological controls are everywhere. Compared to other remaining communist parties, the CCP's totalitarian control is much more exquisite and can be subtle and deceptive.

Because of this, many in the West focus on China's market mechanism borrowed from capitalism. They wrongly believe that economic development has led to political transformation, and that the CCP has become a non-Communist Party, that is, Communist only in name. Like the fable of the Monkey King in the Chinese saga *The Journey to the West*, the CCP also has 72 transformations but its goals of seizing power, defeating capitalism, and achieving communism have never changed. We argue that it is incorrect to call the current system in China legalistic capitalism or state capitalism, or any other capitalism, because capitalism is based on private ownership of the means of production and property. This is not the case in China, and the CCP firmly controls all these. No doubt, the CCP adopts a pragmatic approach to Marxism–Leninism, but it does not change its core tenets, such as class struggle, violent revolution, and one-party dictatorship, which dominates its policies, discourse and propaganda, the Party structure, and its mode of rule and control. If Marxism is the coronavirus, Leninism is the Delta variant, Xiism is the Omicron variant, but none of these variants alters the nature of the SARS-CoV-2 virus.

Indeed, the communist faith in China was somewhat lost for a while after the Cultural Revolution because of the widespread disillusion, but was gradually reestablished through rapid economic growth and a series of political campaigns, particularly Xi Jinping's forced indoctrination. Although we do not know how many truly believe in communist ideology, a 2015 Gallup poll found the number of China's atheists was the highest among the 65 countries surveyed, reaching 61 percent, with only 7 percent of the population claiming to be religious.[169]

As argued, after 1989, Deng and the CCP already had made the United States an archenemy, viewing the U.S. as an existential threat to the CCP's regime security. China unilaterally launched a cold war to undermine the U.S. democracy. As early as 2013, five government agencies and military units joined together to produce a 90-minute internal educational documentary, entitled *Silent Contest*, depicting the United States as a major enemy of China. The documentary explains how the two countries fight behind-the-scenes battles, accusing the United States of waging a silent war against China. The documentary blames the Soviet Union's collapse on the U.S. inciting a "peaceful revolution," and claims the U.S. is employing a similar strategy against China. Even though the U.S. outwardly maintains an appearance of warmth and peaceful cooperation, beneath the surface it always has been trying to destroy China, according to the documentary. It accuses the U.S. of undermining China through political, cultural, ideological, social, and organizational infiltration. *Global Times*, a state-owned newspaper, hails that "the film is an exploration of the belief that the U.S. remains China's enemy and has never stopped its strategies to Westernize and divide China."[170] In the beginning, the documentary announces: "The process of China's achieving a national rejuvenation will definitely involve engagement and a fight against the U.S.'s hegemonic system. This is the contest of the century, regardless of people's wishes." Nothing is clearer than this sentence about why China is the most dangerous regime to world peace, and that war between the U.S. and China is inevitable.

The old and neo-Maoists see the outside world through conspiratorial and ideological glasses, believing that "the imperialists have never given up the wild ambition to eradicate and subjugate us." They create external enemies to consolidate power and strengthen the dictatorship. As with domestic rivals, the CCP will use brutal and ruthless methods to eliminate its external enemies and achieve its goals. The mentality of "the end justifies the means" can lead to warfare, which could bring about a most disastrous war in the world. This makes a strategic competition between two ideologies, two political systems, and two world orders impossible, even if a democracy tries to avoid confrontation with the CCP.

Moreover, the CCP's ideology and practices demonstrate that it is a genocidal and democidal regime. Its nature is determined: It is destined to ruthlessly suppress domestic opposition and expand globally by seeking world dominance. In the process, China could bring vast, irreversible destruction to the world, and it should be regarded as the common enemy of the world's people. The CCP car is going to cause a global car crash that is certain to result in unimaginable horrors and destruction.

Notes

1 姜辉, "'中国之治'的制度基础与文化奥秘," 江淮论坛, no. 1 (2021).
2 Gerry Groot, "The Expansion of the United Front Under Xi Jinping," *The China Story Yearbook* (Canberra, ACT: The Australian Centre on China in the World at the Australia National University, 2015), p. 168.
3 Mao Zedong, "Introducing the Communist," *Selected Works of Mao Tse-Tung*, Vol. 2 (Peking: Foreign Language Press, 1965), pp. 285–296.
4 Mao, "Introducing the Communist," *Selected Works of Mao Tse-Tung*, Vol. 2, p. 288.
5 Mao, "Introducing the Communist," *Selected Works of Mao Tse-Tung*, Vol. 2, p. 288.
6 O.B. Hemmerle, "Lumpenproletariat," *Encyclopedia of World Poverty, Volume 1: A-G*, edited by M. Odekon (Thousand Oaks, CA: SAGE Publications, 2006), pp. 655–656.
7 伊萍, "历史真相- -湖南农民运动的来龙去脉,"华夏快递, November 2014. Available at: <http://hx.cnd.org/?p=104718>. Accessed April 16, 2021.
8 田炳信, "王学泰：游民与运动（上）," 南方网, November 24, 2005.
9 伊萍, "历史真相."
10 伊萍, "历史真相."
11 伊萍, "历史真相."
12 朱开阳, "湖南农民运动是痞子运动," 大纪元, June 24, 2017. Available at: <https://www.epochtimes.com/gb/17/6/23/n9297462.htm>. Accessed April 14, 2021.
13 Mao, "Introducing the Communist," *Selected Works of Mao Tse-Tung*, Vol. 2, pp. 285–296.
14 Mao Zedong, "Report on an Investigation of the Peasant Movement in Hunan," 1927, Available at: <https://www.marxists.org/reference/archive/mao/selected-works/volume-1/mswv1_2.htm>. Accessed April 12, 2021.
15 伊萍, "历史真相."
16 Mao, "Report on an Investigation of the Peasant Movement in Hunan."
17 高中华,韩丽, "中国的革命者个个都应该读一读," 北京日报, January 25, 2021.
18 蔡咏梅, "鲜为人知中共血腥序幕 湖南农民运动烧杀掳掠逼蒋决裂," 阿波罗网, July 02, 2013. Available at: <https://www.aboluowang.com/2013/0702/316548.html>. Accessed April 14, 2021.
19 蔡咏梅, "鲜为人知中共血腥序幕 湖南农民运动烧杀掳掠逼蒋决裂."
20 张朴, "鲜为人知：毛泽东对男女革命同志的性酷刑," 阿波罗网, September 30, 2019. Available at: <https://hk.aboluowang.com/2019/0930/1349373.html>. Accessed April 14, 2021.
21 "红军肃反，红军肃反的背景起因," 知识百科网，March 3, 2020. Available at: <https://www.gdcqhb.com/lswd/arc11873.html>. Accessed April 15, 2021.
22 Jennifer Oldstone-Moore, *Confucianism: Origins, Beliefs, Practices, Holy Texts, Sacred Places* (New York: Oxford University Press, 2002), pp. 54–60.
23 Gao Hua, *How the Red Sun Rose: The Origin and Development of the Yan'an Rectification Movement, 1930–1945* (Hong Kong: The Chinese University of Hong Kong Press, 2018). Insightful histories of the CCP also include Bruce J. Dickson, *The Party and*

the People: Chinese Politics in the 21st Century (Princeton, NJ: Princeton University Press, 2021); and Tony Saich, *From Rebel to Ruler: One Hundred Years of the Chinese Communist Party* (Cambridge, MA: Harvard University Press, 2021).

24 金观涛, 刘青峰, "反右运动与延安整风," 二十一世纪, 1997年4月号,pp. 21–34.

25 杨光，评习近平整风，《中国人权双周刊》第116期，2013年10月18日—10月31日. Available at: <http://biweeklyarchive.hrichina.org/article/11613>. Accessed April 20, 2021.

26 陈彦："理想是怎样失去的？　　　　-高华　　'红太阳是怎样升起的'一书读后," 二十一世纪, 2001年6月号, pp. 143–148.

27 曹瑛, "在延安参加整风運動和七大," 中国共产党历史网, April 1, 2015. Available at: <http://www.dswxyjy.org.cn/BIG5/n/2015/0401/c244516-26783638-2.html>. Accessed April 15, 2021.

28 何方,党史笔记—从遵义会议到延安整风（香港：利文出版社2005年4月初版）.

29 See Gao, *How the Red Sun Rose.*

30 金观涛, 刘青峰, "反右运动与延安整风," 二十一世纪. 一九九七年四月号.

31 杨伊文, "文革幽灵仍在中国大陆游荡,"爱思想网，March 31, 2013. Available at: <https://www.aisixiang.com/data/62604.html>. Accessed April 16, 2021.

32 金观涛, 刘青峰, "反右运动与延安整风," 二十一世纪. 一九九七年四月号.

33 Alexander V. Pantsov with Steven I. Levine, *Mao: The Real Story* (New York: Simon and Schuster, 2012).

34 Pantsov and Levine, *Mao.*

35 胡乔木, 胡乔木谈中共党史 (北京:人民出版社，1999), p. 122.

36 蒙克，"苏联档案解密（上）：还原真实的毛泽东，" BBC中文网, July 6, 2015. Available at: <https://www.bbc.com/zhongwen/simp/china/2015/07/150706_pantsov_mao_zedong_archive_1 >. Accessed April 20, 2021.

37 笑蜀编撰，历史的先声:半个世纪前的庄严承诺（广东汕头大学出版社, 1999）.

38 Gao, *How the Red Sun Rose.*

39 玉清心, "北大才子王实味和他滴血的野百合花," *Epoch Times,* January 30, 2017. Available at: <https://www.epochtimes.com/gb/17/1/29/n8758753.htm>. Accessed April 22, 2021.

40 Mao Zedong, "Talks at the Yenan Forum on Literature and Art," *Selected Works of Mao Tse-tung,* Vol. 3 (Peking: Foreign Language Press, 1967), pp. 69–98.

41 Mao, "Talks at the Yenan Forum on Literature and Art."

42 习近平在文艺工作座谈会上的讲话全文，"香港文汇网，October 15, 2015. Available at: <http://news.wenweipo.com/2015/10/15/IN1510150009.htm>. Accessed April 22, 2021.

43 玉清心, "北大才子王实味和他滴血的野百合花."

44 武德山, "整风中的张克勤反革命特务案," *Epoch Times,* August 14, 2017. Available at: <https://www.epochtimes.com/gb/17/8/12/n9521893.htm >. Accessed April 24, 2021.

45 武德山, "整风中的张克勤反革命特务案."

46 武德山, "整风中的张克勤反革命特务案."

47 武德山, "整风中的张克勤反革命特务案."

48 袁斌, "中共罪行录之十一: 延安整風,"*Epoch Times,* April 27, 2021. Available at: <https://www.epochtimes.com/b5/21/4/27/n12908179.htm>. Accessed April 25, 2021.

49 胡乔木, 胡乔木回忆毛泽东 (人民出版社, 2003), p. 728.

50 崔敏，"李锐:我人生的五个二十年，" 通约智库网，April 28, 2021. Available at: <http://www.tywiki.com/index.php/%E6%9D%8E%E9%94%90:%E6%88%91%E4%BA%BA%E7%94%9F%E7%9A%84%E4%BA%94%E4%B8%AA%E4%BA%8C%E5%8D%81%E5%B9%B4>. Accessed April 25, 2021.

51 李普, "楚狂本色总依然," 爱思想网，January 10, 2007. Available at: <https://m.aisixiang.com/data/12731-3.html>. Accessed April 25, 2021.

52 何方,"'延安整风'与个人崇拜," *Modern China Studies,* no. 1 (2005).

53 杨桂欣，《别了莎菲》，《炎黄春秋》1993年第7期.

54 孙中山，《三民主义》Available at: <https://www.douban.com/note/433973281/?_i=3244980kkdIwQw>. Accessed January 26, 2022.

55 "新中国峥嵘岁月，废除封建土地制度," 新华网， September 04, 2019. Available at: <http://www.xinhuanet.com/politics/2019-09/04/c_1124959932.htm>. Accessed April 24, 2021.

56 "《重审毛泽东土地改革》国际研讨会观察," *RFA*, September 25, 2019. Available at: <https://www.rfa.org/mandarin/zhuanlan/zhongguotoushi/panel-09252019144637.html>. Accessed April 26, 2021.

57 VOA 新闻，"中共功罪评说之五：土改为什么一定要流血？" *VOA*, June 29, 2011. Available at: <https://www.voachinese.com/a/article-20110629-why-does-land-reform-have-to-be-bloody-124729189/783814.html>. Accessed April 26, 2021.

58 VOA 新闻，"中共功罪评说之五：土改为什么一定要流血？"

59 杨奎松，"新中国 "镇压反革命" 运动研究," 史学月刊 1 (2006): 45–61.

60 杨奎松，"新中国 "镇压反革命" 运动研究."

61 杨奎松，"新中国 "镇压反革命" 运动研究."

62 尹曙生，"毛泽东与第三次全国公安会议," 炎黄春秋, May 21, 2014.

63 VOA 新闻， "中共功罪评说之四：'镇反'运动杀了多少人？" *VOA*, June 27, 2011. Available at: <https://www.voachinese.com/a/article-20110627-how-many-people-were-killed-during-the-crackdown-of-the-counterrevolutionaries-124605564/783702.html>. Accessed April 25, 2021.

64 李锐，庐山会议实录 (河南人民出版社， 1996), p. 302.

65 尹曙生，"毛泽东与第三次全国公安会议."

66 谢天奇，"中共"镇反"运动按比例杀人内幕," *Epoch Times*, January 9, 2017. Available at: <https://www.epochtimes.com/gb/17/1/8/n8682051.htm>. Accessed April 26, 2021.

67 高新：决战"泛清真化"与镇压"大回族主义"的历史轮回， 民主中国， October 26, 2018. Available at: <https://minzhuzhongguo.org/default.php?id=86623>. Accessed April 27, 2021.

68 中华人民共和国公安部办公厅编印,党中央、毛主席关于无产阶级专政和肃反问题文件选编, 1958年12月.

69 杨奎松，"新中国 '镇压反革命'运动研究."

70 胡平， "镇反暴露中共的背信弃义和残暴本性," 议报， February 16, 2020. Available at: <https://yibaochina.com/?p=238443>. Accessed May 10, 2021.

71 "中共一大上通过的党纲和决议，" 北京师范大学网. Available at: <http://www.etc.edu.cn/kuayue/keli/zhongxueqita/zhongxuelishi/0201wusiaiguoyundong/0201wusiaiguoyundong/54CCP/danggang.htm>. Accessed April 27, 2021.

72 李肃，"1949之后：背信弃义工商业改造，" *VOA*, February 24, 2008. Available at: <https://www.voachinese.com/a/a-21-w2008-02-24-voa3-58628727/1093738.html>. Accessed April 27, 2021.

73 薄一波,若干重大决策与事件的回顾 (中国党史出版社， 1991).

74 许蕾，"政治运动的动员机制—以'三反'运动为个案," 华中师范大学学报, no. 4 (2004).

75 李肃，"1949之后：背信弃义工商业改造. "

76 爱德华，" 共产党暴政录：三反五反运动," *Epoch Times*, May 8, 2018. Available at: <https://www.epochtimes.com/gb/18/5/8/n10371607.htm>. Accessed April 27, 2021.

77 吴晓波,历代经济变革得失 (浙江大学出版社， 2013).

78 中共中央党史研究室, 建国以来历史政治运动事实 (中共中央党史研究室, 1996).

79 贾章旺, 毛泽东领导下的新中国十七年（上卷）(中国文史出版社， 2019).

80 吴晓波，"历代经济变革得失."

81 爱德华，"共产党暴政录：公私合营（工商改造）," *Epoch Times*, May 12, 2018. Available at: <https://www.epochtimes.com/gb/18/5/11/n10382929.htm>. Accessed April 27, 2021.

82 Chong Koh Ping and Joanne Chiu, "Chinese Liquor Giant Moutai Hits Heady $500 Billion Valuation," *The Wall Street Journal*, February 10, 2021. Available at: <https://www.wsj.com/articles/chinese-liquor-giant-moutai-hits-heady-500-billion-valuation-11612964076>. Accessed May 2, 2021.

83 郭道晖，"'阳谋'背后的权谋——以亲身经历剖析整风反右运动，" 爱思想网，September 9, 2010. Available at: <https://m.aisixiang.com/data/36292.html>. Accessed May 2, 2021.

84 Naranarayan Das, *China's Hundred Weeds: A Study of the Anti-Rightist Campaign in China, 1957–58* (Calcutta: KP Bagchi, 1979).

85 沈志华，"中共八大不提'毛泽东思想'的苏联背景，" 爱思想网, January 14, 2015. Available at: <https://www.aisixiang.com/data/82571.html>. Accessed May 4, 2021.

86 Li Zhi-Sui, *The Private Life of Chairman Mao* (New York: Random House, 2011).

87 萧冬连，谢春涛，朱地，乔继宁，求索中国：文革前十年史 (中共党史出版社出版，2011).

88 金观涛，刘青峰，"反右运动与延安整风."

89 薄一波，"若干重大决策与事件的回顾."

90 罗平汉，"一九五八年全民大炼钢，" 人民网-中国共产党新闻网，July 31, 2014. Available at: <http://dangshi.people.com.cn/n/2014/0731/c85037-25377579.html>. Accessed May 4, 2021.

91 南方周末编辑，"60年消逝词典之经济词语，" 南方周末网，September 9, 2009. Available at: <http://www.infzm.com/content/34490>. Accessed May 4, 2021.

92 南方周末编辑，"60年消逝词典之经济词语."

93 Sheng Hu, *A Concise History of the Communist Party of China*, 1st ed. (Beijing: Foreign Languages Press, 1994).

94 夏明方，灾难记忆与政治话语的变迁．——以文史资料中的灾害记述为中心.《中华读书报》（2015年01月28日 13 版）.

95 Jisheng Yang, *Tombstone: The Great Chinese Famine, 1958–1962* (New York: Farrar, Straus and Giroux, 2013).

96 Frank Dikötter, *Mao's Great Famine: The History of China's Most Devastating Catastrophe, 1958–62* (London: Bloomsbury Paperbacks, 2018).

97 VOA 新闻，"中共功罪评说之八：大跃进和大饥荒饿死多少人?" *VOA*, July 5, 2011. Available at: <https://www.voachinese.com/a/article-20110705-8-great-leap-and-the-great-famine-125025309/784122.html>. Accessed May 5, 2021.

98 VOA 新闻，"中共功罪评说之八：大跃进和大饥荒饿死多少人?"

99 杨继绳，墓碑-中国六十年代大饥荒纪实（香港：天地图书有限公司, 2008).

100 胡乔木，胡乔木回忆毛泽东 (人民出版社, 2003), p. 728.

101 王友琴，"恐怖的'红八月'," 炎黄春秋, no. 10 (2010).

102 中共中央党史研究室，建国以来历史政治运动事实 (中共中央党史研究室, 1996).

103 金 钟，"最新版文革死亡人数，" 开放网，October 7, 2012. Available at: <http://www.open.com.hk/content.php?id=1008#.YSUHt5OxG3I>. Accessed May 6, 2021.

104 李强，"邓小平与反对资产阶级自由化，" 马克思主义研究, no. 03 (2009).

105 中共中央文献编辑委员会，邓小平文选第三卷 (人民出版社, 1983), pp. 36–48.

106 崔敏，"八十年代'严打'的回顾与反思，" 爱思想网，September 23, 2012. Available at: <https://www.aisixiang.com/data/57618.html>. Accessed May 6, 2021.

107 Amnesty International, "China: Amnesty International Briefing," September 1, 1984.

108 "'严打'政策的前世今生，" 中国刑事法律网, July 01, 2010. Available at: <http://www.criminallaw.com.cn/article/default.asp?id=4300>. Accessed May 6, 2021.

109 周斌，"1996年第二次'严打'重拳应对犯罪升级，" 国家人文历史, no. 16 (2013), pp. 27–30.

110 BBC，"档案：邓小平曾说200人死可换20年稳定，" *BBC News*, December 30, 2016. Available at: <https://www.bbc.com/zhongwen/simp/chinese-news-38468353>. Accessed May 7, 2021.

111 玉清心, "'严打运动'冤魂知多少," *Epoch Times*, March 17, 2017. Available at: <https://www.epochtimes.com/gb/17/3/11/n8899967.htm>. Accessed May 6, 2021.

112 文华, "今日中国的百万人被杀案, 新纪元焦点新闻, no. 435 (July 2, 2015).

113 Congressional-Executive Commission on China, *Special Topic Paper: Tibet 2008–2009*, October 22, 2009.

114 BBC, "Xinjiang Arrests 'Now Over 1,500,'" *BBC News*, August 3, 2009. Available at: <http://news.bbc.co.uk/2/hi/asia-pacific/8181563.stm>. Accessed May 7, 2021.

115 "中国计划生育少生四亿多人拆除 '人口爆炸'引信," 中央政府网, November 06, 2019. Available at: <http://www.gov.cn/jrzg/2007-01/11/content_493491.htm>. Accessed May 8, 2021.

116 Rudolph J. Rummel, *Power Kills: Democracy as a Method of Nonviolence* (London: Routledge, 2002).

117 Ben Blanchard, "Xi Jinping's Journey from China Party Elite to Party Leader," *Reuters,* November 15, 2012. Available at: <https://www.reuters.com/article/us-china-congress-xi/xi-jinpings-journey-from-china-party-elite-to-party-leader-idUSBRE8AE0BZ20121115>. Accessed May 10, 2021.

118 Harold Henry Fisher, *The Communist Revolution: An Outline of Strategy and Tactics* (Palo Alto, CA: Stanford University Press, 1955), p. 13.

119 Lin Piao, "Long Live the Victory of People's War," *Peking Review* 8, no. 36 (1965): 9.

120 沈志华, 毛泽东,斯大林与朝鲜战争 (广东人民出版, 2003年11月).

121 杨奎松, "60年前的 '中国道路'," 同舟共进, 1 (2011): 30–33.

122 "在听了××××会议汇报后的讲话," *Marxists Internet Archive*, July 07, 1967. Available at: <https://www.marxists.org/chinese/maozedong/1968/5-325.htm>. Accessed May 8, 2021.

123 林彪, "人民战争胜利万岁—纪念中国人民抗日战争胜利二十周年," 学术月刊 9 (1965): 1–24.

124 钱亚平, "60年来我们援助了谁?" 新华社-瞭望东方周刊, May 24, 2011.

125 何方, "毛泽东搞世界革命扶植杀人魔王," 阿波罗网, March 11, 2016. Available at: <https://www.aboluowang.com/2016/0311/705721.html>. Accessed May 4, 2021.

126 何西阿, "波尔布特:并不遥远的教训," 炎黄春秋, no. 4 (2008).

127 王贤根, 援越抗美实录 (国际文化出版公司, 1990).

128 Conversation Record of Chairman Mao Zedong's Meeting with Pol Pot, Secretary of the Central Committee of the Communist Party of Kampuchea, June 21, 1975. Available at: <https://digitalarchive.wilsoncenter.org/document/122052>. Accessed April 12, 2021.

129 Ben Kiernan, *The Pol Pot Regime: Race, Power, and Genocide in Cambodia Under the Khmer Rouge, 1975–79* (New Haven, CT: Yale University Press, 2002).

130 何西阿, "波尔布特:并不遥远的教训," 炎黄春秋.

131 程映虹, 毛主义革命: 20世纪的中国与世界 (香港: 田园书屋, 2008).

132 杨奎松, "毛泽东对印度支那战争态度的变化(1949–1973)," 毛泽东与莫斯科的恩恩怨怨 (江西人民出版社, 1999).

133 Rudolph J. Rummel, *Statistics of Democide* (Charlottesville, VA: The Center for National Security Law, University of Virginia, 1997).

134 杨奎松, "毛泽东对印度支那战争态度的变化(1949—1973), " 香港中文大学网. Available at: <http://ww2.usc.cuhk.edu.hk/PaperCollection/Details.aspx?id=2897>. Accessed May 4, 2021.

135 VOA新闻, "中共援助缅共闹革命揭秘," *VOA*, November 26, 2001. Available at: <https://www.voachinese.com/a/a-21-a-2001-11-26-14-1-63282182/980191.html>. Accessed May 8, 2021.

136 时宏远, "印度政府为何摆不平印共 (毛)?" 中国青年报, June 30, 2009.

137 程映虹, 毛主义革命: 20世纪的中国与世界..

138 Patrick Ball, Jana Asher, David Sulmont, and Daniel Manrique, *How Many Peruvians Have Died* (Washington, DC: American Association for the Advancement of Science, 2003).

139 中共中央文献编辑室，毛泽东文集第8卷(人民出版社:1999), pp. 117–118.

140 沈志华,李丹慧, "结构失衡:中苏同盟破裂的深层原因," 探索与争鸣, October 1, 2012.

141 吟古, "彭真与赫鲁晓夫的一场激烈舌战，" 看点快报网. Available at: <https://kuaibao.qq.com/s/20200506A0J1E100?refer=spider>. Accessed May 4, 2021.

142 尼基塔·谢·赫鲁晓夫，赫鲁晓夫回忆录(全译本) (社会科学文献出版社出版，2006).

143 Xuetong Yan, "Chinese Values vs. Liberalism: What Ideology Will Shape the International Normative Order?" *The Chinese Journal of International Politics* 11, no. 1 (2018): 1–22.

144 David Brunnstrom and David Lawder, "China Says Has No Intent to Play 'Game of Thrones' but Warns on Sovereignty," *Reuters*, September 24, 2019. Available at: <https://www.reuters.com/article/us-china-usa/china-says-has-no-intent-to -play-game-of-thrones-but-warns-on-sovereignty-idUSKBN1WA04Q>. Accessed May 8, 2021.

145 Brunnstrom and Lawder, "China Says Has No Intent to Play 'Game of Thrones' but Warns on Sovereignty," *Reuters*.

146 Remarks of Secretary of State Antony J. Blinken, National Security Advisor Jake Sullivan, Director Yang and State Councilor Wang at the Top of Their Meeting, March 18, 2021. Available at: <https://www.state.gov/secretary-antony-j-blinken -national-security-advisor-jake-sullivan-chinese-director-of-the-office-of-the -central-commission-for-foreign-affairs-yang-jiechi-and-chinese-state-councilor -wang-yi-at-th/>. Accessed April 20, 2021.

147 程荣, "揭秘:"深挖洞、广积粮、不称霸"的由来," 人民网, May 13, 2016. Available at: <http://m.people.cn/n4/0/2016/0513/c102-6849769_3.html>. Accessed May 8, 2021.

148 沈志华：毛泽东访苏轶闻. Available at: <http://m.aisixiang.com/data/38420-3 .html>. Accessed May 9, 2021.

149 Joint Communiqué of the United States of America and the People's Republic of China, December 15, 1978. Available at: <https://china.usc.edu/joint-communiqu %c3%a9-united-states-america-and-peoples-republic-china-december-15-1978>. Accessed May 10, 2021.

150 Joint Communiqué of the United States of America and the People's Republic of China, February 27, 1972 (Shanghai Communiqué). Available at: <https://china .usc.edu/joint-communiqu%C3%A9-united-states-america-and-peoples-republic -china-february-27-1972-shanghai>. Accessed May 10, 2021.

151 "Sino-Japanese Treaty of Peace and Friendship." Available at: <https://www.fmprc .gov.cn/mfa_eng/ziliao_665539/3602_665543/3604_665547/t18012.shtml>. Accessed May 10, 2021.

152 "Speech by Chairman of the Delegation of the People's Republic of China, Deng Xiaoping, at the Special Session of the U.N. General Assembly," April 10, 1974. Available at: <https://www.marxists.org/reference/archive/deng-xiaoping/1974/04 /10.htm>. Accessed May 10, 2021.

153 Sun Tzu, *The Art of War*, Chapter 1. Available at: <https://www.yellowbridge.com/ onlinelit/artofwar01.php>. Accessed April 24, 2021.

154 袁德金, "毛泽东与新中国军事战略方针的确立和调整及其启示," 军事历史研究, no. 1 (2010).

155 尹曙生, "冤案是怎样酿成的," 炎黄春秋, no. 4 (2015).

156 Jiangling Li, *Tibet in Agony: Lhasa 1959,* trans. Susan Wilf (Cambridge, MA: Harvard University Press, 2016).

157 何清涟, "新疆问题：中国马尔萨斯陷阱的发散效应," 美国之音, March 10, 2014. Available at: <https://www.voachinese.com/a/heqinglian-xinjiang-chinese-migra- tion-20140309/1867614.html>. Accessed May 11, 2021.

158 新疆维吾尔自治区统计局, *2021年6月14日新疆维吾尔自治区第七次全国人口普查主要数据*, June 14, 2021. Available at: <http://www.xj.xinhuanet.com/2021-06/14/c_1127561201.htm>. Accessed October 6, 2021.

159 徐泽荣, "中国在朝鲜战争中的角色," 当代中国, no. 2 (2000).

160 Lianchao Han and Bradley A. Thayer, "The Ubiquity and Subtlety of China's Expansion Compel a Response," *The Hill*, September 7, 2021. Available at: <https://thehill.com/opinion/international/570909-the-ubiquity-and-subtlety-of-chinas-expansion-compel-a-response>. Accessed September 8, 2021.

161 邓小平, "邓小平南巡讲话（全文），" 共产党员网. Available at: <https://news.12371.cn/2016/01/21/ARTI1453342674674143.shtml>. Accessed May 10, 2021.

162 "中央政策研究室主任江金权: 一个国家, 一个政党, 领导核心至关重要," 中国新闻网, November 12, 2021. Available at: <https://www.chinanews.com/gn/2021/11-12/9607753.shtml>. Accessed November 16, 2021.

163 "Wang Yi: China Has No Intention to Play the 'Game of Thrones,'" September 25, 2019. Available at: <https://www.fmprc.gov.cn/ce/ceus/eng/zgyw/t1701346.htm>. Accessed May 12, 2021.

164 何与怀, "个人崇拜加速度——毛泽东个人崇拜的一个历史考察," 中国人权网, February 15, 2018. Available at: <https://www.hrichina.org/en/node/21060>. Accessed May 12, 2021.

165 陈尧, "中国特色社会主义不是国家资本主义," 红旗文稿, no. 23 (2018).

166 "Resolution of the Central Committee of the Communist Party of China on the Major Achievements and Historical Experience of the Party over the Past Century," *China Daily*, November 17, 2021. Available at: <https://www.chinadaily.com.cn/a/202111/17/WS61944b49a310cdd39bc75c01.html>. Accessed November 20, 2021.

167 Vladimir Ilyich Lenin, "Critique of Imperialism," in *Imperialism, the Highest Stage of Capitalism* (Moscow: Progress Publishers, 1963), p. 109.

168 Mao Zedong, *Comment on the Open Letter of the Central Committee of the CPSU(IX)*, By the Editorial Departments of *Renmin Ribao* (People's Daily) and *Hongqi* (Red Flag), July 14, 1964. Available at: <https://www.marxists.org/reference/archive/mao/works/1964/phnycom.htm>. Accessed May 12, 2021.

169 Gallup, "Losing Our Religion? Two Thirds of People Still Claim to Be Religious," June 8, 2015. Available at: <https://www.gallup-international.bg/en/33531/losing-our-religion-two-thirds-of-people-still-claim-to-be-religious/>. Accessed January 19, 2022.

170 Huang Jingjing, "'Silent Contest' Silenced," *Global Times,* November 17, 2013. Available at: <https://www.globaltimes.cn/content/825489.shtml>. Accessed May 12, 2021.

3

XI AND THE XI DOCTRINE

Continuing with the analogy of a car crash, let us now examine the driver of China's "car," Xi Jinping, who is a particular menace to the Chinese people and international stability. Global financier George Soros captured this point well in his 2019 speech to the World Economic Forum in Davos, Switzerland, when he declared, in a stark and crystalline characterization, that "Xi Jinping [is] the most dangerous opponent of open societies" because "China is not the only authoritarian regime in the world but it is the wealthiest, strongest and technologically most advanced."[1] Soros is correct about Xi, the fifth-generation CCP leader. Unfortunately, many Western China-watchers and politicians misread Xi, before and after his rise to power, hailing him as China's Mikhail Gorbachev.[2] That is, some consider Xi to be a revolutionary figure who could favorably change China's political trajectory. In the decade of his rule, Xi has failed to meet such a grandiose expectation. Western China-watchers' wishful thinking is rooted in a profound, long-lived misunderstanding of the CCP's nature and of Xi himself. This results in misinterpretation and misjudgment of Xi's intentions and threats. He has taken the course of Stalin and Mao, instead of Gorbachev. Xi Jinping indeed has become the world's most dangerous man.

To demonstrate this, we address three major issues: what makes Xi the free world's most dangerous opponent, including his personal history and his "Red DNA," or Red Guard fanaticism and paranoia; his ideology, rooted in Maoism; and the Xi Doctrine's seven major implications for China and the rest of the world. These seven implications are, first, the recognition that Xi's "Chinese Dream" is actually a form of the socialist imperialism described in Chapter 2; second, China's global expansion is designed to create a new world order dominated by the CCP; third, the PLA is not a professional military but an arm of the CCP; fourth, the CCP has become a digital dictatorship, which augments its ability to stay in power; fifth, its infiltration of Western societies for intelligence

DOI: 10.4324/9781003283614-3

collection and influence is massive and ubiquitous; sixth, the gross human rights abuses against Muslims in Xinjiang, including the use of concentration camps, reveal the depths to which the CCP will go to crush potential dissent; and, lastly, Xi's suppression of the pro-democracy movement in Hong Kong and violation of the 1984 Sino-British agreement demonstrate that China will tolerate no other centers of power.

3.1 Xi as an Individual: The World's Most Dangerous Man

Only a few men other than Xi have risen to the top of the CCP, which is no small feat, and it indicates that Xi is exceedingly ambitious. He is truly a dangerous driver of the CCP car. Born in 1953, Xi spent his formative years as a radical Red Guard during the Cultural Revolution. He believed in carrying out the CCP's violent proletarian revolution around the world to "liberate mankind." He was proud of his father's strong Party credentials, but when Xi was about nine years old, misfortune befell his family, affecting him until young adulthood. These events influenced the formation of his beliefs, values, identity, and character, and the development of his interests and abilities. Analyzing what happened during this period helps to explain why Xi has become so dangerous.

3.1.1 Xi as a Young Man: His "Red DNA" and Red Guard Mentality

Mao Zedong's authority remained largely unchallenged during his lifetime. This is primarily because he ruled through terror before and after the CCP seized state power. China's second-generation leader, Deng Xiaoping, rose and fell three times in his political career, and his low was the Cultural Revolution, when he was publicly purged, denounced, demoted, and humiliated as one of China's chief "capitalist roaders." Mao even made Deng promise that he would never try to reverse the verdict of Mao's purge against him. For that reason, Deng's authority could not reach Mao's exalted status.

Then power passed to the CCP's third-generation leader, Jiang Zemin, who came from a CCP veteran's family. His father was killed during the Anti-Japanese War (1937–1945), but Jiang was a technocrat trained by the Soviets, with no military experience. He came to power as Deng Xiaoping's concession to another CCP leader, Chen Yun, after the 1989 pro-democracy protests that caused Deng to order a bloody massacre. Jiang's vanity and hyperbolic personal style often made him an object of ridicule.

The fourth-generation CCP leader, Hu Jintao, was the weakest. He did not have a "Red DNA" background—his father ran a tea store. During the Great Cultural Revolution, Hu's father was persecuted and died in his fifties soon after the revolution ended. Like Jiang, Hu was a technocrat and the CCP's princelings considered him to be an "outsider." According to his confidant, Hu never expected to become the Party's top leader. His dream was to become a vice president of his alma mater, Tsinghua University. Hu's calm personality and introverted disposition affected his ruling style of consensual decision-making with the regime's governing body.

Before Xi came to power, he was regarded as a "*Zhonghou*" (忠厚 honest, kind, and generous) person, which sometimes means a pushover or someone who is incompetent in the context of Chinese politics. Xi faked this impression of weakness to fool his rivals and friends, to clear roadblocks and gain support to move up the CCP's leadership pyramid. He practiced "*Taoguang yanghui*" (韬光养晦) perfectly—that is, keeping a low profile and biding his time—and hid his intent. He told many people that he was just a person to "*tinghe*" (听喝的), a servant waiting to be called upon. But in October 2007, in a straw vote CCP senior officials selected him to lead.

His father, Xi Zhongxun, co-founded the guerrilla Shaan-Gan-Ning revolutionary base, with the capital at Yan'an, named for the provinces of Shaanxi, Gansu, and Ningxia. The senior Xi headed the Soviet government of the border region, and later became a member of the CCP's national leadership, assisting Premier Zhou Enlai. However, in 1962, Mao Zedong purged him for using a fictionalized biography of Liu Zhidan, Xi's comrade and co-founder of the Shan-Gan-Ning base, to oppose the Party. The book was written by Liu Zhidan's sister-in-law, Li Jiantong (李建彤), to commemorate Liu but triggered a factional fight among Party leadership because it exposed indiscriminate killings in the region by a PLA general, Yan Hongyan. Yan reported it to Kang Sheng, who was Mao's confidant overseeing internal security, intelligence, and the Party's ideology apparatus.

In this power struggle, Mao sided with Kang and the issue escalated as being anti-Mao and anti-Party—the most serious charges. Xi Zhongxun was forced to step down from the position of deputy premier. In late 1962, he was confined to a house in Beijing's suburbs for self-reflection and self-criticism as a special student in the CCP's Central Party School. In 1965, he was demoted to Henan province to be a deputy manager of a mining machinery factory. In an unusual outcome for a clique leader accused of being "anti-Party," the senior Xi's charges were determined to be an "internal contradiction" in nature, allowing him to stay in the Party.

During the Cultural Revolution, he was persecuted. The Red Guards dragged him to denouncement meetings, where he was humiliated and tortured. For "protection," he was sent to a military garrison in Beijing for solitary confinement from 1968 to 1975. After his release, he was sent to another factory in Luoyang, Henan province, until his verdict was reversed in 1978 and he was assigned to be the Party chief in Guangdong. There, he played a critical role in China's economic opening and development.[3]

The purge against Xi Jinping's father lasted more than 16 years. As many as 16,785 cadres and citizens were implicated; of them, 229 were killed, 75 were driven mad, and 53 were severely disabled.[4] Because Qi Xin, Xi Zhongxun's wife, refused to make a clean break with him, she was blacklisted by Kang Sheng and persecuted. She was sent to the May Seventh Cadre School, a labor camp system established during the Cultural Revolution, for seven years of manual labor while being investigated, according to her own account in a documentary of Xi Zhongxun.[5]

When Xi's father was labeled as a leader in an anti-Party clique, the Xi family lost many privileges. Xi was 13 years old when Mao launched the Great Cultural Revolution. Xi's parents became targets again, and he suffered for his participation in the Cultural Revolution. All of these circumstances may have traumatized Xi—but also hardened him, and his beliefs. The Red Guards ransacked his family's home, and the family moved to the Central Party School where his mother worked. During this time, Xi's older sister, Qi Qiaoqiao, was sent for re-education at a production corps in Inner Mongolia; their other sister, Qi An'an, went to a Shanxi rural village. Xi went to the neighboring Shaanxi province. All of them were minors when they were sent away. His younger brother, Xi Yuanping, stayed with his mother in the May Seventh School, but when he was refused admission to high school he became an apprentice turner in a factory. A half-sister, Xi Heping, killed herself because of the unbearable persecution inflicted by the Red Guards.[6] According to a 2000 interview, when he was governor of Fujian province, Xi Jinping said that he rarely cries, but he wept in public when he heard of Heping's death.

In that interview, Xi told the story of how he chose a political career. He got in trouble because he offended "revolutionary rebels," a term for those who answered Mao's call to attack capitalist roaders in the Party. "I always had a stubborn streak and wouldn't put up with being bullied," Xi said.

> I offended the revolutionary rebels and they blamed me for everything that went wrong. Everyone thought I was the ringleader, so Kang Sheng's wife, Cao Yi'ou, ferreted me out as a family member of the "reactionary gang" and I was less than 15 years old then. They said that I deserved to be shot 100 times. I thought, 100 times was no different from one time. There's nothing to be afraid of after a hundred times.[7]

The revolutionary rebels tried to scare him by taking him to a police station. They planned to send him to a juvenile detention center, but because it was full he was spared this humiliation and volunteered to go to Shaanxi rural area for re-education, even though he was underage for this. Xi did not reveal how he had riled the revolutionary rebels, and he rarely talked about his experiences during the Cultural Revolution. Yet from various sources we can piece together what might have happened to him. In 1960, he went to the August First School (八一学校), named for the date of the PLA's founding. This was a boarding school for children of high-ranking CCP officials, established by PLA marshal, Nie Rongzhen in 1947 before the Party seized power. Even though Xi's father was purged, it had been determined a case of "contradictions among the people," meaning that the elder Xi could be corrected and reformed. This determination allowed Xi Jinping to stay in the elite school.

In May 1966, the first wave of Red Guards appeared.[8] Formally named The Red Guard to Defend Chairman Mao, they required that all members of their first incarnation come from families of high-ranking CCP officials in Beijing's middle and high schools. This group later was called "Old Red Guards" or "Veteran Red Guards" (老红卫兵). All Red Guards must pledge their loyalty to Mao. Any student could join a Red Guard group or organize one, as long as they came from the families of the "Five Red Categories" (红五类)—namely, poor and lower-middle-class peasants, workers, revolutionary military personnel, revolutionary cadres, or revolutionary martyrs. Children who came from families classified as the "Five Black Categories" were not allowed to join the Red Guards. They included children of landlords and rich farmers, counterrevolutionaries, bad influencers or bad elements, and rightists. These groups were seen as enemies or potential threats to the revolutionary cause.

"Red Princelings" formed the Red Guards not only because they had channels to the top and could obtain information fast, but also because they were fanatical believers in Maoism, zealously holding that they were natural successors of the Red Revolution. They were determined to carry out Mao's revolution to victory. "Chairman Mao has defined our future as an armed revolutionary youth organization," said one Red Guard leader.

> So if Chairman Mao is our Red commander-in-chief and we are his Red Guards, who can stop us? First, we will make China Maoist from the inside out, and then we will help the working people of other countries make the world Red … and then the whole universe.[9]

In other words, the Red Guards were members of Mao's cult—his shock troops. Mao's instigation made the Red Guard movement become reality, and later grew it out of control. In fact, Mao used the Red Guards to start the Great Proletarian Cultural Revolution (1966–1976): They were the first to answer his call to participate. Mao laid the foundation for this by reminding them to "never forget class struggle," to incite violence. He made it clear that in order to ensure the Party and country remain Red, it is necessary to train successors to the revolutionary cause. Because the "Old Red Guards" grew up in top communist families, they were indoctrinated with the CCP's violent revolutionary ideology from childhood. They believed in their Red pedigree and judged others based on bloodline and class standing, which in Communist China determine one's values, worldview, political attitude, and moral character.

As the Cultural Revolution unfolded, Mao goaded this group of Red Guards to "Destroy the Four Olds and Cultivate the Four News," a campaign that, on the surface, aimed to erase any symbols of China's pre-communist past and replace them with Maoist ones. But in fact, Mao's real intent was to use the Red Guards in radical, violent ways in the Party's internal power struggle. During this stage, the Red Guards primarily targeted those they perceived to be enemies or bad elements in society. Anyone, including family members, who fell into the Five Black Categories would be a target of their "Red Terror." In Beijing and surrounding districts, they detained, tortured, and killed many people. The Ministry of Public Security and local police stations provided names of those they should attack. From there, they incited Red Terror in Shanghai and other cities.

The rampage culminated in August 1966, which became known as "Red August." That month, the Red Guards started their effort to annihilate a specific class of people, setting up detention centers, torture chambers, labor camps, and prisons. Their atrocities were no less appalling than those of their parents in the CCP's armed struggle to seize state power. Many witnesses documented the horrific crimes against humanity committed by these Red terrorists. The Daxing Massacre is one example: From August 27 to 31, the Red Guards rampaged the Daxing District in a Beijing suburb, murdering 325 people from families in the Five Black Categories. Whether a person actually belonged in one of these categories was often immaterial to an accusation and its consequences. The youngest victim was 38 days old. In all, they wiped out about 22 families.[10] According to a report released by the Beijing Municipal Government on November 5, 1985, in the Red August death toll reached 10,275. The Red Guards ransacked 92,000 homes and kicked 125,000 households out of the city.[11]

As the Cultural Revolution spread and deepened according to Mao's design, many parents of the Old Red Guards also were targeted. New factions of the guards ferreted them out and publicly denounced them, causing the veteran Red Guards to unite to defend their parents and protect themselves. As the result, the Old Red Guards formed the Capital Middle-High School Red Guards United Action Committee, shortened for "*Liandong*" (联动). This organization aimed to oppose the Central Cultural Revolution Group (CCRG; 中央文革小组), the group Mao assigned to lead the Cultural Revolution. Mao's wife, Jiang Qing, controlled the CCRG. The Old Red Guards opposed denouncing revolutionary veterans without reason. Deng Xiaoping's daughter, Deng Rong, was one of the leaders of the organization, and the Red Guard organization in Xi Jinping's school was a core member of the "*Liandong*."

In late 1966 and early 1967, the *Liandong* clashed with other Red Guard factions supported by the CCRG, and the Ministry of Public Security rounded up some of its members. *Liandong* broke into the ministry compound and occupied part of it four times, demanding the release of comrades. The group's activities disrupted Mao's plan, so the CCRG ordered a crackdown against it. *Liandong* soon was labeled a counterrevolutionary organization. Its members were detained and bases destroyed. *Liandong*'s last stronghold was Xi Jinping's August First School. On January 25, 1967, more than 30,000 revolutionary rebels raided *Liandong*'s base in the school. Thirty-two leaders and key members were caught, and afterward the school was shut down.[12] Although Mao later released the detained *Liandong* leaders, they were not allowed to organize and their cause lost steam soon after. But many of them continued their revolutionary efforts by "beating up hooligans," an excuse for factional fights against Red Guards the CCRG supported. *Liandong*'s activities did not end until 1968.[13]

Even though Xi Jinping never explained whether he participated in Red Terror atrocities, his childhood friend, classmate, and a professional Go player, Nie Weiping's (聂卫平) memoir revealed that Xi was a member of the Old Red Guards.[14] Xi was admitted to the junior high department of the August First School in September 1965 and assigned to Class 4, according to his Chinese language teacher at the time.[15]

When the Cultural Revolution started, Xi had nearly completed his first year of junior high school. The school was a hotbed for zealous Red princelings and young militants from families of prominent CCP officials. They believed they were destined to continue their parents' revolution and achieve the realization of communism by liberating all of mankind. The school's curriculum was tailored for that purpose. That is, its culture reinforced Maoist ideology. Xi spent six days a week there and must have shared his friends' outlook. If he did not, he would not have survived the school, where the political culture demanded that one become either a revolutionary or counterrevolutionary—and any revolutionary must actively participate in the Cultural Revolution.

At the time, Xi's parents had not been targeted and labeled as "*heibang*" (黑帮), or "black gangsters." His school was a key Red Guard base and hub for *Liandong*. So it is probable that he joined the school's Red Guard organization and participated in its activities. Xi was 13 years old, and so it might be thought that he was too young to take part in the Cultural Revolution.[16] But in reality, the most zealous Red Guards were these younger teenagers. Wang Nansheng, a Red Guard leader in a Beijing junior high school and son of a PLA general, has said: "At that time, high school students [Red Guards] had more fighting power than college students, but junior high students were the best."[17]

Li Cheng, a scholar at the Brookings Institution, thinks Xi was not an active member of the Red Guard movement because Mao purged his family before the Cultural Revolution.[18] Youqin Wang, a leading scholar on the Cultural Revolution at the University of Chicago, interviewed Chen Qiuying, Xi's Chinese language teacher at the August First School, who said because Xi's parents were detained at that time, Xi was a so-called child of "*heibang*." Xi was beaten in school and once "paraded" through the streets.[19] After carefully examining Chen's interviews, we find that Chen Qiuying did not specify the time when Xi encountered his predicaments. In other interviews, Chen indicated Xi was bullied by a Physical Education (PE) teacher, not Red Guards. Chen said Xi was bullied during the violent struggle (武斗), which generally refers the stage of Red Guards' factional conflicts between 1967 and 1968.[20] But even though he was demoted, Xi's father still was considered a revolutionary cadre who worked as a high-ranking Party official in a key state-owned mining machinery factory, responsible for the safety technology and power production sections. He was not denounced until early 1967.[21] Xi may have been looked down upon, but by no means was he excluded. His father was a national leader who made a mistake and temporarily left his position. Thus, Xi Zhongxun's status did not affect whether Xi Jinping joined the Red Guards at the early stage of the Cultural Revolution. On the contrary, he probably was deeply involved in *Liandong* and Red Guards' street fights, and so got himself in trouble because of his views and actions. Since Xi was younger than Bo Xilai and Zhu Jiamu (朱佳木), he was more likely to be a follower than a leader, and therefore less known in 1966. Bo and Zhu were leaders of the Old Red Guards and Zhu Jiamu, a *de facto* big brother to Xi Jinping, currently advises him. Bo was a "boy king" in the Central Party School compound, and Xi reportedly was one of his sidekicks during the Cultural Revolution. We believe that Xi very likely became a minor Old Red Guard leader among his peers by 1968.

Nie Weiping befriended Xi when the CCRG dissolved the August First School. When the students were transferred to other schools, Xi and Liu Weiping, whose father was a general in the PLA Air Force, were sent to Beijing No. 25 School around 1968. Nie recalled that he was a Go nerd and originally belonged to "*Xiaoyao*" (逍遥) sect, a group of students who adopted a passive attitude toward Red Guard factions and refused to side with any of them. But because of Xi and Liu, Nie sided with the Old Red Guards. "At that time, everyone in the class looked down on us and dared not interact with us. We also looked down on them," he writes.

> We had a lot of contact with the Old Red Guards outside the school. This was mainly due to the ties Xi Jinping and Liu Weiping had. Under the influence of the two of them, my feelings clearly turned to the Old Red Guards.[22]

According to Nie Weiping, one day in 1968, a sudden message called all Old Red Guards to go "crashing," that is, to destroy the bad elements who gathered in Beijing 38th Middle/High School. Xi Jinping, Liu Weiping, Nie Weiping, and several hundred other Old Red Guards showed up. In the end they were defeated in the fight and Liu Weiping, who was younger and slower, was beaten up, resulting in a severe concussion.[23] Liu later became a PLA general and served as a deputy chief of staff of the PLA's General Logistics Department.

Other than Nie's account, no information has surfaced so far about Xi's whereabouts and activities from early 1967 to early 1968. During this time, the Red Guards from Shaanxi province went to his father's factory on January 4, 1967, to denounce and physically take Xi Zhongxun back to Shaanxi. They paraded him through many cities and forced him to confess that he was a leader of an anti-Party clique. In one of his letters to Mao Zedong on February 2, 1967, the elder Xi wrote that he was taken to Xi'an, the capital of Shaanxi, on January 11 and put through a denouncement session twice, which turned to violence. As a result of the physical abuse, he lost hearing in one ear. Mao ignored his letters.[24]

This treatment must have driven Xi Jinping to more firmly side with *Liandong* and oppose the CCRG. The Old Red Guards in *Liandong* believed that the

CCRG failed to follow Mao's line. Their parents were true revolutionaries and the subject of the revolution, not the object or target. Most of the children of high-ranking Party officials held this view. Since all classes in China's schools were suspended to carry out the revolution between June 1966 and the end of 1967, Xi and his fellow students very likely engaged in the Red Guards' rampage against "The Four Olds" and "Five Black Categories," and the factional fighting. Xi Jinping himself also might have been targeted because of his father's capitalist roader status or his own *Liandong* activities. After many denouncement sessions and a year of torment, Xi's father felt that his health had deteriorated to the point that he might die, and Xi senior wrote letters to Mao, Zhou Enlai, and the CCP's Standing Committee, seeking help. Zhou ultimately sent a plane to pick him up and put him in a garrison to protect him. Although he continued to be investigated by case officers in the task force, the Red Guards no longer could abuse him, which may have saved Xi Zhongxun's life.

About this time, Xi Jinping was labeled a counterrevolutionary and denounced in his mother's working unit—the Central Party School—along with the former head of the school, Yang Xianzhen, according to one source.[25] Xi Zhongxun's biography, which Xi Jinping has endorsed in principle, does not mention this. Xi Jinping's interview mentioned that he offended the revolutionary rebels in the Central Party School, though he would not say when or why, and they labeled him as a reactionary student and treated him as such. But from the timeline in his own account, it is likely that he got in trouble around late 1968. Yang Ping, who befriended with senior Xi during his second tour in Henan in 1975, says that Xi Jinping was labeled a counterrevolutionary because he uttered a few words against the Cultural Revolution. Xi himself claims that it was Kang Sheng's wife, Cao Yi'ou, who punished him in order to hurt his father, a theory that no one has publicly corroborated.[26] His mother publicly accused Cao of persecuting her, but there are no records to show that Qi Xin was denounced in the Central Party School. What likely happened is that Xi was involved in *Liandong* factional fights and *Liandong* was targeted by the CCRG for crackdown. Xi might have echoed *Liandong*'s position about the Cultural Revolution and expressed his discontent with the CCRG. The "Six Articles of Public Security," promulgated on January 13, 1967, stipulated that anyone who uttered something or acted against the CCRG and the Cultural Revolution would be deemed a counterrevolutionary.

It is likely that Xi clashed with "revolutionary rebels" from non-elite families, who supported the CCRG in the Party school where he lived, or he simply expressed his views about the theory of Red bloodline and the Cultural Revolution. According to Xi, they believed he was the ringleader of troublemakers in the school compound, blaming him for anything bad that happened, and they detained him for a while in late 1968. Then they tried to figure out what to do with him, debating whether to send him to a re-education camp for children of "*heibang*," meaning literally "black gangsters," in a juvenile center. He implied that he went through denouncement sessions. In the end, he volunteered to go to the Shaanxi rural area for re-education. Xi Jinping's younger brother, Xi

Yuanping, wrote an article in 2013 to commemorate their father, saying that in 1968 his elder brother was 15 years old and was implicated in their father's case and detained several times for interrogation by authorities. When he came out, Xi Jinping was very weak and his body was covered with lice. He was sent to their aunt's home in Fuping, Shaanxi, and it took some time for him to recover. Their aunt fed him a bowl of fresh goat's milk each day.[27]

But Xi Yuanping did not mention how his brother was implicated and why their two older sisters were not. In a 2004 television interview with Xi, the official explanation was that Xi was labeled as a "reactionary student" and sent to "Xuexiban (学习班)," a re-education camp at the time.[28] As we have stated, after Mao used the children of CCP veterans to start the Cultural Revolution, he turned on the parents of the Old Red Guards. Mao's actions greatly affected the Old Red Guards. If their parents were to fall, they would lose their privileges and status. They formed *"Liandong"* to counter the CCRG's action, and physically clashed with the "rebel Red Guards" (造反派红卫兵) from non-elite families, upon whom the CCRG relied to target top-level capitalist roaders. They even attacked state agencies such as the Ministry of Public Security. We know Xi participated in at least one of these clashes.

Xi was happy to leave Beijing. In a 2004 television interview, he explained how he felt at the railway station when leaving Beijing: "Everyone is crying, but I am laughing. I would be crying if I don't leave. I don't know if I'm going to live or die, if I don't walk away from here."[29] In his 2000 interview he said that he left Beijing because Shaanxi was his father's base and there would be more people to protect and help him. Instead of being denounced, he would be the one to host denouncing meetings.

But Xi Jinping overestimated the situation. The harsh living conditions in the rural village and poor points given him under the socialist work point system on his production team made him dislike agricultural work. He said they lived like Shantingtong cavemen and he refused to go to work in the beginning when everyone else went. Later he found a way to loaf on the job. He learned to smoke to find an excuse to take a break, Xi said.[30] After three months, he returned to Beijing but was caught as a drifter and detained for half a year, forced to do manual labor. At the time, no one dared to openly refuse to go to work as Xi did because the person with this behavior would definitely be punished severely. It was surprising that Xi was not. This shows his rebellious mentality which was so abnormal at that time. Xi Jinping was the only one who dared to challenge the re-education system. This defiant attitude and audacious behavior were only present in a few die-hard Old Red Guards who believed they possessed "Red DNA." This is likely the underpinning of Xi's character and ideology.

Eventually, Xi's aunt and uncle persuaded him to return to his village in Shaanxi and change his reckless and unruly behavior so he could make it out of that remote place, which he did. He learned to adapt to rural life. But he knew how to secure a personal advantage by cultivating good relations (搞关系) with people in important positions, which allowed him within three years to complete the whole process of joining the Communist Youth League of China (CYLC), the Communist Party, be promoted to the party chief of his production brigade, and sent to Tsinghua University. This was extremely rare and almost unique among his peers. He befriended a Party chief of his production brigade, who pushed for his admission into the Communist Youth League of China (CYLC). Xi even convinced the commune's CYLC chief, Liu Mingsheng, to believe in him after five days of conversation and became his "sworn follower" who burned Xi's dossier that contained negative records including whatever Xi did during the Cultural Revolution, at the risk of punishment.[31] Liu confirmed this in an interview.[32] Yang Shizhong, another local party cadre, also admitted that he assisted in destroying the information of Xi's political clearance for his party membership sent from Beijing without authorization.[33] These actions are significant because they violate the CCP's procedures and actually could disqualify Xi's party membership. Several times, Tao Haisu, the county's CYLC chief, recommended that his superior recruit Xi to become a government cadre. He helped Xi to secure a position in which Xi demonstrated his leadership ability. That got him to be admitted into the CCP, and soon after, Xi was appointed as a Party chief of his production brigade.

We believe Xi Jinping's experience in Liangjiahe village largely shaped his subsequent ruling style. Xi's main achievement at the time was the so-called biogasification of Liangjiahe brigade, which was just a publicity stunt. In 1974, Xi saw a newspaper report about a methane-generating pit campaign in Sichuan and persuaded a county cadre to lead a team which included Xi himself to go Sichuan to learn about it. Upon return, Xi launched his own campaign and built dozens of the pits in his brigade, and then boasted that it solved peasants' problems of lighting, cooking, and heating. This move immediately lifted Xi to a lofty height. The provincial methane site meeting was held in Liangjiahe, where Xi was lavished with awards and titles such as Mao Zedong Thought Activist and model youth. But the truth is that methane-generating pits are not sustainable in Northern China because of the cold temperature and are costly to build and maintain. Xi's biogas project was a typical hype commonly made during the Cultural Revolution. Yet it was a precursor of many of his initiatives today, which are launched in the heat of the moment, in the name of the people to gain political capital for himself.

Within a year or so, Xi was recommended to attend Tsinghua University in 1975. Working hard, gaining peasants' trust, joining the CCP, going to university—this was the best way for young people sent to rural areas to escape dire conditions, but only a few of the luckiest succeeded, as Xi did. He had no intention of staying there forever. From Tao's 2017 interview about his relationship with Xi, it was obvious that Xi was politically ambitious.[34]

At the beginning of his rural life, villagers or nearby peasants would stop to chat with Xi and other young people from Beijing. The most important question that Xi and his roommates would ask was, "What is your class background?" If they were poor peasants, they were welcome to stay, but they were hastened out if they were rich peasants. The youngsters also chased away beggars, and even allowed their dogs to bite them, because, according to Xi, beggars were "bad elements" or "deadbeats." Locals called the Beijing students cruel.[35]

Xi and his family suffered in the Cultural Revolution, but his experience is not unique. Many others suffered no less than he. Neither Xi nor his father blamed Mao for their suffering. They blamed "bad people" in the CCRG. For example, Yang Ping, a young man who befriended Xi Zhongxun during his second tour in Luoyang in 1975, writes that during a visit, Xi Zhongxun tested his son to see how many of Mao's essays he could recite.[36] It is said that Xi passed the test by reciting two essays: "On Contradiction," at 23,250 words, and "On Practice," which has 9,340 words.

Yang also wrote that Xi Zhongxun asked Xi Jinping to recite Mao's entire four-volume "Selected Works" because the elder Xi reportedly could recite it even backward. This may be an exaggeration, but it shows the loyalty and devotion of the father and son to Mao and Maoism. Their loyalty is rooted in the myth that Mao Zedong saved Xi Zhongxun's life in 1935 when he and other leaders were about to be buried alive during the CCP's suppression of counterrevolutionaries. Xi Zhongxu was arrested and tortured by his own comrades on trumped-up charges. Mao stopped it, releasing Xi and others. Later, Xi recalled that the CCP base in Shaanxi was

> encircled and suppressed by the Kuomintang's heavy troops from outside, and at the same time was endangered by the "left" line inside, and many outstanding Party members, cadres, intellectuals and lower-level military commanders were shot and buried alive. ... If Chairman Mao arrived four days late ... if he didn't call the execution off, I would have died long ago, because they (the leftists) had already dug a pit to bury Liu Zhidan and us alive.[37]

Scholar Gao Xin said that he was not sure if Xi Jinping participated in the Red Terror activities, but all Xi learned in his second and third years of junior high were Mao Zedong's works, including poems and quotations, and the *People's Daily* editorial. This is why Xi often makes mistakes when he cites the Chinese classics, but never does when citing Mao's quotes or poems.[38]

No doubt, Xi's experiences during the Cultural Revolution shaped him in many ways, but all signs indicate that, rather than reflecting on the political system and Maoism, he blamed certain individuals, such as Kang Sheng and his wife, or even Mao's wife Jiang Qing, for his and his family's misfortunes and the country's turmoil. Tao Haisu revealed that Xi enjoyed gossip about the CCP top echelon and disliked Jiang Qing. In a letter to his roommate, Xi talked about Jiang and the letter was discovered by an official who threatened to report its content to the superior. Of course, to oppose the Cultural Revolution and the CCP Central Committee was regarded as a grave matter. Through the work of a mutual friend, the cadre was given two military coats, which were rare at that time, to calm down.[39]

From his repeated bragging about his father's revolutionary history—such as being the chairman of the Shaan-Gan-Ning Border Region Soviet Government at age 19—we can deduce that Xi is proud of being "born Red," a popular belief among the "*Hongerdai*" (红二代), or the second generation of the Party elite. Nearly all "*Hongerdai*" were Old Red Guards involved in creating the Red Terror during the Cultural Revolution. They believed the theory of bloodline— if the father is a hero, the son is a real man. If the father is a reactionary, the son is a bastard (老子英雄儿好汉，老子反动儿混蛋). They worshipped Mao and were brainwashed by Maoism, particularly the class struggle ideology, and had a strong sense of superiority because of what their parents did to win the revolution.

They believed it was their right and duty to be Mao's natural successors and to ensure the country would continue the revolution to the end. Like China's emperors, he who conquers the country should perpetually rule it. This is where Xi's worldview is grounded: Mao's absolute power, political trickery, power grabs, and hegemonic ambition inspired him. Like Mao, sources reveal that Xi has a strong imperial complex or mentality. He loves to study the history of Chinese empires, and the Chinese emperors' trickery in controlling their subjects (驭人术). Xi's most favorable emperor is Emperor Yongzheng of the Qing Dynasty. According to historians, he was extremely shrewd and cruel, strictly exercised the imperial centralized power, used harsh measures to "rectify" or kill his officials, closely surveilled his court as well as his subjects with secret agents, carried out large-scale literary inquisitions to control thought by deliberately extracting words or phrases from intellectuals' writings and arbitrarily punishing them for their speech. But at the same time, he gave small favors to lower-caste people. It seems Xi is indeed learning from Yongzheng.

When Xi graduated from Tsinghua University, he supposedly was assigned to work in a chemical factory but had no desire to do so. He or his family arranged for him to work for General Geng Biao, an old friend of his father's. It was a typical backdoor move for someone able to network with higher echelons. In 1982, Xi asked to be transferred from the PLA to a local government because the CCP decided that in the future it would promote more younger people to its top echelon. He went to Zhengding county of Hebei province as a deputy Party chief. Xi knew it was a big gamble, and he told Tao this could enable him to shape a big career or do the grand things that he wanted as a youth.[40] Through his family's connections, Xi knew the CCP wanted to select high-ranking officials from lower-level government positions. His plan was to move up the chain of command, with the goal of grasping power for himself and changing China— and the world—through Marxist-Maoist ideas.

In May 2021, the CCP's top theoretical journal *Qiushi* (Seeking Truth) published Xi's article, "Make Good Use of Red Resources, Inherit the Red Gene, and Pass on the Red Country from Generation to Generation Forever." The article is excerpted from Xi's speeches during visits over the past eight years to sites of great significance to the Party-state.[41] Xi explicitly drew from Mao's era to create a new dictatorship. When he came to power at the end of 2012, Xi felt that the CCP had lost control of the ideological domain. He demanded that the CCP dare to draw swords to eliminate dissent. His rule is similar to the Red Terror of the Cultural Revolution. That is, it has wiped out China's civil society and turned the country into an Orwellian dystopia.

Patricia Thornton contends that the Xi family's suffering during the Mao era made him reject the Cultural Revolution.[42] In fact, Xi Jinping gradually reversed the verdict on the Cultural Revolution and defended Mao's "legacy." By doing so, Xi aims to justify his own dictatorship and prevent the Chinese people from repudiating the CCP or Mao. This is why, when he assumed power, he issued "Two No Repudiates" (两个不能否定):

> The historical period after reform and opening up cannot be used to repudiate the historical period before reform and opening up, and the historical period before reform and opening up cannot be used to repudiate the historical period after reform and opening up

which simply means that no one should negate Mao, nor Deng, nor himself. Xi argues that repudiating Mao would lead to repudiating the CCP, ultimately causing the political system to collapse.[43]

But Xi deliberately forgot that Deng Xiaoping later regretted his decision not to repudiate Mao, saying that it was a mistake. In essence, Xi is repudiating Deng and embracing Mao. Xi's reversal of the negation of the Cultural Revolution can be found in the recently modified *Brief History of the Chinese Communist Party*. The older version named Mao as the person responsible for the disaster of the Cultural Revolution, citing Mao's arbitrariness and personality cult within the Party, where he held too much power. It stated that the lack of democratization and the rule of law within the Party and the country makes it difficult to correct top leaders' errors. In Xi's 2021 edition, these points disappeared.

Interestingly, the new edition adds that the Cultural Revolution was a setback for the CCP but has proven that the Party can correct its mistakes. The older edition does not contain this. It quoted Deng Xiaoping saying the Cultural Revolution must be negated thoroughly; the new version deleted part of Deng's quote, distorting his original remarks. A "peaceful evolution" of foreign hostile forces was a factor in launching the Cultural Revolution, the new version states. Clearly, it aims to fit today's politics.[44]

Gao Wenqian, a China-watcher and former CCP insider, offers some insights into Xi's psyche. Gao points out that Mao has been a specter hanging over China for generations and his great political legacy—the Cultural Revolution—controls the CCP's "way of thinking, ruling modes, discourse style and path choice."[45] Even though the *Hongerdai*, as represented by Xi Jinping, had very different experiences, they grew up in the same environment. They grew up drinking "the wolf's milk" of the CCP culture and regarded Mao as the spiritual godfather. They have inherited Mao's hostile mentality and his push for class struggle and worldwide revolution through violence. Gao thinks that Mao's Cultural Revolution legacy and the CCP official ideology are of the same origin and mutually dependent.[46] Gao Xin believes that Xi's ruling model came directly from Mao's Cultural Revolution legacy.[47]

A 2022 article assessing Xi, which was quickly censored in China, claims that Xi's inferiority complex is his Achilles' heel.[48] However, we contend that Xi has a dual or multiple personality—an inferiority complex on the one hand and arrogance and self-importance or superiority complex on the other. Xi's inferiority complex comes from his father's purge, his own persecution in the re-education study camp, and forced labor in the detention center, and possibly his status as a worker-peasant-solider university student, who were looked down upon after the Cultural Revolution. At the same time, his family and personal experiences as a teenager drove him to reinforce his "Red DNA," hardened his belief that he was "Redder" than others, more revolutionary because of his father's heroic contributions to the CCP. Through his own radical revolutionary actions, he has tried to prove the purity and superiority of his Red lineage in order to right the wrong he and his family suffered, to be accepted back into the Red princeling circle and return to the CCP's power center. The fact that his father helped to save the Communist Party by creating the Shaanxi-Gan-Ning Soviet base also gave him the capital to justify his sense of supremacy. This gave rise to his arrogance and conceit. This superiority complex may fuel his political campaign to save the Party, including formally demanding adherence to communist ideology to ensure that the communist country for which his father fought would never change.

However, unlike Mao, who emerged through the fiercest internal power struggle and whose authority none dared to challenge, indeed, Xi once was a victim of it, Xi has far less authority to rule. His experience of being physically and mentally abused made him depressed, causing paranoia about his security and unsettling him in his possession of power.[49] This makes him unpredictable and perhaps even more dangerous than Mao, because the power and resources Xi controls today are far more than Mao had. Like Mao, Xi appears obsessed with power and violence, zealously militaristic, and in a race to become the world's leader. He believes, as Mao taught, that the end justifies the means. Mao would launch nuclear war even if half the population was wiped out, and Xi would hold on to power and return to China's past imperial glory and greatness at all costs, including engaging in warfare.

3.2 Xi's Ideology

Understanding Xi's ideology begins with Mao, who had a famous comment: "To overthrow a political power, it is always necessary first of all to create public opinion, to do work in the ideological sphere."[50] This is the motto for the CCP's ideology and propaganda. Xi takes Mao's "supreme instruction" to heart. He knows the importance of ideology and control of public opinion. Domestically he aims to achieve the goal of creating one leader, one party, one nation, one ideology, and one culture in China. Internationally, he wants to create the alternative order of socialism with Chinese characteristics to replace liberal democracy. Again, this is based on the communist ideology of liberating the whole of mankind, as well as the Chinese imperial mentality: There cannot be two suns in the sky and no two rulers on the earth.

Significantly, the first thing Xi did as China's leader was to enhance the CCP ideology with his own characteristics. He cracked down on dissenting ideologies, censored public opinions, and wiped out the remaining space for free speech in China. Xi frames himself as a savior of the CCP who is on a mission to lead China back to the right path. In reality, Xi perceives that his legitimacy has been challenged, both from within and outside the system. To consolidate power and deal with his insecurity, he needs to create enemies to maintain a coherent ideology and control the country. By creating enemies, he can enhance his status and give new authority to himself, as Mao did.

Xi first faked an ideological crisis, claiming that hostile forces had overtaken the CCP's ideological front and China's public opinion domain, using platforms such as the internet to vigorously promote the so-called "universal value." Xi claimed that hostile forces aimed to "compete with us for positions, for people's minds and hearts, and for support of the masses, and ultimately [to] overthrow the leadership of the CCP and the Chinese socialist system."[51]

For the first time, Xi raised the ideological issue to the level of regime security, saying that the CCP's ideological and political security relied on the internet. He instructed the CCP to put the internet under its absolute control. According to Xi, anyone who advocates universal values and "distorts" CCP history is China's enemy. Soon the PLA newspaper published an article repeating the rhetoric that hostile countries—implying the United States—did not want to see a strong socialist China and were conspiring to intensify the spread of bad ideas to infiltrate China, interrupt its development, and shake up the CCP leadership.[52]

The focus on the United States as the enemy is alarming for U.S. security and international stability. In February 2021, a county Party chief revealed Xi's secret talk in which Xi claimed that "the biggest source of chaos in the world today is the United States," and "the United States is the biggest threat to our country's development and security."[53] Xi's ideology is based on this judgment, similar to Mao's claims that "imperialism will never abandon its intention to destroy us" and "the East wind prevails over the West wind."[54] Xi's doctrine is based on hostility toward the U.S. because, as the leader of democracies, the U.S. is a major challenge to his dictatorship and the last obstacle to achieving the CCP's centennial goals.

Xi must revive Maoism fully in order to justify his own dictatorship and to prevent the Chinese people from questioning one-party rule, which often starts by criticizing Mao. Xi intends to make Maoism come to life again to consolidate his power and ensure that the Red Party-state never changes color. Indeed, he has mimicked Mao in most aspects to establish his own historical status or a legacy on par with Mao's. In Xi's mind, Mao was the greatest leader, and Xi puts himself on equal footing with him.

Perhaps the most telling document that captures Xi's ambitions was generated in May 2013, shortly after he came to power. The CCP Central Committee issued a directive, Document No. 9, on the ideological situation. This brief from the CCP's General Office required that the Party "ensure the leadership of the news media always be in the hands of those who are in line with Comrade Xi Jinping and the CCP Central Committee."[55] It banned any discussion of seven topics that the CCP perceives as threats: universal values, media freedom, civil society, civil rights, the CCP's historical nihilism, crony capitalism, and judicial independence.

Xi has launched a series of ideological campaigns with a grand strategy that seeks to suppress any ideas deviating from the CCP's ideology. He aims to regain the Party's total control over China and its people. To keep people's thoughts in line with the CCP's ideology, Xi's suppression has become increasingly violent. First, he targeted liberal-minded leaders, intellectuals, and university professors. Then he went after human rights lawyers, who were rounded up, forcibly "disappeared," detained, arrested, tortured, or sometimes killed. Xi began a "content clean-up campaign" to ban information the regime deems "harmful." He has made Tibetan Buddhists, Uyghurs and other Muslims targets, branding them as separatists, terrorists, and religious extremists who put regime security at risk. He has put two million Uyghurs and other Muslims in internment camps and constructed a new religion embracing his ideology. As a result, Xi has largely silenced dissenting voices in today's China.

3.2.1 Xi's Ideology Is Neo-Maoism for China and the World

Xi's ideology, officially termed "Xi Jinping Thought," centers on "socialism with Chinese characteristics for a new era." Socialism is the first stage of communism in the CCP's ideology. Under Xi, many mixed principles comprise this ideology. It was amended into the CCP's Constitution in 2017, and in 2018 was incorporated into the preamble of the PRC's Constitution. Then in 2021, Xi Jinping Thought was written in the CCP's Third Historical Resolution. In the past, only Mao and Deng were able to do this. But despite its hyperbole and the CCP's phraseology, it can all be boiled down to a single sentence: Suppress internally and expand globally to enable the CCP to rule perpetually to dominate the world and achieve the goals of communism.

As we argued in Chapter 2, each of the CCP's paramount leaders comes up with his own guiding ideology for the Party-state to follow. All claim it is the Sinicization of Marxism–Leninism. In other words, their ideology, though with different names and focuses, represents Marxism–Leninism adapted to apply to Chinese circumstances in specific time periods: Mao's "Continuing the Revolution under the Dictatorship of the Proletariat," Deng's "Socialist

Market Economy," Jiang's "Three Represents," and Hu's "Scientific Outlook on Development." This cherry-picking pragmatism toward Marxism is a hallmark of the CCP ideology and is used to justify its leaders' goals and to gain "legitimacy" among its followers. It results inevitably in far-fetched theories and interpretations through the process of what the Chinese term "cutting the feet to fit the shoes."

Xi's ideology holds that the world has entered a new era and is undergoing major changes unseen in a century.[56] That is, the current global configuration and international order are undergoing profound changes, as is the global governance system. Revolutionary changes have started, enabling the world's center of gravity to shift to China. To use Xi's words, "The East is rising and the West is sinking" (东升西降). In his mind, the U.S. and other democracies in the free world are declining and China is rising. This offers China a rare opportunity to create a new world order.

In the Chinese government's official narrative, Xi's ideology focuses on the kind of socialism with Chinese characteristics to uphold and develop, and how to do so. The ten "make clears" (明确 mingque, which means to clarify and affirm) summarized in the CCP's Third Historical Resolution form a theoretic basis for socialism the CCP must advance. These are, first, maintaining the CCP as the highest force for political leadership and Xi as the core leader with absolute authority to rule China; second, achieving China's great socialist modernization and national rejuvenation; and third, maintaining economic growth to gain performance legitimacy; fourth, building a socialist system that fully instills communist ideas in all areas; fifth, continuing to improve socialism through strengthening the CCP's ideology; sixth, furthering the socialist rule of law, which aims to disguise dictatorial oppression; seventh, upholding and improving the socialist economic system, with Party-state domination; eighth, building world-class armed forces that obey the Party's command and can win major wars; ninth, enabling China's socialist diplomacy to focus on superpower confrontation to gain global dominance; and tenth, strengthening the CCP itself.

Officially, the other key parts of Xi's ideology are the "Fourteen Upholds," which explain how to carry out Xi's socialism with Chinese characteristics. These are: upholding Party leadership over all work; taking a people-centered approach; deepening reforms; providing a vision for development; running the country for the people; governing the country based on law; abiding by core socialist values; improving living standards through development; fostering harmony between people and nature; having a holistic approach to national security; maintaining absolute Party leadership over the military; advancing the principle of "one country, two systems" and reunification; building a shared, common destiny for mankind; and sustaining full, rigorous governance over the Party.

Xi's ideology essentially is neo-Maoism. Despite its grandiose terminology, the theory behind Xi's ideology and the plan for its implementation are to maintain and augment communist dictatorship through terror and lies, disguise repression under the cover of law, and control China's society to enable the CCP's perpetual rule. Internationally, the goal is to further communist ambitions for domination and U.S. defeat, while using economic growth and benefits as a lure to gain legitimacy and belief in China's ruling model. Fundamentally, Xi's ideology is Mao's continuing communist revolution under the dictatorship of the proletariat. Like Mao, Xi fears loss of power, so he frames his narrative that revolutions can betray themselves, as the Soviets did, threatening the survival of the Party and Party-state. These threats stem from multiple sources, including endemic corruption and the potential evolution of the CCP into a post-communist entity. To combat these threats, the CCP must return to its founding principles. Xi is a Maoist fundamentalist but, unfortunately for the world, his ideology is more deceptive and dangerous than Mao's.

Xi promotes his ideology as a perfect combination of the basic tenets of Marxism with China's specific realities and fine traditional culture. It includes the foundational, scientific principles of socialism as created by Marx and Lenin.[57] The CCP's propaganda apparatus boasts that Xi's ideology is 21st century Marxism, that Xi is the new heir of Marxism-Leninism-Maoism, and his ideology is a continuation and further development of their ideas. Xi often urges CCP members to stick to Marxist historical materialism to firm up their faith. He has said, "Marx's and Engels's analysis of the basic contradictions in capitalist society is not outdated, nor is the historical materialist view that capitalism is bound to die out and socialism is bound to win," and that human society will enter the communist society.[58]

The other critical part of Xi's socialism with Chinese characteristics is that it purportedly has integrated the superiority of Chinese traditional culture, or imperial cultures of past dynasties. Xi and the CCP claim that Chinese civilization is the only civilization in the world that has continued uninterrupted for thousands of years, making great contributions to the progress of human civilization. The CCP inherited this superior culture from Confucius to Sun Yat-sen, and thus sustains the unique spiritual identity of the Chinese nation. Clearly, Xi inserted hyper-nationalism into his ideology to act as the legitimate heir of Chinese culture and to restore China's past imperial glory through his dream of rejuvenating the Chinese nation. In other words, Xi attempts to wrap the CCP's revolutionary ideas with China's superior culture to advance Chinese supremacy, essentially recreating a revolutionary soul of Chinese socialist culture to increase the regime's soft power. Carefully examining Xi's rhetoric, we believe that his Chinese socialist culture does not have fine traditional Chinese cultural ethos but decayed feudal imperialist dross. For example, with the emphasis on Confucianism, Xi intends to include elements of etiquette in a highly hierarchical system, such as rules between the ruler and his ministers, which constantly reinforce the idea of the supremacy and absolute power of the ruler. No one should challenge his authority, which is similar to the absolute rule of the Chinese monarch. All the monarch's actions are correct. Additionally, Confucius's idea of the commonwealth under heaven is also used to seek China's global hegemony through Xi's community of common destiny for mankind. Ironically, more than other dynasties, the CCP has done the greatest destruction of Chinese traditional culture, by eliminating languages, cultures, religions, and history of ethnic groups.

Under Xi, economic development continues to be an important way to build legitimacy. The socialist market economy is turning more into a state-dominated economy, with policies to make state-owned enterprises stronger, bigger, and better. China claims this effort is to "serve national strategic goals and adapt to high-quality growth," but in reality, the government wants to ensure its monopoly over the economy through mergers and consolidation of state-owned enterprises, with limited private participation to decorate its economic reform, and also by taking profitable businesses from the private sector. It allows the Party-state to secure control of the country's economy. Economic security is a key component of Beijing's regime security. The CCP fears that if the private sector gains a sufficient share of the economy, it may use its resources to demand political rights and reforms that could weaken the Party-state's power. In other words, Xi has elevated economic performance to the level of regime security, and a state-dominated economy can ensure this outcome. This is Beijing's real intent, not to improve the efficiency and pro-ductivity of enterprises.

This socialism with Chinese characteristics is a perverse hybrid of a partial market economy and the communist planned economy. The Party-state con-trols every aspect of China's economic activities. Even though some private ownership exists, these are nominal and, in a sense, ornamental. The CCP owns the state and is the state, giving the Party total control of economic activi-ties. Fundamentally, socialism with Chinese characteristics is akin to Adolf Hitler's odious ideology of national socialism. It can control private or market activities not only through the Party-state's economic intervention but also through political, judicial, and social controls. Behind the so-called market mechanism is the Party's total control, including price controls and the maxi-mization of profits to achieve political goals and ensure economic security. Xi has made clear that public ownership must dominate China's economy. Of course, the "public ownership" is, in fact, Party ownership. This makes the CCP the world's wealthiest political party. All of its assets and resources are used to advance the communist cause globally. Therefore, Xi's socialism is the worst form of Marxist socialism, more dangerous than its antecedents among totalitarian ideologies.

The most important component of Xi's ideology is the CCP's absolute control of the Chinese people and society. "The Party exercises overall leadership over all areas of endeavor in every part of the country," it claims. Moreover, "The leadership of the Communist Party of China is the most essential feature of socialism with Chinese characteristics."[59] Xi believes that only absolute control can ensure regime security, a lesson apparently learned from the collapse of the Soviet Union and Eastern Bloc countries.

As China's leader, Xi advances socialism through a five-pronged approach, what he calls the "overall layout," a blueprint to integrate economic, political, cultural, social, and ecological construction into a coherent whole. As we have discussed, economic construction aims to ensure the Party-state's ownership dominates China's economy. The political construction refers to implementing socialist consultative democracy. Xi insists this is a true form of democracy, just like electoral democracy, because "the essence of people's democracy is that the people get to discuss their own affairs."[60]

The irony is that Xi—along with previous CCP leaders and even China's Constitution—emphasizes that the people are the master of the nation, but clearly under China's so-called consultative democracy the people are not allowed to decide their affairs. In fact, they cannot even discuss their affairs. Any criticism or discussion of sensitive subjects, such as political or civil rights, or Xi's dictatorial leadership style, is to "speak ill of the CCP Central Committee's major policies," a transgression that could put the speaker in prison. Xi has wiped out an emerging civil society and eliminated free speech in China. Since he assumed power, many individuals have been arrested and jailed for criticizing CCP policies. Reporters Without Borders ranked China fourth to last out of 180 countries on its 2021 World Press Freedom Index. The organization has ranked China near last place since 2015.[61]

Xi's idea about social construction claims to center on ensuring and improving people's livelihood. The people-centered approach is the most deceptive part of his ideology, because Xi claims that everything the CCP does is to maintain social justice, raise the standard of living, and ensure people's happiness. In our view, all of these intend to secure the CCP's perpetual rule. Xi once said, "Those who win the hearts of the people win the world, and those who lose the hearts of the people lose the world. The support of the people is the strongest foundation of the Party's governance."[62] Xi has revised this to say the main contradiction in the new era is "between unbalanced and inadequate development and the people's ever-growing needs for a better life."[63] He acknowledges that unbalanced and inadequate development could cause social conflict, and economic development alone may not be sufficient to solve China's problems. All-around social progress—including "demands for democracy, the rule of law, fairness and justice, security, and a better environment," addressing regional imbalances and structural flaws in development—should be implemented to solve this contradiction.

On the other hand, Xi's social programs have gained some favor with the population. His construction of an ecological civilization is calculated for effect that he cares about the environment. It is based on his idea that "clear waters and green mountains are as good as mountains of gold and silver." However, Xi's true intent is to address a problem that may threaten regime security: Predatory rapid economic development has profoundly damaged China's environment and risks people's health, which could seriously affect the sustainability of economic growth. In the past, many protests in China were triggered by environmental concerns, so Xi has put forward the thought of building an ecological civilization with sustainable construction and environmental protection. Despite his rhetoric, China remains the largest polluter in the world. In 2019, its greenhouse gas emissions were an estimated 13.92 billion tons, twice as much as the United States. Between 2000 and 2018, its annual carbon emissions nearly tripled, and now account for nearly a third of the world's total greenhouse gases linked to global warming.[64] This is because China has fallen into the trap of its economic miracle and performance legitimacy, which the CCP must sustain. China's transition from the world's manufacturing factory to an innovation center is hardly attainable because of system defects. Between economic stagnation and environmental protection, China always will choose economic development, and so it will continue to pollute.

Xi believes in his ideology's "historic significance" to the world. He intends to guide not only the Party-state but also the world. Comprehending his real intent will help us understand the China threat. In the following sections we will examine the implications of Xi's ideology for the world. It is true that Beijing claims it will not impose the China model on other countries and, at least on the surface, Xi's ideology does not advocate world revolution. However, the ideology is undoubtedly based on the Marxist-Leninist-Maoist idea of destroying the old world order. Xi has urged the Party to return to its founding mission—which includes using a proletarian revolutionary army to overthrow the *bourgeoisie*, establishing a proletarian dictatorship, eliminating class, abolishing private ownership, and confiscating all means of production. The ultimate goal of Xi's socialism is to win the "great victory of socialism" and achieve a communist society, and it does not matter how this goal is reached. Not mentioning world revolution does not mean that Xi has abandoned such an approach. Openly advocating for violent revolution would backfire, but it does not mean Xi has given up the idea. By launching high-tech-based warfare of information, psychology, public opinion, and economic enticement, he may be able to achieve his goal without firing a shot.

3.3 The Xi Doctrine

Xi's ideology is pernicious, caused by what we term the "Xi Doctrine." This is his plan to ensure CCP rule within China and its triumph globally, supplanting the U.S. as the world's dominant power. Although Xi has never made statements that clearly elaborate on his doctrine, from his remarks and writings and the Party-state's official documents, we can peel the fancy veneer off his rhetoric, such as a "global community" and "common prosperity," to uncover his true intent. For Xi, the world has entered an era in which the CCP's rule in China cannot be challenged. The world must recognize and embrace China's rise as a superpower. The CCP must lead China to achieve its national rejuvenation—or the Chinese Dream—and lead the world to build a common destiny for mankind under a new order of socialism with Chinese characteristics. Any effort to prevent these goals is considered hostile and must be defeated. Eight principles define the Xi Doctrine:

1. The CCP must rule China perpetually and ensure regime security at all costs, and other countries must respect the regime and its ruling model.
2. To rule China perpetually, the CCP must have absolute control of every aspect of Chinese society.
3. China must maintain high economic growth under socialism with Chinese characteristics.
4. Only the CCP can lead China to achieve its national rejuvenation, restore China's past glory and honor, maintain its territorial integrity by annexing Taiwan and the South China Sea, and return China's international status to its rightful position as the center of the world.
5. China's rise and the West's decline is an inevitability, and the U.S. is the biggest threat to the CCP regime and its mission; therefore, China must defeat the U.S. in this great-power confrontation.
6. China will use force, or unlimited warfare, globally to defend what it perceives as its core interests, including its development and ideological interests.
7. The "Rule of China," or China model, offers the world a better course than capitalism and democracy, and it should be expanded globally as the shared common destiny for mankind.
8. To achieve this destiny, China must lead global governance with a China-centered world order of socialism with Chinese characteristics that displace the existing liberal order.

From these principles, we can see that Xi's objectives have both domestic and international components. Domestically, they are to ensure the CCP's perpetual rule through repression, terror, fear, and surveillance, while utilizing rhetoric about economic growth and the Chinese Dream of national rejuvenation to mobilize the population into believing in the Xi Doctrine and prepare it for sacrifices that will be necessary when China's confrontation with the U.S. intensifies. Xi will make certain that no one can challenge his leadership.

Ensuring CCP regime security is the core of the Xi Doctrine, the most critical objective in China's foreign policy. One statement that China repeats in its foreign relations is that each country has the right to choose its social system and development path, independently and autonomously, which means the world must recognize the legitimacy of the CCP's dictatorship and its perpetual rule of China. No color revolutions are permitted, and neither is the peaceful evolution of the regime.

In the international realm, the objectives are to use ideological, economic, diplomatic, military and other means to expand China's power, create a China-centered world order, and supplant the United States as the dominant power. The ideological means are the foundation upon which other slogans and concepts are based, such as "socialism with Chinese characteristics" and the creation of a "common destiny of mankind." These aim to weaken U.S. strength and world leadership, expand China's power, and advance a new world order. For states of the global south, China advances its model for growth and modernization, which combines repressive political rule with CCP-led crony capitalism—all supported by China and requiring China's goodwill to sustain. The ideological tools serve as a mask to conceal Chinese control. In effect, the great-power confrontation is a contest of competing ideologies.

The economic means include the AIIB and BRI, investment and infrastructure creation, and China's dominance of the global supply chain and market shares to expand its power through economic might. China aims to lure other countries, particularly developing countries, to accept its new world economic order, which would change the existing order and international financial system. The goal is to clinch China's long-term economic security by securing strategic resources, materials, and markets while undermining the U.S.-led, free-market economy.

The key objective of China's diplomatic mechanisms is to persuade other countries to side with it and not the U.S. This is a traditional avenue for expanding power, such as creating bases in Djibouti and Pakistan as the start of what will become a global network of intelligence and military bases. China entices countries with economic interests, such as promised investments, and bribes the elites in those countries to gain control.

Finally, the military instrument—China's newly modernized conventional weapons and expanded nuclear arsenal, strengthened space combat capability, advanced cyber weaponry, and other asymmetrical and unlimited war expansion—will help to cement China's political, economic and influence gains, and further its expansion to include seizing Taiwan and annexing the South China Sea. This will create a showdown with the United States. The military elements of the Xi Doctrine include an alarming proclamation of undisguised threats to use force or wage an unlimited war to secure the CCP's overall security and global expansion. China will use its "wolf-warrior" style to legitimize its territorial expansion, target the U.S. as its greatest threat and the cause of the world's major problems, and ultimately evict the U.S. from its seat as the global leader. To achieve these objectives, Xi has accelerated the PLA's centenary goal eight years ahead of schedule. Below we discuss five major implications of the perilous Xi Doctrine to demonstrate the China threat.

3.3.1 The Chinese Dream Is One of Socialist Imperialism

To comprehend the employment of the Xi Doctrine, we must recall the concept of socialist imperialism introduced in the previous chapter. In 2010, PLA Colonel Liu Mingfu, a retired professor and former director of the Institute of PLA Building at National Defense University, published *The China Dream: Great Power Thinking and Strategic Power Posture in the Post-American Era*. The

China Dream that Liu proposed was advanced two years ahead of Xi Jinping. In the book, Liu analyzes America's global dominance and advocates the need for China to overturn it. China's dream, according to Henry Kissinger's summary of the book, is to become number one in the world, thereby restoring its historical glory.[65]

That is the main theme of Liu's book. "The world is too important to hand it over to the United States," he writes, and "China must build the world's most powerful military force to compete with the United States for the 'world championship.'"[66] Liu openly urges that China's rise doesn't need to be peaceful. He sets up an analogy of this ultimate fight as a sporting game, a hundred-year "marathon contest." In the book's preface, Liu Yazhou, a former PLA lieutenant general and political commissar of the National Defense University, writes that the 21st century is the century of China–U.S. confrontation. The country that creates more attractive results for world development, is stronger, and moves faster will win the necessary influence to lead the world and determine its future course.

The fact is, Liu's view represents the CCP's unspoken official position, and even that of the mainstream Chinese public: China must rise to be the world's number one country at all costs. Peaceful rise is just a cover for its true strategic intent; the CCP believes that "political power grows out of the barrel of a gun." That means world hegemony grows out of the barrel of a gun. Under Deng Xiaoping, Jiang Zemin, and Hu Jintao, the CCP hid its intent because China was still weak compared to the United States. Now Xi Jinping believes that China is strong enough to openly challenge U.S. dominance. Influenced by Liu's book, he announced the "Chinese Dream" as soon as he became Party chief in November 2012.

Xi's ideas have evolved. He once defined the greatest Chinese dream as realizing the nation's rejuvenation in modern times. Later, he added that the key to realizing the Chinese Dream is to achieve the CCP's two centenary goals. In addition, a strong and prosperous country, a rejuvenated nation, and people's happiness are part of the Dream. Xi later claimed that in the final analysis, the Chinese Dream is the people's dream. Then his propaganda apparatus further broadened the Dream beyond the Chinese to the world, because the Dream is one of peace, development, and "win-win" cooperation for China and its partners. It benefits people around the world. Xi's shared destiny of mankind community and the BRI is the international expression of the Chinese Dream.[67] But no matter how Xi and the CCP frame it, it is a dream of world hegemony, a dream to restore China's imperial glory as the most powerful empire. There are three components to this rejuvenation.

First, national rejuvenation is Han Chinese-centric since they comprise about 92 percent of mainland China's population. Included in this rejuvenation are the 40–50 million Han Chinese or Chinese descendants in the Chinese diaspora. In China's official narrative, the Chinese Dream supposedly includes all ethnic peoples, such as Tibetans, Uyghurs, and Mongolians, whose territories are occupied by China and who live under the CCP's rule. Despite the CCP's efforts, through forced assimilation and disguised genocide, most of these people refuse to identify with Chinese ethnicity. But any advocacy for self-determination or autonomy is considered to be separatism and subversion of Party-state power, which is always punished harshly. There are more than 50 ethnic groups other than the Han Chinese in China, and clearly the CCP would shut down their rejuvenation.

Since the Cultural Revolution, the Chinese people's faith in the CCP has diminished. Although Deng's economic development helped to restore some confidence, most people do not take the communist faith seriously. The CCP needs new rhetoric to fool the masses and strengthen the faith of the communists. National rejuvenation worked well in the past. It worked for Sun Yat-sen, Mao Zedong, and so far, for Xi. This narrative takes advantage of deeply rooted Han-centric nationalism, or national pride, racial and cultural superiority, and a strong sense of being hurt by the CCP historical narrative of a "century of humiliation," from the First Opium War of 1839–1842 to when the CCP seized power and founded the PRC in 1949. Of course, the CCP forgets to mention that the Party has been a primary reason for the Chinese people's tremendous suffering.

Second, in China's official narratives, realizing China's rejuvenation means the country must overthrow imperialism, feudalism, and capitalism. The complete reunification of the motherland is a requirement for the "great rejuvenation of the Chinese nation." If China fails to achieve unification and gain territorial integrity, there will be no real rejuvenation or realization of the Chinese Dream.[68]

This means China will do anything to ensure that Tibet and Xinjiang remain under its control, including putting more people in concentration camps or forced labor, or luring them with economic aid. It means that China must take over Taiwan, with or without force, before 2049, even if it triggers a war in the region or armed conflict with the U.S.—even a nuclear war. Xi has threatened Taiwan:

> The fact that the two sides of the strait have not yet been completely reunified is a trauma left by history to the Chinese nation. The Chinese on both sides of the strait must work together to seek national reunification and heal the trauma of history.[69]

China's rejuvenation also requires a full annexation of the South China Sea, including its militarization, reclamation, and monopoly of natural resources. It is evident that China's great rejuvenation is all about the great debilitation of other countries and peoples.

Third, Xi's historical narrative of the great rejuvenation has implied a kind of revenge against those perceived to be the perpetrators of China's century of humiliation. This is not unique to China. For example, the animus that Russia has against the West arises from its feeling that it was taken advantage of after the end of the Cold War. What is unique to China, however, is the ubiquity of the sentiment and the fact that the CCP will never stop reminding the Chinese people of the humiliations China has endured.

In sum, Xi's Chinese Dream employs retaliation to motivate the Party and population to dominate the world, while using racial and cultural supremacy and economic development as bait to construct a new form of imperialism at the expense of the interests of the Chinese people, ethnic minorities, and other countries.

3.3.2 China's Global Expansion Seeks to Create a New World Order

This section examines Xi's hegemonic ambitions as a component of the Xi Doctrine. Particularly important are the CCP's stance to "lead the reform of global governance" and BRI as it relates to the Chinese Dream, and the threat to the liberal international order. Xi's community of common destiny for mankind, which has been hailed as "the direction forward for human society," intends to break the existing international order and establish one according to the CCP's design. This is the continuation of the communist Red Revolution to achieve global dominance, but with the invocation of the Chinese culture's "Datong World" and "peace-loving" to sugarcoat the PRC's dominance.

3.3.2.1 The New World Order of the Xi Doctrine

The liberal world order poses a fundamental challenge to the CCP's domestic rule and global expansion, and as its power grows, China has begun to advocate a new order. However, Beijing does not want to destroy the old order immediately; it still needs to take advantage of some institutions, such as the United Nations, accepted principles of sovereignty, free trade, global investment, and technology transfer, to become stronger for its showdown with the U.S. At the moment, China has been working to change the liberal world order, not to build a completely different system.[70] But in the end, the Xi Doctrine will drive China to impose socialism with Chinese characteristics to replace the liberal order.

Gu Xuewu, director of the Global Research Center at the University of Bonn, claims that China hopes to establish a world order that is "politically multipolar, functionally multilateral, and ideologically diverse," under which several great powers, including China, would dominate the world, decide the global agenda, and accept different forms of governance.[71] These views parrot China's official position and take at face value the CCP's narrative. They fail to see Xi's real intent. It is true when Xi says in speeches that China benefits from the existing order and does not want to overthrow it and start over. He pretends to be a strong advocate of multilateralism, multipolarity, and political diversity. One cannot find any error in Xi's authoritarian declaration that his Chinese Dream is the World Dream.

The problem is that Xi's rhetoric never matches his conduct—and even his rhetoric sometimes contradicts itself. A "community of common destiny for mankind" was first put forward in 2012, during the CCP's 18th Party Congress. Since then, the CCP's propagandists have promoted it across the world. *People's Daily* claims that "the community of common destiny for mankind" is the alternative for the world's order, and that the reason a new order is needed is that the old international order has gone wrong and with many problems in the world, people long for a new order to bring peace, prosperity, fairness, and justice to the world. That is why China formally put forward the "Community of Common Destiny for Mankind" initiative and its plan for building a new international order in the new era.[72] In his 2014 remarks at the Fourth Conference on Interaction and Confidence-Building Measures in Asia (CICA), Xi stated: "Keep up with the progress of the times, for one cannot physically have entered the 21st century and his head still stays in the past, remaining in the old era of colonial expansion, in the old frames of Cold War mentality and zero-sum game."[73] This was an attack on the U.S., implying that the existing world order is outdated. Xi's foreign minister, Wang Yi, has attacked the U.S. many times for "rehashing the Cold War mentality."[74]

Xi's own words shed more light on this. On February 17, 2017, he spoke at the CCP's National Security Work Symposium, saying, "It is necessary for China to lead the international community to jointly create a new world order that is more just and rational."[75] In 2018, Xi demanded that China "lead the reform of the global governance system" when speaking at the Central Foreign Affairs Work Conference.[76] At a study session of the CCP Politburo, he explained why China must do this, stressing that the fundamental purpose of China's push to reform the global governance system is to realize the Chinese Dream and reach the CCP's goal of rejuvenating the nation.[77] China claims the Western world order and governance system are not only unfair but cannot meet today's challenges.

According to Chinese government scholars, China's position on the world order has evolved from being an opponent from 1949 to the early 1970s, to becoming a participant between the 1970s and 1990s, to being a builder from the 1990s to 2012, and now leading. In other words, China opposed the world order before the Nixon–Mao reconciliation, and then participated in it when China took the UN seat from the Republic of China (ROC). When China's "economic miracle" took place, it became a major contributor to the world order, and now, under Xi, China dominates or leads in reshaping the world order. As mentioned in the previous chapter, the 2008 financial crisis brought on by the subprime mortgage debacle made Chinese communists believe that their turn had come, and so they abandoned Deng's "*Taoguang Yanghui*" strategy to mask China's intent and decided to "lead global governance system reform," a euphemism for creating a new world order. The deception coincides with Xi's claim that China will defend the existing order while creating a new one.

The new order does not need to be created by completely tossing everything in the old. It could be developed on the basis of the old order. It includes both the absorption and transformation of reasonable elements in the old order, such as the United Nations and the negation of its unjust elements. They also believe that some rules and institutional arrangements are, in fact, advantageous to China and should be kept. That is why the CCP advocates the establishment of a new order while maintaining the existing one.[78]

Obviously, China intends to fundamentally change the world order to create a China-centered one, but it does not want to do so openly and immediately for fear of effectively countering its ambitions and losing what's valuable in the existing order. In its staged approach to becoming the top superpower, China must advocate multilateralism and multipolarity to disrupt the current world order by weakening U.S. global leadership and increasing its own influence. It also advocates for political diversity to ensure that its one-party rule is not threatened by any color revolutions or by peaceful evolution. This is the reason that Xi insists upon what he terms "double leads" (双引领)—lead to establish a new global order that is more equitable, and lead to ensure international security.[79]

3.3.2.2 Community for a Common Destiny for Mankind: CCP Rule by Another Name

According to China, because of the West's liberal world order coming to an end from internal and external pressures, the world has called for China to construct a new, fair, rational, and equitable order.[80] Therefore, the CCP hastened the birth of the idea of a community of shared future for mankind. The official narrative defines the idea as a community with lasting peace, universal security, common prosperity, openness and tolerance, and a clean and beautiful world. It claims the idea is a "scientific system with rich contents."[81] But behind these superficial words hides the CCP's grand strategy to reshape the world according to its ideology.

It is useful to examine what Chinese government scholars have said about the idea. Because of the nature of the CCP's ideology, any interpretations must come from the same script, reflecting the top leader's view. Government scholars, therefore, are the CCP's propagandists; what they say represents the CCP's official position.

An official Chinese scholar declares that, from the theoretical point of view, the "community of shared future for mankind" or "common destiny of mankind" lies in opposing Western centrism and Western superiority, the hierarchy of civilizations, and the clash of civilizations. The justification for this is that the community built and led by capitalism is "a homogenous type of civilization" that stereotypes and degrades other types of civilizations as being backward, uncivilized, and ignorant. This mentality sets up a zero-sum game, a belief that there is no escape from wars between emerging powers and existing powers. The new framework can avoid it.[82] These messages make it clear that the community of shared future for mankind is designed to oppose the Western world order based on liberal democracy and universal values, and to replace it with a China-centered world order based on Marxist ideas and values.

In April 2021, Xi delivered a keynote speech at the Boao Forum for Asia Annual Conference, in which he once again elaborated on his idea of the community of shared future for mankind with four initiatives: first, consultation on an equal footing to create a future of shared benefits; second, openness and innovation to create a future of development and prosperity; third, solidarity and cooperation to create a future of health and security; and fourth, commitment to justice to create a future of mutual respect and learning. Xi specifically pointed out, "We must not ... allow unilateralism pursued by certain countries to set the pace for the whole world."[83]

This rhetoric sounds great on paper to any peace-loving country and people. But if we examine it more carefully, Xi is continuing to attack the U.S. and appears determined to displace it as the world's leading superpower. The CCP's conduct falls far short of its rhetoric. The world needs only to look at how the CCP treats ethnic peoples such as Tibetans and Muslims in China to understand the consequences of a community of shared future for mankind. China never considered the Uyghurs and other Muslims to be equal even before Beijing began imprisoning them in internment camps. Cooperation to create a future of health and security is also unfortunately absurd. Xi's mishandling of the Covid-19 pandemic has caused more than five million deaths at the time of this writing, and the world has not heard an apology from him or the CCP. There is little cooperation from China in the international community's effort to determine the origin of the virus. We can imagine what the world would be like under a China-centered order. Since the CCP's launching of the "community of a shared future for mankind," it has created a few institutions and think tanks to propagate the idea globally. The Party-state has sneaked the term into UN resolutions several times, to create the impression that it has been generally accepted by the international community.

3.3.2.3 The BRI: An Instrument for a New Communist World Order

China calls its BRI a great practice of building a community of shared future for mankind.[84] Undoubtedly, the BRI is the implementation of the idea. An examination of the BRI can shed some light on how a China-centered world order would appear.

Xi announced the BRI as a way to build an economic belt of the Silk Road on September 7, 2013, and a month later added a way to build a 21st century maritime Silk Road. This was less than a year after he proposed to "build a community of common destiny for mankind," and since then, all of these have been propagandized as "providing the world with the 'Chinese solution' and 'Chinese wisdom.'" So far, 140 countries and 32 international organizations have joined the BRI.[85] In Africa alone, more than 10,000 Chinese companies are participating in the BRI.[86] The BRI originally was a move by Chinese trade authorities to get rid of China's overproduced goods and surplus capital from its export trade. Xi made it into a geopolitical strategy, combined it with the "Marching West" strategy, and turned it into a great struggle with the United States for world dominance.

By examining domestic Chinese messaging about the BRI and interviewing insiders, we find that after Xi announced the community of common destiny for mankind, he needed specific measures to make it materialize, so he rushed to put forward the BRI without his agencies completing an assessment of the idea. CCP strategists, researchers, and scholars later came up with many justifications to support the BRI. For the CCP, the BRI is the best way to counter the U.S. pivot to Asia policy without a head-to-head confrontation. In the beginning, they claimed that through the Obama administration's rebalance to Asia and the Trans-Pacific Partnership (TPP), the U.S. intended to contain China militarily and economically. The BRI would enable China to move westward into the Middle East, Central Asia, and Africa, and by doing so, China could break the U.S. encirclement and strike the U.S. at its weakest points where its power and influence were fading. Thus, to gain the upper hand over the U.S., the CCP employed a strategy of "using the rural areas to encircle the cities."

The CCP argues that China can use newly gained land power to balance its sea power and resolve the difficulty of passing through the Straits of Malacca. Many scholars hold the view that whoever controls this passage will dominate seaborne trade from Asia to Europe. It will allow China to contain the rise of potential rival India and secure China's frontier Muslim region by eliminating any potential security threat from "Uyghur terrorists" once and for all. More importantly, it will help China continue to expand economically by providing new markets to absorb its overproduction capacity and a better return for its $4 trillion in foreign reserves, and in the process, it will create a booming economy in the less-developed Western regions. It also will secure much-needed materials such as oil, natural gas, and minerals, enabling China to sustain its long-term growth.

With time, the BRI has been shaped into a full-fledged grand strategy—a great practice for materializing the community of common destiny for mankind. By doing so, China has decided that it will expand its land and sea power at the same time, its soft and sharp power, and its economic and political power. In his book, Xi specifically says the BRI is an important path for building the community of common destiny for mankind, composed of the "five connectivities:" policy, infrastructure, trade, capital, and people-to-people exchange.[87] Each connectivity has a deeper meaning than what the word describes. Policy communication and consultation are not limited to economic development projects and require BRI countries to choose to side with China politically. Infrastructure connectivity means physically linking BRI countries with China and with each other, including through highways, railroads, and undersea cables. Impeded trade makes the BRI into a trading bloc, and capital connection means an RMB currency zone with the hope of replacing the U.S. dollar. Linking people's hearts and minds means winning people's support for China's agenda through education, culture, health, and tech transfer.

When Western media questioned the motive of the BRI, China's official media outlets denied the BRI is a tool for China's expansion, insisting it is not geopolitics related to security but geoeconomics concerning development. They denied any military intent of the BRI. But Cai Xia, a former professor at the CCP Central Party School who trains Party officials, revealed the military's role in the BRI. She writes:

> China's vigorous expansion of Xi's military reform also runs in tandem with Xi's vaunted BRI. A few years ago, I was invited to participate in the selection of "best curriculum" for military, ideological, and political education, and I attended the lecture competitions for a week. Quite a number of the lectures were about "how to use the military to" keep the Belt and Road on course (保驾护航).[88]

Clearly, supporting the community of common destiny for mankind and the BRI is a PLA-designated mission. The PLA's acquisition of military bases overseas, such as in Djibouti, has been documented by international researchers and is hard for China to deny.[89] The CCP propagandists will use other excuses, such as peace-keeping, asset protection, and counterterrorism, to continue China's military expansion in BRI countries. However, no one has spoken so well about the real goal of China's new colonization of BRI countries as the CCP itself. The CCP criticized the Soviet's global expansion policy in 1970, stating:

> The Soviet Revisionist renegade group says that it provides "assistance" to the Asian, African and Latin American countries, but in fact, under the guise of it, all it does is to put some countries in these regions into their sphere of influence and compete with U.S. imperialism for the neutral zones. Through the export of arms, capital output and unequal trade, the Soviet Revisionists plunder the resources of those countries, interfere in their internal affairs, and wait for an opportunity to seize military bases.[90]

The CCP further cited Lenin to criticize the Soviet policy:

> To the numerous "old" motives of colonial policy, finance capital has added the struggle for the sources of raw materials, for the export of capital, for spheres of influence, i.e., for spheres for profitable deals, concessions, monopoly profits and so on, economic territory in general.[91]

The Soviet social imperialists were following the path of capitalist imperialists, the CCP claimed.

What was condemned during the Cold War is now embraced, since this is what China is doing through the BRI. The BRI is China's "one stone, many birds" grand strategy in an attempt to create China-dominated international relations and a China-centric world order. It uses economic development as a disguise, as well as bait to increase its sphere of influence. Originally, China's paranoia about its regime security made it overreact to a U.S. pivot to Asia, resulting in a rushed, somewhat irrational decision—a decision based more on perceived geopolitics than on economic calculation. But plundering resources to ensure China's long-term energy security and the security of other strategic resources means that predatory exploitation of BRI countries' markets is on Beijing's agenda.

Scholars such as Nadege Rolland and Eyck Freymann argue that the BRI is the modern version of the ancient Chinese imperial tributary system. Under this system, BRI countries exchange their political vassalage to China for "money and access to Chinese goods and technology. BRI is Xi's attempt to use that past model to build China's future glory."[92] This argument has some truth to it. The ancient Chinese concept of "the world" and the states is mixed. China always has been proud when world nations pay tribute to the emperors (万邦来朝). This China-centered mentality reflects its ambition for world dominance and therefore the BRI.

Even though Xi removed his mask concerning China's intention to pursue world dominance, there is still a concern in Beijing that it will backfire if China openly acknowledges the BRI's geopolitical component. Xi wears layers of masks, and he would not take off the mask of "peace-loving" and "economic development." During a debate on The March West, the BRI's precursor, China's strategists suggested not formalizing the initiative because it could alert the U.S. to China's intentions and make its implementation difficult. Discussions on this point seem to lead to a consensus that quiet implementation would be preferable. The BRI provides additional cover. Now, Chinese government scholars openly admit that the BRI aims to break away from the liberal international order and advance one based on Xi's common destiny for mankind. The complaints the CCP listed, in addition to economic unfairness, include unequal political relations and universal values.[93] No doubt, the BRI is China's geopolitical grand strategy and its attempt to destroy the current world order and create a new one based on communist ideology, and ultimately achieve its imperial rejuvenation of the Chinese nation by becoming the world's hegemon.

3.3.3 The People's Liberation Army: The CCP's Private Army Is Preparing for War

The Xi Doctrine calls for an urgent arms race to achieve his dream of making China the greatest military power in the world and preparing for a war with the U.S. Even though every CCP leader made a strong effort to modernize the military, Xi's move has made it more dangerous. This section explains the manner in which he has done so. Unlike most armies, China's PLA is owned by the Party, to which it pledges absolute loyalty. The Party chief commands both the CCP and the PLA. This principle of "Party commanding the gun" requires that each generation of leaders must first control the power of the PLA in order to control the Party.

Xi has launched a cult of personality campaign, which made the PLA openly pledge absolute loyalty to him. For example, the army's new motto is, "The PLA must always do the following: All major matters must be decided by Chairman Xi, all work must be done to answer for Chairman Xi, and all actions must be taken under the direction of Chairman Xi."[94] This never happened before, not even under Mao's rule. It can be explained only by Xi's paranoia about security and that he might not have sufficient authority over the PLA. Xi's secret weapon to tame the PLA is his anti-corruption campaign.

When Xi became Party chief, systemic corruption rampaged the PLA and officer promotion was priced to the highest bidders, which seriously affected the military's overall combat effectiveness. The corruption started in the 1980s when the military budget was cut, and the PLA was told to support itself with commercial activities. Later, when Jiang and Hu tried to curb PLA corruption, it was too late.

Xi uses this past as an excuse to clean up the PLA and insert his confidants into it. The Chinese military has investigated more than 4,000 corruption cases and issued disciplinary action on more than 13,000 officers. At least 69 generals were purged.[95] Xi forced more than 200 PLA generals to retire early, replacing them with younger generals who are loyal to him. By doing so, Xi broke the institutionalized military promotion system and made the PLA less stable and more aggressive. His ambition to become the greatest leader of China—and of the world—motivates him to build an army that can defend and expand the Red Empire. Xi knows that a corrupt general will not be a good combat commander. In Chinese history, a seriously corrupt army almost always loses on the battlefield.

Additionally, the arms race has accelerated. As a critical component of Xi's Chinese Dream, completing the PLA's modernization has been a CCP priority. But "modernization" is a euphemism for building the most powerful military force, one that could fight a war against the U.S. In 2016, the CCP issued the "Outline of the Thirteenth Five-Year Plan for Army Construction and Development," in which it set a three-step strategy to reach the goal of a strong military by 2049. But within a year, Xi was unhappy with the progress. In October 2017, at the 19th CCP National Congress, Xi formulated a new three-step development strategy for national defense and army building, emphasizing the need to ensure that mechanization is achieved by 2020. He stipulated that major progress must be made to improve information warfare and strategic capabilities, in order to achieve China's national defense and military modernization by 2035, and to shape the PLA into a world-class military by the middle of this century, 15 years ahead of the previously set schedule. However, in October 2020, Xi once again accelerated his military modernization goal in the CCP Central Committee's proposal for formulating the Fourteenth Five-Year Plan (2021–2025) for "National Economic and Social Development and the Long-Range Objectives Through the Year 2035." For the first time, he added a third centenary goal, one for the PLA that demands its completion in 2027, its 100th anniversary.

This acceleration, according to the official media, is because regime security has been elevated to an unprecedented height, and the PLA must speed up its military modernization in theory, organizational structure, personnel, and weapons and equipment, to safeguard the rejuvenation of the Chinese nation.[96] In addition, the goal requires the PLA to accelerate the military's effectiveness, by prioritizing quality and efficiency, increasing joint exercises, and ensuring simultaneous improvement of might and economic strength.[97] The road map for the PLA was to achieve significant progress in mechanization and information operations by 2020, reach the PLA centenary goal in 2027, achieve modernization in 2035, and then complete the building of a first-class military in 2049.

Based on China's domestic messaging, the PLA's centenary goal is rapidly and drastically improving its combat capability, including its strategic strike power to defend the regime's core interests, which include "sovereignty, security, and development interests" against hostile forces such as the U.S. According to Chinese propagandists, the goal is to ensure that by 2027, the PLA will be able to "promptly, effectively and resolutely strike back against all actions that endanger our sovereignty, security, and development interests, and ensure that even an inch of our territory is indispensable and that all foreign interventions be defeated."[98] In other words, the PLA should be able to win armed conflicts against Taiwan, the South China Sea, India in the Himalayas region, and Japan in the East China Sea. In 2020, Xi for the first time elevated development interests to the same level as regime security and instructed the PLA to defend them across the globe. It was an important shift, indicating that China will use its troops overseas to expand its global economic interests, when it deems necessary.

China amended its National Defense Law in 2020, inserting Xi's ideology and authorizing the PLA's global reach by codifying military activities to curb any separation from China and to defend China's development interests. It means that China can use force against countries for sanctions imposed against Chinese companies, such as Huawei, or for any other measures that are perceived as ways to contain China's development or block its rise and "great rejuvenation." We submit that the law specifically targets the United States and came about in response to a U.S. government policy shift, to prepare China for armed conflict with the U.S. and its allies, despite the CCP's deceptive declaration of the law's defensive nature. The CCP now can cite the law as a cover to launch military action against Taiwan or to annex the South China Sea.

As China's economy has been deeply integrated into the global market, its economic interests cover all corners of the world. Its global supply chain, energy and raw materials, and key investments can be disrupted and damaged by states or by natural disasters. China will take military action to protect these development interests. Since China relies so heavily on imported energy and overseas markets for many goods—as Japan did before World War II—it is likely that economic factors could drive China to start a war to ensure its energy supply, overseas markets, and investments.

Interestingly, the shift, or "strategic arrangements for overall development and security," according to the *People's Daily*, was "personally planned and finalized" by Xi.[99] Stressing this point indicates that Xi controls the CCP's agenda and discourse and shows his aggressive mentality. With this far-reaching decision, he has abandoned Deng's *"Taoguang Yanghui"* strategy and is preparing for a potential war against the U.S. This shift alone should end any debate about China's intention once and for all.

On July 1, 2021, the CCP's centennial celebration, Xi again expressed his hostility, by warning the U.S. and other Western democracies that the Chinese people will never allow any foreign forces to bully, oppress, or enslave them. Anyone who dares try to do that will have their heads bashed bloody against a Great Wall of steel forged by over 1.4 billion Chinese people, he warned. He also announced that the CCP had achieved its first centenary goal and is moving closer to the second.[100] Most Westerners may not fully grasp Xi's meaning. The phrase "have their heads bashed bloody" (碰得头破血流) is the CCP's belligerent language that means thoroughly defeating the enemy or annihilating the enemy. It is a war cry, long used in pep talks before PLA soldiers go into battle. Xi also vowed to complete the "great cause of motherland's unification," a euphemism for seizing Taiwan.

This is not simply Xi's bluff or CCP propaganda. China has been building up its military power, or militarizing the country for the ultimate showdown with the U.S. About the time that Xi issued his war cry, a Chinese official magazine, *Naval and Merchant Ships*, published a detailed plan for launching a surprise attack to conquer Taiwan. According to the article and an accompanying video, this would be a three-stage operation. First, ballistic missiles such as DF-16 short-range missiles would break through Taiwan's missile defense system and destroy the island's control and command centers, airports, early-warning radar, and anti-air missile bases. Then H-6 bombers and J-16 fighter jets would strike naval ports. Second, China would launch cruise missiles such as the Eagle-91 and Changjian-10 from land, warships, and submarines to bombard Taiwan's military bases, arsenals, radar systems, communications infrastructure, and key highways. In the third stage, surface ships and land-based rocket forces would jointly launch a fierce shelling to clear any remaining obstacles for the PLAN Marine Corps and amphibious landing force to reach the island.[101]

This detailed outline should not be taken lightly. China has been bullying and provoking Taiwan for years, but the provocations greatly intensified in 2020 and 2021. In October 2020, when the CCP Central Committee was discussing the new strategy, PLA fighter jets invaded Taiwan's airspace 27 times, setting a record. Around the time that China deployed 150 of its fifth-generation, stealth-fighter J-20s, specifically targeting Taiwan and Japan, the CCP propagandists claimed it was the last warning to Taiwan before China would take military action to seize the island.[102] Soon after, the PLA deployed in the south-east coastal area Dongfeng-17 missiles, making this China's first operational hypersonic weapon system and one of the world's first to be put in full deployment.[103]

A PLA spokesperson boasts that the army has sufficient capability to defend the national security and territorial integrity of the motherland and directly defeat any form of "Taiwan independence" separatist activities. China's military expert, Ni Lexiong, has revealed that J-20s are deployed in Wuhu, Anhui, and Anshan, Liaoning, close to Taiwan and Japan, respectively. According to Ni, these powerful precision weapons will be used to "bomb Taipei first."[104] China's threat to use force against Taiwan signals its determination to become the top superpower. Its hostility is directed at the United States.

Additional research finds that China has begun constructing more than 100 silos for intercontinental ballistic missiles (ICBMs), a major expansion of Beijing's nuclear capabilities.[105] State Department spokesperson Ned Price told a regular news briefing it appeared China was deviating from decades of nuclear strategy based on minimal deterrence.[106]

Editor-in-chief Hu Xijin at *Global Times*, a CCP mouthpiece, posted on *Weibo* on May 27, 2021, that in view of the U.S.'s intensified strategic containment of China, the most urgent task is to "continuously and rapidly increase the number of nuclear warheads and Dongfeng 41 high-range, high-survivable strategic missiles in the arsenal."[107] He also said, "We must be prepared for a high-intensity showdown between China and the United States" and that "the number of our nuclear missiles must be so large that the American elite will tremble when they even think about military confrontation with China."[108]

China has made numerous such nuclear threats against the U.S. in the past. Cai Xia, the former CCP insider and professor at a top CCP training school, writes in her paper that the Chinese Navy displayed its nuclear submarine-launched Julang-3 (JL-3) intercontinental missile from the deep sea near Yantai to demonstrate its determination against the U.S., and that the "CCP has embarked on the path of militarism conspiring to wage war, and they regard the United States as their most threatening enemy."[109]

In July 2021, the *Six Military Strategies*, a Chinese military online channel, openly advocated for abandoning China's early commitment not to use nuclear weapons against a non-nuclear country and preemptively destroying Japan with nuclear bombs to prevent Japan from sending troops to help defend Taiwan. Because Japan is the only country ever to suffer a nuclear attack, such an attack by China "will get twice the result with half the effort."[110]

China's aggressive threats of nuclear attacks and its vigorous military expansion indicate that Xi is serious about waging war against the U.S. and its allies. What makes him so dangerous is that he has inherited Mao's mentality that an atomic bomb is a paper tiger and, like Mao, he maintains that China could survive a nuclear war even if half of its population were killed. The CCP believes in deception and conspiracy as the best strategy for war. The Old Red Guards' fanaticism, concentrated power, and absolute loyalty to the military could drive Xi to seize a window of opportunity and conduct a surprise attack against U.S. interests or the U.S. homeland.

China's arms race is much more comprehensive and extensive than it reveals. In an interview with *Financial Times*, Stuart Peach, head of NATO's military committee, told the reporter: "It is quite shocking how quickly China has built ships, how much China has modernized its air force, how much it has invested in cyber and other forms of information management, not least facial recognition."[111] This is why NATO leaders have sounded the alarm for the first time that China poses "systemic challenges" to the rules-based international order.

Xi has demanded the PLA comprehensively strengthen its training and intensify the preparation for war. He has made the PLA complete its reorganization, mimicking the U.S. command system. Xi also supposedly curbed any paid services rendered by the PLA, including the armed police, removing a hotbed for PLA corruption to enable it to focus on warfighting. For five years, Xi has issued a training mobilization order, insisting that the focus is on training for war. He has doubled the PLA budget during his tenure, from 670.3 billion yuan to 1.35 trillion yuan—that alone is alarming but does not count the concealed military budget, so actual defense spending is much greater.[112]

Xi's propagandists claim that only with the sovereignty of the South China Sea in China can the world share the Chinese Dream.[113] But China's sea power has gone beyond Taiwan and the South China Sea. Today China owns and operates 95 ports outside the PRC, apparently readying to expand and protect its interests and achieve the Chinese Dream.[114] As PLA Colonel Liu Mingfu points out: "The great rejuvenation of the Chinese nation must go hand in hand with a rich and powerful army." Liu contends that China-U.S. relations have entered the final stage of the game. He believes it is a dangerous stage and that it is naïve to claim that war between the two will never come.[115]

With accelerated military buildup, war preparations, and intensified confrontation with the U.S. military, the danger of war is imminent. The danger is not only whether China will wage war against other countries, but how it will fight the war. By now, most China-watchers in the West are familiar with the book *Unrestricted Warfare* by two senior Chinese military colonels, Qiao Liang and Wang Xiangsui. When the book was published, Li Datong was the managing editor of *Freezing Point*, a section of *Youth Daily*. Li recalls that initially, only 3,000 copies of the book were printed and few showed interest in it. One of his reporters approached him about the book, claiming it was filled with tricks that hit the U.S. below the belt. After reading the book, Li said his flesh broke out in "goosebumps" because of the book's collection of no-holds-barred tactics. He sent his reporter to interview the authors and ask particular questions such as, "What if the U.S. uses the same unlimited warfare?" When the interview was published, his chief editor called to scold him that he should know better than to publish such a highly sensitive subject, something that should be discussed only internally. Within an hour, Li got a call from Zhongnanhai, the central headquarters for the CCP, and was instructed to send a copy of the book because the chief wanted to read it. Later, Qiao told Li that about 100 PLA generals asked him for copies and the publishing house could not print enough to meet the demand. Now every PLA officer at the regimental level and above has the book, Li said. He believes that unlimited warfare is a generally accepted tactic for today's art of war.

We argue that China has accelerated its goal in the military buildup and is preparing for a showdown with the U.S. in its attempt to achieve world dominance. It is not just a one-time misjudgment of the current situation, but a consistent, long-term goal that the CCP has been pursuing, accelerated by Xi's guiding ideology of winning an ultimate socialist victory and achieving "great rejuvenation" of the Chinese nation. The fact that the PLA pledges absolute loyalty to Xi and would be willing to wage unrestricted war against its enemies makes it extremely dangerous to world peace, even though its combat capability has never been tested, nor has its less-advanced weaponry.

The PLA is neither a paper tiger nor an invincible force, but its nature of being violent and aggressive cannot be underestimated, particularly considering that a new generation of younger officers, who are ultra-nationalistic and fanatic neo-Maoist ideologues, is eager to get promoted through military actions. Xi's attempts to build a more hierarchical, tightly controlled system, similar to a pyramid gang organization, means the positions of members determine the privileges and resources allocated to them. Members may spend their lives trying to move up the hierarchy. Competition is fierce because of the sheer number of officials, and few actually can be promoted. It is a situation described by a Chinese saying: "There are too many monks and too little gruel." This system is likely to brew military fanatics, as well as corruption, which is the key to understanding the Party-state's military affairs.

No doubt, much of Xi's rhetoric and many of the CCP's moves are posturing at this point, to show China's determination to deter the U.S. and its allies from defending Taiwan or other global interests, and to compel the U.S. to withdraw from Asia-Indo-Pacific. "*Bitong*" (逼统) is the phrase often used today in China's domestic messaging, which means to use all levers to push Taiwan to the corner including pushing for no countries to have diplomatic relations with the island country, forcing it to surrender or submit to China's demand for unification. But if "*Bitong*" fails, Xi will not hesitate to use force to "liberate" Taiwan. He dares to do so because, like Deng, he believes China's market is too big for Western capitalists to ignore. Despite the atrocities the CCP commits, foreign capitalists will return and business as usual will continue. The CCP and its military have passed the point of "integrating but hedging" by taking advantage of U.S. goodwill and its engagement policy, and by deceiving U.S. decision makers. A new U.S. strategy of robust confrontation must be put in place quickly to reverse China's advance if the U.S. wants to remain the world leader.

3.3.4 The CCP Is a Fully Digital Dictatorship—Weapons of Mass Surveillance, Repression, and Indoctrination

The Xi Doctrine requires a digital dictatorship to carry it out, which makes it an exquisite dictatorship, or precision dictatorship as Chinese activists call it. This is because it uses advanced technology, including digital information technology and social networking, on top of the traditional apparatus to track, detect, predict, and eliminate any dissent and opposition, organized and unorganized, planned or spontaneously occurring. The regime relies on this to surveil, deter, repress, and manipulate its population. It is capable of using artificial intelligence (AI), Big Data, advanced neural science and other mind-control technologies to carry out mass indoctrination and win the minds and hearts of domestic and foreign populations. The CCP has successfully built an Orwellian nightmare that helps keep it in power. Truly, it has made totalitarian control over people cheaper. Orwell imagined scores of Winston Smiths laboring in the Ministry of Truth—all are now replaced by IT, which does Smith's job far better than Orwell could have imagined. Digital dictatorship with Chinese characteristics is a paradigm shift, which poses a grave threat to open societies by unbalancing the power between democracies and autocracies. In this section, we examine China's digital dictatorship, how it operates, and why it is proliferating around the world.

3.3.4.1 All-Dimensional and Informatized Public Security and Prevention System

As explained in Chapter 2, the system was devised in the early 1990s in response to the Tiananmen protests and collapse of the Soviet Union and its Eastern Bloc allies. It accelerated after the Arab Spring or the Jasmine Revolution in 2011. The system is a combination of total information awareness and operational capability enhancement designed to predict, detect, and eliminate any threats and risks to the regime, in the name of crime prevention and control. China under Xi's leadership views civil and political rights as an existential threat to regime security, and uses crime control and prevention, or "public security," to carry out a repressive policy against human rights and civil society activists. The Party-state considers any dissent to be a crime against the regime, and charges such as "provoking quarrels and making trouble," speaking ill of the CCP's policy, "inciting subversion of state power," "subverting state power," or any economic crimes are used for crushing criticism of the Party-state. The system weaponizes technology to achieve a super police state by controlling every aspect of society and its people. To hide the repressive nature of the system, China has adopted the democratic phrases of "rule of law" and "crime control and prevention" in a veiled attempt to rewrite its abusive narrative in a form acceptable to Western democracies.

Under Xi, the system has been elevated to the top strategy for regime security. It has shifted from comprehensive social control to digitalization and informatization, which means the system is upgraded from high-definition, man-powered surveillance and control networking to big data, machine learning, and other AI-based smart systems. These improvements have made the older version, which is centered on surveillance video networking as the main feature, to become the new-generation mechanism centered on data networking.

The system includes three main platforms—Safe City, Skynet, and Sharp Eyes—to place digital shackles on citizens. In fact, what China has created while the world was not watching is the largest, most sophisticated and repressive super police state, like nothing the world has seen beyond the pages of a dystopian novel. China's weapons of mass surveillance and repression have shown their ability to exert absolute control over populations, as evidenced by the mass detention and control of millions of Uyghurs and other Muslims in Xinjiang Province.

Integrated into the all-dimensional and informatized public security and prevention system is China's social credit system, which became fully operational in 2020. The social credit system scores people in China according to their business, social and daily behaviors, including their online behaviors and speeches. Data about people's lifestyle, health, education, hotel reservations—collected from facial recognition, surveillance cameras, grid inspectors, mobile payment apps, police records, and other channels—is fed into the social credit system. People who score low are labeled as "dishonest persons subject to enforcement (DPSE)." As of November 8, 2019, there were 15.85 million DPSEs, and authorities had denied 34.77 million DPSEs from buying air tickets and 6.29 million from obtaining high-speed train tickets.[116]

The CCP's weaponizing of financial credit ranking aims to keep everyone in line with Xi's ideology and policy, and also to try to change people's behavior, making totalitarian repression an accepted norm. If people have trouble grasping the significance of the social credit system, Netflix's original *Black Mirror* has an episode titled "Nosedive," which describes what it is like to live in a world with social ranking. Netflix's fictionalized episode supposedly examines futuristic technology, but it is a daily life for 1.4 billion Chinese.

3.3.4.2 The Great Firewall of China

As part of total societal control, the PRC also uses its Great Firewall—its control of the internet within China as well as social media outlets such as WeChat, Weibo, TikTok, and internet service providers—to censor information, surveil netizens, and report them to the authorities. The Great Firewall is the world's most extensive and sophisticated information control system. It blocks website content, monitors individuals' internet access, uses humans and bots to spread China's lies and fake news, and engages in ideological warfare to demonize universal values and democracy. Through the Great Firewall, China possesses a monumental internet censorship machine that is fully integrated with its mass surveillance systems such as Skynet, Safe City, Sharp Eyes, and the social credit system—making it the most repressive information and mind-control system the world has ever witnessed. Effectively, the Great Firewall has sealed the country and fostered ignorance among many citizens. Therefore, penetration of the Great Firewall should be a key U.S. response to defeat China in the ideological struggle.

The PRC essentially has two Great Firewalls, internal and external, which complement each other. The former is a network and content censorship system that prevents Chinese citizens from posting online content the regime perceives as "inappropriate," "anti-CCP," or "speaking ill of the leader or central policy." China's internet industry, service providers, tech companies, websites, and telecommunication firms are required to self-censor and self-regulate, and are subject to government intervention. They are required to surveil netizens and report illegal activities. All must follow the CCP censorship rules. The external Great Firewall controls people's access to websites abroad and their content.

In 2012, before Xi came to power, Ma Deyong, a professor at Nankai University, conducted surveys on China's social media. These showed that among Chinese netizens, only 6.2 percent were pro-CCP leftists, 38.7 percent were pro-democracy liberals, and 55.1 percent were centrists. However, 97.5 percent of Chinese internet users believed that "no matter who is China's leader, his power must be restricted," and 97.2 percent of internet users agreed that "the current unfairness in Chinese society is very serious." More than 90 percent agreed that "everyone has the right to criticize the government."[117]

The first thing Xi did upon assuming power was to wipe the internet platforms and online opinion pages where people could express their views. The CCP, under Xi, has enhanced the most advanced Great Firewall to censor, surveil, and repress dissent. Today nearly all spaces for free speech are gone, despite the fact that as of December 2020, the number of internet users in China had reached 989 million, the number of mobile internet users had reached 986 million, and the internet penetration rate was 70.4 percent.[118] Xi clearly comprehends the importance of the internet. In a study session with his Politburo members in January 2019, he said: "Without internet security, there would be no national security; if we cannot overcome the internet obstacles, we won't be able to secure our long-term rule."[119] That is why he has put the internet under absolute centralized control, with over 60 agencies to oversee all online activities in China.[120] Xi's digital dictatorship not only controls information, surveils people, and represses dissent, but, more critically, it uses all available advanced technologies to carry out mass brainwashing and indoctrination to achieve mind control. Xi has largely succeeded in controlling China. A Harvard University study of a long-term view of how Chinese citizens view their government released in 2020 shows that 95.5 percent of respondents were either "relatively satisfied" or "highly satisfied" with Beijing.[121]

3.3.4.3 The Globalization of Digital Dictatorship

China's digital dictatorship has expanded globally under the Xi Doctrine. We believe it poses a grave danger to the liberal world order and open society by providing an unprecedented model for population control and mind control powered by technology, which can track, detect, deter, and eliminate any opposition. Not only can China's digital dictatorship keep dictators in power; it can empower them to challenge and defeat democracies globally.

In 2015, China launched the $200 billion Digital Silk Road (DSR) project as a complement to its BRI. The DSR has become a core component of the

BRI. Xi emphasizes that it is necessary to utilize the BRI as an opportunity to strengthen cooperation with other countries, especially developing countries, in terms of digital infrastructure construction, the digital economy, and network security to build the Digital Silk Road.[122]

As a result, China's optical cable industry has flourished, with production and sales accounting for more than 50 percent of the global share. Huawei Marine has become one of the world's important submarine cable system integrators, with the ability and experience of transoceanic submarine cable general contracting and delivery. Huawei Marine has completed 105 projects, with a total of over 64,000 kilometers of submarine cables. Huawei has become the world's major contractor for submarine communications cable projects, laying one-third of new submarine optical cables in the world. Huawei completed the first cable connecting Latin America and Africa at the end of 2019.

Huawei also is working to lay the first 5G submarine optical cable from China to Chile.[123] In addition, despite U.S.-imposed trade restrictions, Huawei and ZTE have increased their share of the global market, according to the Dell'Oro Group report. Both also increased their share of telecommunications equipment in 2020. Huawei's global telecommunications equipment market share was 31 percent, and ZTE accounted for 10 percent of the world shares.[124] China's ability to control DSR and BRI countries' telecommunication infrastructure, and their markets, with its digital economy will allow China to lay the foundation for introducing its digital governance model to these countries and creating a new digital order.

In fact, China has sold digital technology to foreign regimes for decades. For example, Singapore bought and used Chinese facial-recognition technology and cameras for street corners.[125] It even integrates the technology into its national identification system to verify individuals for private and government services. Singapore's SingPass is like China's One-Card Pass.[126] It is reported that there is a growing appetite in the world for China's advanced surveillance products. Southeast Asian countries such as Malaysia have employed China's body-mounted camera with facial recognition technology for police to spot suspects.[127] Security forces in Ethiopia surveil dissidents and reporters using products supplied by ZTE.[128] Other African countries have imported AI behavioral analytics products from Huawei to spy on journalists and activists.[129] In Venezuela, with the help of ZTE, the Maduro regime has deployed a digital social control system, centered on the "carnet de la patria" or "fatherland card" to track citizens' social, political, and economic behavior. Dissidents and activists are detected and persecuted with China's digital technology.[130] China provides and finances technology for Ecuador's mass surveillance system.[131] Argentina also has installed China's facial recognition camera system.[132] The global demand for China's cheap but effective digital dictatorial technology is growing. Its technology, systems, and products are in all continents. A Brookings Institution report finds that at least 18 countries use Chinese surveillance and monitoring systems, and at least

36 governments have held Chinese-led training and seminars on "new media" or "information management."[133]

The world pays little attention to China's cultural imperialist expansion through "new media" as part of the digital dictatorial governance model that has invaded many developing countries. For example, StarTimes, a Chinese electronics and media company, first set up its shop in Africa in 2007 and now has become one of the most important media companies in the continent. StarTimes has business operations in 37 African countries, and 20 subsidiaries. StarTimes offers TV program relay, digital terrestrial, satellite television, and internet-based video services. It built a cable network connecting 10,112 rural African villages in 23 countries with satellite TV services as part of China's "foreign aid" projects. The company has signed contracts with more than 20 African governments to provide its services. As of 2021, it has 13 million high-quality household users with spending power, 27 million new-generation mobile video consumer users, and more than 10 million social media, multi-platform, multi-channel users. They watch 23 Chinese mainstream media channels, including CGTN, CCTV-4, CGTN-F, CGTN-D, and CNC. They may view 43 StarTimes-produced content channels, including the Kung Fu Channel and the Chinese Film and Television Foreign Language Channel, covering almost all types of news, movies and TV shows, sports, children's entertainment, and music, in 11 languages, including English, French, Portuguese, Swahili, and Hausa. StarTimes's user base will allow the company to expand its business beyond media products, with digital payments and online shopping.

StarTimes continues expanding its African business to connect cities and villages to provide more of China's soft brainwashing content and other Chinese products to reach all corners of African society. It even uses traditional CCP propaganda strategies such as traveling entertainment teams to reach out to as many African people as possible. A vice president of the company revealed that StarTimes uses "video caravans" with LED projection equipment to travel to many rural areas, showing China's propaganda content to audiences with an average of 500 to 1,000 people per show.[134]

We can imagine that when more AI-based precision indoctrination content is placed through companies such as StarTimes, China will gain enormous power and influence for its global political, social, and economic agenda. No doubt, China's digital dictatorship protects its one-party state and is now propping up dictators around the world. These regimes now have unique capabilities beyond the barrel of a gun to control their populations and perpetuate their power. China has waged three global wars of public opinion, psychology, and law for two decades, now led by the nascent PLA Strategic Support Force (PLASSF). This should be conceived of as a form of China's A2/AD strategy in an ideational guise, rather than a military one. This, in turn, gives the Party-state geopolitical advantage in fierce, all-fronts warfare against the free world. It is time we recognize the threat of these weapons of mass surveillance as powerful tools against open society.

3.3.5 CCP Infiltration Is Massive and Ubiquitous

Infiltration strategy is as old as Chinese history. Qi Shihuang, China's first emperor, used it to defeat six other warring kingdoms and unify the country. His prime minister, Li Si, bribed the elites with gold and precious gems, and employed tricks to divide the kings and their advisers. When these failed, he assassinated them and then dispatched his army to conquer them easily. China has successfully adopted and implemented this strategy. China's infiltration presents greater threats than did the Soviet Union, as the Trump administration's Secretary of State Mike Pompeo rightly pointed out when he spoke in Prague in August 2020. Pompeo believed "the CCP is already enmeshed in our economies, in our politics, in our societies in ways the Soviet Union never was."[135] This situation reflects China's long game of deep, all-front infiltration and penetration into Western societies for technology know-how, capital access, and political influence. It is partly the result of a U.S. engagement policy that tried to integrate the PRC into the existing world order. Under Xi Jinping, China's infiltration has become more aggressive and intensified.

For example, tremendous efforts were made to influence American elites to counter perceived U.S. peaceful evolution with great success, resulting in China winning each year's most favored nation debate and securing permanent trade status, gaining access to the vast U.S. market. More importantly, China's deception as a benign power and willingness to be integrated into the international community enabled it to take advantage of the openness of American society. The same infiltration occurred in other democracies. In November 2020, Di Dongsheng, deputy dean of the School of International Relations at Renmin University of China, boasted on a TV show that the CCP can fix any issue with the U.S. quickly because it has old friends at the top of America's inner circle of power and influence.

China's multifaceted, industrial-scale, people's war-style infiltration into the free world cannot be underestimated. Many other states conduct influence operations, but the fundamental difference is the CCP "follows the mass line" to mobilize the whole population and use state resources to implement its plan, aiming to not only collect information and peddle influence, but also to sabotage and undermine perceived enemies. China carries out such infiltration through espionage, political interference, and influence operations, or through other forms of covert, coercive, and corrupt operations.

After the Tiananmen protests in 1989, the CCP's infiltration focused on changing the views of people throughout the world on the CCP and neutralizing democracies' opposition in order to ensure regime security. Xi has shifted to a more aggressive, hostile, offensive approach, aiming to undermine democracy and universal values and to create a China-centered world order. The world has not seen malign infiltration operations of such scope and magnitude before. Books and investigative reports have exposed China's infiltration, but what has been made public is the tip of an iceberg because of its clandestine nature. This section attempts to examine some aspects of China's infiltration, to shed light on the operations.

3.3.5.1 The United Front Work—The CCP's Massive Circle of Friends

China has many channels to conduct political warfare through influencing foreign elites and gaining "friends in high places." But one of the main ways is the United Front Work (UFW). The UFW is one of Mao's three "magic weapons" to win the Party's victory. The CCP survived and grew from a few dozen members to become the largest political party in the world. In its own view, this was largely because of its UFW, which enabled the Party to deeply infiltrate the Koumintang government and influence decision-making and provide critical information to the CCP.

As a general strategy, the UFW exists as a formal part of the CCP to advance its interests and undermine, neutralize, and defeat its enemies, often working through front organizations and clandestine agents or proxies to mask the CCP's involvement. Whether operating through the formal United Front Work Department or as an informal "united front," they target elites through a collection of front organizations, academe, media, and business, with a goal of influencing politics and policy and shaping perceptions about China and the CCP. The UFW's mission is to target individuals and organizations outside of the CCP's system to become allies, supporters, and sympathizers for China's reunification, and now the Chinese Dream.

In the 1980s, under Deng, the CCP set forth with two unified fronts—the National Patriotic United Front and the International Anti-Hegemony United Front.[136] Even though the CCP later did not openly advocate for the Anti-Hegemony United Front, it has always stayed in the shadow of its strategy and policy implementation. As relations between great powers evolved after the Tiananmen protests and the collapse of the Soviet Union and Eastern Bloc, the U.S. became the world's only hegemon. The CCP perceives that the U.S. is determined to do everything to block China's rise as a great power and therefore the U.S. is its greatest foe. Xi has escalated the tension to the highest level by internally accusing the U.S. of being the main source of world chaos and the greatest threat to China.

Although the CCP has not announced it, there exists a *de facto* international anti-U.S. united front. No matter how hard China tries to hide its strategic intent with rhetoric and narratives, this anti-U.S. united front opposes the existing liberal world order led by Washington. As one of China's well-known commentators, Guo Songmin, has said, China must use the International Anti-Hegemony United Front to defeat former Secretary of State Michael Pompeo's "alliance of democracies."[137] Xi uses an analogy—"concentric circle" (同心圆)—to describe the UFW's mission. If we use this analogy, the National Patriotic United Front is the first circle and the International United Front is a second, larger circle.

The first circle consists of Chinese citizens and the Chinese diaspora and their organizations; the second circle consists mainly of foreigners.

The CCP often assigns oversight of the UFW to the member of its Standing Committee who heads the Chinese People's Political Consultative Conference (CPPCC). At the time of writing, it is Wang Yang. He is responsible for formulating UFW strategy and policy, recommending it to the Standing Committee and the paramount leader, coordinating agencies that have any UFW portfolio, and ensuring UFW policy implementation after it is proved. UFW agencies under Wang Yang include the CPPCC, the United Front Work Departments at central and local levels with ethnic commissions and religious affairs bureaus, the State Council's Office of Overseas Chinese Affairs, the Federation of Industry and Commerce, and the All-China Federation of Returned Overseas Chinese. Although the UFW of Taiwan, Hong Kong, and Macau also are under Wang's oversight, Xi directly controls overall Taiwanese affairs, and PSC member Han Zheng is responsible for Hong Kong and Macau through the State Council's Offices of Taiwan and Hong Kong Affairs.

Since 2012, Xi has doubled down the efforts to empower the UFW by reforming the UFW Department, and he has assigned two deputy national leader-level officials to the agency. He demands the entire Party, government, and society should carry out a UFW people's war, which he calls the Grand UFW (大统战) strategy. The Party-state has accumulated massive resources that can be used to strengthen the UFW. "Now, the historic position of our Party, the internal and external situations it faces, and the mission and tasks it shoulders have undergone major changes," Xi has said. "The greater the changes, the more we must develop the United Front and carry out the work of the United Front."[138]

At the beginning of January 2021, the CCP issued its newly revised "Regulations on the United Front Work of the Communist Party of China." It defines the UFW's missions, guidelines, policy, and structure. Specifically, the regulations state that the UFW is an alliance of those who support the CCP's domestic and global agenda. The job includes political party relations, ethnic relations, religious relations, class relations, and relations with compatriots at home and abroad. There are 12 category targets for the UFW, including democratic parties, people without party affiliation, non-Party intellectuals, ethnic minorities, religious believers, private entrepreneurs, people studying abroad who have returned home, compatriots in Hong Kong, Macao, Taiwan and their relatives on the mainland, overseas Chinese, Chinese who have returned from overseas and their relatives, and other people who need to unite—all of whom are elites from all walks of life.[139]

The mission for the overseas UFW includes five elements, aimed at indoctrinating anyone of Chinese origin with Xi's ideology; convincing them to support the Chinese regime; using them to reach out to foreigners to advance the CCP's agenda; using them as a cover for China's influence operations; persuading Chinese abroad to achieve the Chinese Dream; supporting China's territorial claims; and joining in China's effort for the community of common destiny for mankind.[140]

The danger is the sheer number and key positions of the Chinese diaspora in the world, which could present a new challenge to democracies. They take advantage of open societies and often operate in gray areas, working as agents of the CCP. The 2018 World Migration Report indicates that as of 2015, about ten million people from the PRC were living abroad.[141] Altogether, there are around 60 million Chinese people living around the world. China continues to be one of the top emigration countries. Its own data show there are over five million Chinese living in the U.S., and over one million in Japan.

Among those in the U.S., 54 percent of adult Chinese hold university degrees and 51 percent of them work in technology or management sectors. There are more than 300 members in the National Academy of Sciences, American Academy of Arts and Sciences, National Academy of Engineering, and National Academy of Medicine. There are more than 320 Chinese professors at the eight Ivy League universities in the United States. More than 200,000 alumni who graduated from 39 first-tier universities in China work in high-tech companies or institutions in the United States. About one-third of AI researchers in the U.S. are from China.[142] There are also several members of Congress of Chinese origin, and many musicians, actors, and artists. Similar demographics can be found in other developed countries. In addition, China sends tens of thousands of students to developed countries to seek higher education degrees. According to the 2020 China Study Abroad White Paper, in 2019 there were nearly one million Chinese students studying abroad—363,341 in the U.S., 192,984 in Australia, 143,412 in Canada, 107,260 in Japan, and 95,090 in the UK.[143] All of these represent an enormous pool of resources and networks for China's UFW to exploit.

The UFW has gone far beyond the reunification issue, as demonstrated by the fact that most countries where the CCPNR set up chapters have no diplomatic relations with Taiwan and support "peaceful reunification." China does not need a massive network to lobby these governments on the issue. Ironically, the CCP insists that reunification is China's affair and that no foreigners should interfere; yet, the CCPNR hires foreign politicians, such as former Australian prime ministers Gough Whitlam and Bob Hawke, to serve as key members.[144]

Our arguments demonstrate that front organizations for the UFW are a repressive tool of the CCP, not normal public diplomacy groups. The UFW covers areas so extensive it is likely beyond anyone's imagination. For example, the Western Returned Scholars Association (Overseas-Educated Scholars of China, 欧美同学会 中国留学人员联谊会) is a subsidiary of the CCP Central Secretariat but managed by the UFW Department. Through its layered branches, it carries out many covert activities. Years ago, when Xi ordered China to set up high-end strategic think tanks, the Western Returned Scholars Association was among the first organizations to set up shop in the United States.

It is important not to exaggerate the threat of China's infiltration, but it is equally important not to underestimate such a threat, simply because most of China's covert activities have yet to be uncovered. The CCP is a highly secretive organization; so are its front organizations. Many signs indicate the UFW has evolved from a defensive posture to an offensive one, and it attempts to convince foreigners to disrupt, manipulate, and undermine the civil and political functions of other countries, particularly democracies. This is the fifth column of the CCP to establish its new world order.

The extensive infiltration operations carried out by the UFW and other agencies present the biggest challenge to the U.S. and other Western countries because the West does not have the mechanism or organizational structure in place to handle this type of infiltration. The sheer number and industrial scale of China's operations can overwhelm any of the West's counterintelligence agencies. There may not be an appropriate mechanism to discover and deal with such insidious subterfuge through legitimate nongovernmental organizations in the gray areas where China operates. These include the campaign by 122 diaspora organizations that demand the U.S. government lift the ban on WeChat, or the nearly 200 organizations that protested against Asian hate, or the campaign to demand the U.S. Congress apologize for the mistreatment of Chinese workers in the 19th century.

3.3.5.2 Political Infiltration

China's political infiltration operations target foreign politicians and other elites who can influence policy making. These operations are primarily carried out by its agencies that handle foreign relations, such as the Ministry of Foreign Affairs and CCP International Liaison Department. Each has its own focus and front organizations. The UFW Department also conducts such operations, but more often relies on the Chinese diaspora. We believe it is the CCP Politburo's PSC Leading Group on National Security and Leading Group on Foreign Affairs that oversee political infiltration operations. Xi heads both groups, and both are, in fact, one office with two names.[145] Technically, it is not the National Patriot United Front that conducts non-Chinese infiltration but the unofficial International Anti-U.S. United Front. In practice, however, political infiltration operations are carried out by multiple agencies and through many channels.

The Ministry of Foreign Affairs has a large number of diplomats in more than 180 countries, who often carry out illegal and covert activities under the cover of diplomacy. In addition, it has the Chinese People's Association for Friendship with Foreign Countries, Chinese People's Institute of Foreign Affairs (CPIFA), China Public Diplomacy Association, Association of Former Diplomats of China, Council for Promoting South-South Cooperation, and the China Arms Control and Disarmament Association as representative of allied groups. The Chinese Institute for Foreign Affairs alone so far has hosted more than 4,000 delegations and 30,000 foreign dignitaries from parliaments, think tanks, and news media. The CPIFA boasts that it maintains close contact with prominent politicians, diplomats, and businessmen from more than 120 countries and has more than 20 bilateral dialogue and exchange platforms.

The International Liaison Department is more secretive. Many of its front organizations remain unknown. It focuses on influencing political leaders throughout the world. As of 2021, the International Liaison Department maintains regular contact with more than 560 political parties and organizations in more than 160 countries.[146] The China Center for Contemporary World Studies (CCCWS), One Belt One Road International Think Tank Cooperation Alliance, China International Exchange Center, and China Economic Cooperation Center (CECC) serve as the department's windows to the outside world. It has China Hualian International Trading Company as its front organization, a holding company that is 100 percent controlled by the CECC.

The UFW network reaches out to foreigners mainly through the Chinese diaspora and their organizations. In fact, each central and local agency has a foreign affairs office, and each has its own GONGO or GONGOs and other front organizations, depending on the nature of their work. All may carry out foreign infiltration operations. The UFW Department also has the Huaxing Economic Consulting Service Center, which owns other companies in China and abroad.

The PLA's overseas political infiltration is primarily carried out by its Political Department's Liaison Department. Its front organization is the China Association for International Friendly Contact (CAIFC). The CAIFC claims to be an organization to promote people-to-people understanding between China and foreign countries, under the dual leadership of the Ministry of Foreign Affairs and the Ministry of Civil Affairs. But researchers have figured out this is a front organization to conduct infiltration operations.[147] The CAIFC's current president is Chen Yuan, a son of CCP veteran Chen Yan. Its leadership team reveals the ownership since its vice presidents are from the Liaison Department of the PLA's Political Department. Deng Rong, the youngest daughter of Deng Xiaoping, has served as a vice president for decades. She reportedly created a front organization, the China Arts Foundation. It is also reported that the Liaison Department owns CEFC China Energy, a $44 billion Chinese conglomerate. CEFC China Energy has the China Energy Fund Committee, which finances many overseas projects.

Even though the CCP uses multiple agencies and channels for its political infiltration, there is a pattern of "bringing in" and "going out." "Bringing in" means to invite targeted elites to China, offering free trips, free tours, free entertainment for conferences, forums, lectures, or for pleasure, depending on the needs of individuals and their families. In the process, the CCP further tracks, analyzes the person, and tailors a specific plan to entrap them for various uses. For decades, the CCP has designated agents to maintain close contact with key American political families.

"Going out" means the CCP sends delegations to, or sets up shops or front organizations in, targeted countries to work on specific political elites through different high-level dialogues, or regular contact to make "friends," with a goal of influencing politics and policy, shaping perceptions about China and the CCP, or recruiting for intelligence work. For example, under Xi the International

Liaison Department has significantly stepped up its political infiltration efforts by sending official delegations to dozens of countries to brief the political and think tank leaders about Xi's thoughts and achievements, so that they see the merits of the China model and might be willing to form a "new type of political party relations" with China. China's so-called "briefing delegations" are meant to "educate" foreign politicians and political parties about CCP policies and China's governance. These delegations are the CCP's global sales force to export Xi Jinping Thought and the China model to the world. Within a few months of the CCP's 19th Congress, the International Liaison Department sent nearly 30 propaganda delegations (*Xuanjie Tuan*, 宣介团) to 80 countries.[148]

"Going out" also includes sending the CCP's agents or proxies to form political parties or join countries' existing parties and win elected offices. For example, the number of legislators with Chinese connections is growing in democracies. All "going out" and "bringing in" activities are aimed at winning the CCP more "endorsers, supporters, and fellow travelers," as Song Tao, the head of the International Liaison Department, points out.[149] But the CCP also uses the occasions to spot and recruit politicians or organizations for deeper infiltration.

These operations have enabled China to form a wider circle of friends. But the consequences of its growing number of friends with influence are damaging to Western interests. The catalyst is often financial enticement. China has rewarded its foreign supporters with business deals, bribery, and other corruption. Key politicians and their family members and friends, from both democracies and developing countries, are all targets. If any Chinese business deal involves those people, it is likely that it is a "special deal," meaning part of the CCP's infiltration operations. Propaganda briefings have far less persuasive power than money. The list of prominent political families who supposedly are in China's pocket is reported to be extensive, including the Bush family, the Clintons, the Bidens, Elaine Chao's family, the Trumps, the Feinsteins, the Pelosis, and the Obamas. The CCP has an absolute monopoly over China's economic activities, including its private sector. Therefore, deals are easily arranged, drawing more and more world political figures and their families into China's circle of friends.[150] As we have discussed, this tactic is nothing new and was successfully used by Qin Shihuang when he sought hegemony by defeating six competing kingdoms in the late 3rd century BC.

Following the CCP's money trail, we should have a more accurate assessment of the extent and effectiveness of its political infiltration. Using industrial-scale corruption to influence international politics is the most prominent feature of China's political infiltration— call it "infiltration with Chinese characteristics." It works well for businesses to influence domestic politics. That is why all CCP agencies with a political infiltration portfolio have set up front companies. The challenge is to keep these deals disguised and fully deniable, covered up with layered legitimate business. The West has not yet fully understood and appreciated this massive hidden infiltration. In our assessment, this is a single most effective tactic to infiltrate a country, and it represents an existential threat to the international liberal order. The free world has no tactics to really counter it.

A third pattern is using a classic "honeypot" operation to lure politicians and other elites and gain access to influence them. It is rumored that all CIA station chiefs and ambassadors may have had Chinese mistresses. Nixon's mistress, Marianna Liu, may have had some influence on his decision to go to China.[151] *Mother Jones* reported in 2017 that Angela Chen, a New York businesswoman who also goes by the names Xiao Yan Chen and Chen Yu, bought a $15.8 million penthouse in a building owned by Donald Trump in order to gain access to him. Chen reportedly is an operative for the PLA's Liaison Department that specializes in political and psychological warfare, and the chairperson for the front organization, the China Arts Foundation.[152] U.S. Sen. Dianne Feinstein (D-CA), chairwoman of the Senate Intelligence Committee, hired a Chinese spy as her office director who worked for her for 20 years.[153] The latest example is Chinese agent Fang Fang, or Christine Fang, who worked with U.S. Rep. Eric Swalwell (D-CA).[154] In sum, the CCP's global political infiltration has gone far beyond a conventional approach, particularly with its industrial-scale use of economic and financial incentives to gain broad political control. This is clearly worrisome because it could corrupt democratic systems from within.

3.3.5.3 Infiltration for Intelligence Collection

China has developed a massive intelligence collection network. Traditionally, the Ministry of State Security and the Second and Third Departments of PLA's General Staff are the main agencies that conduct espionage infiltration under the PSC Political and Legal Leading Group. However, Xi set up the PSC National Security Leading Group and oversees all that is related to regime security, including espionage. Because Xi is a strong believer of Mao's mass line, his espionage strategy appears to put equal emphasis on professional and non-professional intelligence collection. In other words, a people's war for espionage is employed, which has made it impossible for Western counterintelligence to defend against it. To do this, China passed its National Intelligence Law in 2017, updating it in 2018. This law stipulates that all organizations and citizens shall support, assist, and cooperate with national intelligence work and keep the secrets that they know. The state protects individuals and organizations supporting and cooperating with national intelligence work.[155]

This means that every Chinese citizen and company has a legal duty to help the Party-state to spy, no matter where they are. For example, tech giants such as Huawei and Tencent, which owns WeChat with 1.24 billion users, and ByteDance's TikTok, which has over 1 billion users, must submit the data they collect overseas if the Chinese government asks for it, despite Huawei's claim that "Huawei's subsidiaries and employees outside of China are not subject to the territorial jurisdiction of the National Intelligence Law." But the intelligence law and several other security-related laws have similar requirements and are not limited to Chinese territory. The fact is China already began its "long-arm" laws to prosecute people who are suspected of committing so-called crimes against China abroad, which means it intends to apply the law without geographic restriction.

The MSS has 34 provincial, 333 district, and 2,844 county bureaus. Their primary job is to recruit intelligence assets and use any means to collect intelligence for the CCP. Other agencies have their own intelligence networks. Xi's holistic regime security and grand strategy demand the entire Party-state actively participate in espionage and infiltration activities. The ways that the CCP conducts espionage infiltration have become more diversified. Their organizational structure has reformed and evolved, and their operational models and finances have also morphed. However, despite the massive efforts to gain access to all aspects of targeted countries, China's infiltration operations always focus on 16 areas of security with the goal of achieving the Chinese Dream of great national rejuvenation. The urgency of the CCP's centenary goal drives its aggressiveness, and espionage infiltration has risen sharply in the past few years.

However, China's non-traditional espionage infiltrations—massive cyberattacks to target government agencies, companies, universities, individual researchers, and overt and covert big data collection—present much a greater threat to open societies. China has hired the world's largest number of hackers to conduct these operations, enabling it to acquire an astronomic volume of intelligence information and invaluable technological secrets. In the U.S. alone, hundreds of billions of dollars are lost each year to this cyber espionage.[156] Examples include the 2015 U.S. Office of Personnel Management data hack, resulting in the loss of 22.1 million records of federal employees.[157] Additionally, multiple sources indicate that Beijing has stolen many secret documents of advanced U.S. weapons systems, such as the C-17, F-22, and F-35, and used the information to develop the PLA's advanced weapons systems such as the Chengdu J-20 and Shenyang J-31 stealth fighters and electromagnetic catapult launch systems.[158] Despite China's 2015 promise to stop cyberattacks, it continues to carry out these activities.

3.3.5.4 Infiltration of University Campuses

The CCP understands well that the children of targeted countries are key to its infiltration operations. Whoever controls today's children and young adults will hold the future of a country. China also understands the power of language and culture; in particular, it considers the Chinese language and cultural education as a key strategy to ensure that overseas Chinese keep their roots. It believes that the "root-keeping project" of teaching the Chinese language to overseas Chinese youths is the most popular and effective way to infiltrate the Chinese diaspora. Meanwhile, spreading the Chinese language to foreign youths also can be a stepping stone in their communities. At the time of writing, there are about 20,000 Chinese schools, hundreds of thousands of Chinese teachers, and millions of overseas Chinese youths who are learning Chinese.[159] However, these schools are not only for language learning; the UFW also uses them as bases to organize parents for political and other covert activities.

China's Ministry of Education and its Office of Chinese Language Council International aggressively promote its infiltration operations through Chinese language and culture education. According to Chinese official media, more than 70 countries have incorporated Chinese language teaching into their education systems, and more than 4,000 foreign universities have Chinese language programs and courses.

More dangerously, China uses its money to buy its way into prestigious Western universities. A U.S. Education Department investigation revealed that China was among the top donors giving billions of dollars to U.S. universities as gifts or contracts.[160] More cases, such as Charles Lieber, chair of Harvard's Department of Chemistry and Chemical Biology, who secretly received large sums of money from China, have surfaced in recent years, showing that the CCP has deeply infiltrated Western universities with purposes beyond the indoctrination of Western youths. Stealing technology and co-opting talent are among China's goals. China has devised more than 200 talent recruitment programs to "gather the best and brightest minds under heaven" to help it overtake the high-tech industry.

3.3.5.5 Media Infiltration

China's infiltration into Western media is a key component of its global expansion strategy. Rooted in its Marxist–Maoist ideology, the CCP sees media as a critical weapon to mobilize and manipulate the population to believe in and follow them. Chinese official narratives often cite an old Chinese saying to stress the importance of media: "The three-inch tongue is mightier than a million soldiers."[161]

Currently, the PSC Leading Group for Propaganda and Ideology, headed by Wang Huning, oversees media infiltration planning and operations. Specifically, the CCP Central Committee's External Propaganda Office and the State Council's Information Office—one agency under two names—manage the daily work of overseas media infiltration. Although the office was set up in 1991 to offset the negative impacts of the Tiananmen protests and the collapse of the Soviet Union, it now strives to create a new world media order, or new order of international communication in which China controls the power of discourse. Xi feels strongly that negative views of China are a result of his propaganda machine not telling China's story well, and he insists that China's power in international discourse must match its current composite strength and rising status.

For Xi, China needs greater discourse power to create a world media order that favors his community with common destiny for mankind. Only when the CCP controls the global narrative can it ensure the communist regime's security and expand its global reach. To tell China's story well means convincing the world that the CCP's one-party dictatorship is superior to democracy; that Marxism works; that socialism with Chinese characteristics is great; that no human rights abuses or internment camps exist in Xinjiang; and that everyone is happy with the CCP's governance and supports its policy. To achieve this, Xi wants China to build a strategic communication system with distinctive Chinese characteristics and to improve the appeal of Chinese culture, the likability of China's image, and the persuasiveness of China's discourse to guide public opinion worldwide. But the real ambition is to change from a defensive, reactive media practice to an offensive, wolf-warrior style of propaganda in order to build a new world media order.[162]

For more than two decades, China employed a whole set of plans with information warfare strategies to conduct overseas media infiltration. One of the first steps China took was to control the overseas Chinese media, which it holds as a special branch in the global communication system, since the media already have spread across five continents and are influential with the Chinese diaspora. According to a Chinese government count, there are 1,019 overseas Chinese media outlets, including 390 newspapers, 221 magazines, 77 TV stations, 81 radio stations, and 250 online media platforms, distributing content in 61 countries and regions. The CCP believes that "overseas Chinese media have always played a special role in balancing international public opinion and clearing up the host country's mainstream society's misunderstandings and prejudices against China."[163] They can be used to "guide" international public opinion.[164] For that reason, China poured large sums of money into buying them. A Hoover Institution investigative report, *Chinese Influence and American Interests: Promoting Constructive Vigilance*, documented how the CCP acquired media outlets and changed their views and content afterward. The report concluded that when China completed its acquisitions, there were only a few Falun Gong media outlets left.[165] The Chinese language media outlets are largely part of the CCP propaganda apparatus, focusing on brainwashing the Chinese diaspora. Sometimes the content created by overseas Chinese media is also used for domestic propaganda.

A parallel step is to strengthen China's media presence in the world. This operation actually began in the 1950s, right after the communists seized state power. In 1955, Mao instructed the CCP *Xinhua News Agency* to send more reporters abroad "to control the globe so that the whole world can hear our voice."[166] In 2008, China invested about 45 billion RMB in expanding its global media platforms, the equivalent of $9.3 billion. All of the media such as CCTV, *Xinhua*, and the *People's Daily* expanded rapidly under the central government's control.[167] Local CCP media outlets and those that are marketized media (for-profit) also sent reporters abroad. Today, *Xinhua* has become the largest media outlet in the world. In 2019, when the International Olympic Committee (IOC) recognized *Xinhua* as one of its four official international news agencies, alongside *The Associated Press*, *Reuters*, and *AFP*, it cited the agency's 16,000 staff members in more than 200 offices around the world, working in eight languages, with three more languages about to be added. These outlets produce more than 7,000 news items a day and have more than 19,000 subscribers.[168] According to CGTN's website, this media platform launched in December 2016 has production centers in Nairobi, Washington, DC, and London. People in more than 160 countries and regions can watch its content. Through its apps, YouTube, Facebook, Twitter, Weibo, and other social media platforms, CGTN can deliver its content to more than 150 million followers across the globe. CGTN claims to have 1.2 billion audiences, including 30 million households in the U.S.

Cheng Kai, a former insider of China's media network, reveals that these outlets are not only the CCP's propaganda apparatus, they also are used for intelligence collection. Traditionally, the MSS inserts spies into *Xinhua* or *People's Daily* to use journalistic credentials as a cover to collect information. When he worked at *People's Daily* in the 1980s, the newspaper had about 40 overseas offices and Cheng says half of those employed were MSS agents. They rarely wrote news stories. Non-MSS reporters must write intelligence reports for the CCP leadership from time to time, but their main work is producing communist propaganda, according to Cheng. When Cheng headed *Hainan Daily*, he was ordered by the provincial Party committee to issue 20 reporter credentials to MSS and MPS agents without knowing who they were. He reasonably concluded that the Chinese media, or media "under the leadership of the Party," really are not pure news media.[169]

Another of China's media infiltration strategies—to "borrow a mouth or throat to speak out"—complicates the situation further. This strategy means hiring non-Chinese journalists to speak for China and using third-party media outlets to propagandize on Beijing's behalf, particularly established individuals and recognized news brands. China also signs agreements with Western mainstream media outlets to pay for publishing its propaganda content on their platforms. These news outlets have a vast readership or audience in the CCP's target countries, and are regarded as reputable, credible sources of information. Inserting CCP propaganda content is the most cost-effective way to infiltrate Western media and manipulate public opinion. One common practice is to pay mainstream newspapers to insert pages of China's propaganda. Alarmingly, many reputable newspapers willingly lend their names and cooperate with Beijing's deception of the public in exchange for money.

Infiltration in foreign correspondent corps in China and using every lever possible—including visa sanctions, exclusive interviews, and monetary payments—to neutralize them from criticizing China has been ongoing for years. Beijing effectively put these corps under control and far less critical articles came out in recent years. Under Wang Huning, the CCP's external media infiltration has expanded to movies, arts, music, and other cultural areas worldwide, to create an image of China as a peaceful country with superior culture. Beijing targets celebrities such as Yo-Yo Ma and prestigious music organizations such as the New York Philharmonic, the Philadelphia Orchestra, Chamber Music Society of Lincoln Center, and the Juilliard School. The Philadelphia Orchestra ran into financial hardship in 2011 and China jumped to its rescue by offering the orchestra a strategic cooperation agreement. Since then, it has performed numerous times the "Ode to the Red Flag," a symphony that praises the CCP and its violent revolution.[170] Hollywood is another example of how China's infiltration has affected American values.

However, behind all these, communist media outlets have further morphed into a new integrated media supported by artificial intelligence, machine learning, big data, and other advanced information technologies, which are mingled with Western media content and can reach many international audiences without users' awareness. This is the imminent danger of the CCP's deep media infiltration, which is largely missed or underestimated by Western China-watchers.

3.3.5.6 Economic Infiltration

The CCP's economic infiltration may be the least discussed and exposed area. China clearly has had a grand strategy to build a new economic order since Deng Xiaoping, with a goal of displacing the U.S. as the world's manufacturing factory and innovation center. To achieve this, it has been infiltrating the world business community for management knowledge, markets, capital, technology secrets, and talent. The ultimate goal is to control strategic materials, energy, global supply chains, and the world's economic lifeline.

The CCP claims that the Chinese diaspora is the "third largest economy in the world." In some countries in Southeast Asia, Chinese businessmen even control the economic lifeline of these countries. They have played a critical role in China's rapid economic growth. The CCP continues to rely on them as its foot soldiers to infiltrate the world business community. The best evidence may be the CCP member database, leaked by an unknown individual onto Telegram, a privacy messaging app, in September 2020. The database contains nearly two million CCP members, working in 79,000 foreign companies, universities, and government agencies, which include Boeing, Volkswagen, Pfizer, AstraZeneca, ANZ, and HSBC, and consulates of Australia, the UK, the U.S., and European nations. While not all Party members are intelligence agents, they have vowed to remain loyal to the CCP and to do whatever the Party asks—even if it means giving up their own lives. It is likely that many of them serve as the CCP's eyes, ears, and mouths, under a duty to collect information and steal technologies, particularly those who are placed by Shanghai Foreign Agency Service Corporation, a state-owned employment agency that provides service for foreign entities in Shanghai. This type of agency traditionally is a front for the MSS or has close ties with it.

China's global tech giant Tencent has more than 60,000 employees, and one in six is a CCP member. The company's rule is, where its business develops, the Party organization and Party work must follow up. Tencent has 14 general Party branches and 275 Party branches, managing more than 11,000 Party members. The 11 members of the company's Party committee and 3 members of the Disciplinary Committee are core executives of the company. In addition, there are 10 full-time and 724 part-time Party officials.[171] Huawei, ZTE, and other tech giants have similar Party organizational structures and compositions. Unlike companies in democracies, the CCP can control each of them and order them to do its bidding. They are indeed a formidable army for the CCP's economic warfare against the world.

China's geo-economic strategy is to lure developing countries, particularly those that have joined the BRI, with its China model—rapid economic development under political dictatorship. Xi claims that China's governance model offers a new option for countries that want to speed up their development while preserving their independence. But Indian scholar Ayjaz Wani counters Xi by pointing out that "Invest, indebt, incapacitate" is the true China model. Many other scholars have discussed China's debt trap. In 2021, Laos signed a 25-year concession agreement with a Chinese company, allowing it to build and manage its power grid, including electricity exports to neighboring countries.[172] Sri Lanka took Chinese loans to co-develop the Hambantota Port. When it could not repay, Sri Lanka had to lease the port for 99 years to China in return for $1.1 billion.[173] The Maldives, Pakistan, and many African countries are all deeply in debt to China.

The CCP is applying the strategy of economic dependence in Hong Kong and Taiwan. Since it took Hong Kong back from the UK in 1997, Beijing has made great efforts to create a highly integrated, interdependent economic community with the island city. It first dispatched a huge number of state-owned enterprises and personnel to Hong Kong. As of 2018, Hong Kong had over 4,200 companies from the mainland, accounting for a growing share of Hong Kong's business in key sectors.[174] At the same time, China has been working to further control Hong Kong's economy by fully integrating it into the Pearl River Delta Economic Zone. When Hong Kong's people demanded political rights, Beijing used economic levers such as banning mainland tourists to Hong Kong to create divisions in society and suppress protests.

The same strategy has been used in Taiwan. According to statistics from Taiwanese authorities, from January to November 2020, Taiwan's exports to the mainland amounted to $136.7 billion, accounting for 43.8 percent of Taiwan's total exports, a clear upward trend. Taiwan's imports from the mainland amounted to $58.417 billion, or 22.5 percent of total imports. For years, China has been Taiwan's largest export market and its share continues to rise, despite the Tsai administration's effort to reduce its dependence on a single market and move its exports to Southern Asia. That is why Beijing media outlets keep saying that "Taiwan cannot get rid of its dependence on the mainland. If the mainland uses economic means, it will be more ruthless than military means."[175]

China also has created strong economic ties with Australia and is Canberra's top export market. But when China is displeased with Australia's political position, it uses economic weapons to punish the country. As a result, Australia's non-iron ore exports to China have slumped by 40 percent over the past year.[176] China has used this weapon against South Korea, Norway, and other countries as well.

In the next 15 years, China's economic infiltration will heavily focus on technology. Xi Jinping believes that industrial change and a scientific and technological revolution are reshaping the global economic structure and China must seize the opportunity. Xi has tied his Chinese Dream of the great rejuvenation of the Chinese nation with the new world economic structure. He has launched a campaign to achieve this critical strategic goal of becoming the world's "primary center for science and technology, and commanding heights for innovations."[177]

To further this end, the Chinese quietly put money into startups in Silicon Valley and Route 128, the Boston Technology Corridor. By infiltrating the U.S. hi-tech sector, China can obtain what Xi calls the "chokehold technologies" and talent from the West. Additionally, foreign companies' dependence on China allows Beijing to compel them to further China's interests. In December 2021, China's vice foreign minister, Xie Feng, warned U.S. businesses that they cannot make a fortune in silence and must push the U.S. government to end its ideological conflict with China.[178]

If China will control the world's economic lifelines as well as people's minds through its advanced digital dictatorship, it can place the totality of liberal democracy in grave danger. This may be an ultimate fight between techno-democracies and techno-autocracies. Whoever wins will dominate the world. China's infiltration of the world is comprehensive and premeditated, with the aim of creating a China-centered world order. It utilizes hybrid warfare at the moment but will continue to intensify its tactics as democracies try to resist China's efforts. At any point, China very well may turn its hybrid warfare into unlimited or unrestricted warfare.

3.3.6 The Abuse of China's Muslim Minority Populations

The Chinese province of Xinjiang is the locus of some of the world's worst human rights abuses. The internment of mostly Kazakh, Kyrgyz, and Uyghur Muslims has received some attention—far less than what it deserves—from the world's news media, United Nations, and human rights organizations.[179] But there is an additional aspect of this gross human rights abuse that has received almost no attention. In Xinjiang, China has created the world's largest gulag to support its cotton and textile industry. Echoing the gulag prison system of the Soviet Union, or the earlier history of the PRC and its actions in Tibet against Tibetans, this horrific system punishes and banishes inmates, re-indoctrinates them while working them brutally to make money for the state.

This contemporary slavery, what we term a "cotton gulag," provides much of the labor that allows Xinjiang to produce 84 percent of China's cotton output.[180] Xinjiang is the primary supplier and worldwide exporter of cotton apparel products, which accounts for about 43 percent of the region's total exports. The profit from these sales is used to reinforce the forced labor front of the cotton gulag.

Today's Xinjiang is home to the highest percentage of China's prisoners per capita, and the largest population in internment camps. These inmates serve as a key labor force in every link of China's cotton chain, from reclamation of cotton fields and construction of irrigation systems construction, to planting, harvesting, and processing cotton, and producing garments.

Citizen Power Initiatives for China, an organization with which both authors are affiliated, has published a report based on direct evidence from data published by the CCP, Chinese companies, and witness testimonies—all of which show that inmates in prisons and re-education camps in the region are forced to work in the cotton and garment industry.[181]

It is China's longstanding policy to use prisoners as forced labor, and since the CCP took power it has been shipping prisoners from the interior of China to Xinjiang to do hard labor and "contribute to Xinjiang's economic development" in the harsh desert environment. Many died in the process. Since the launch of "The Crackdown on Violent Terrorism Campaign," a government response to the July 2009 Urumqi Unrest, more Uyghur prisoners have been added to the prison population.[182]

As a result, Xinjiang has a disproportionately high concentration of prisons in comparison with other provinces in China. Excluding Uyghur re-education camps, there are over 80 prisons in Xinjiang, compared to a mere 25 in Shandong Province, even though the latter has a population more than four times larger. Xinjiang has mega-prisons, each with many satellite prisons. For example, the Change Prison has 11 satellites.

This absurd ratio underscores a system of ethnic disenfranchisement initiated by the CCP that, while being propagated as a supposed means of re-education for criminals, actually functions as a way to inhumanely punish inmates, eradicate Islam in China, and provide a renewable source of unethical but cheap forced labor for the cotton and textile industries. Though the exact figure is unknown, it is estimated there are 500,000–800,000 prisoners incarcerated in Xinjiang, who are routinely forced to reclaim land for cotton fields and participate in other aspects of the cotton value chain, including work in garment factories.

In 2014, the Chinese government began to implement a multifaceted strategy to maintain political stability in Xinjiang. Xi wanted to use economic performance to legitimize China's rule over the region by creating jobs to reduce "religious extremism," "separatism," and "terrorism," and to expand China's influence westward and globally under the BRI.[183] A component of this strategy involves the development of the vertical integration of China's garment manufacturing sector by moving textile and garment factories from the coastal provinces closer to cotton production hubs in Xinjiang, and the detention of large numbers of Uyghurs in "re-education camps," "vocational schools," and "skill training centers," where they are re-indoctrinated and provided skills training. They are then forced to work in barbed wire-enclosed and heavily guarded cotton/textile/garment facilities.

Over a million Uyghurs are held in the "re-education camps" and vocational schools, and many are forced to work under the new textile/apparel expansion plan. As of 2018, 2,200 new cotton/textile/apparel companies were set up to participate in the program. Xinjiang Lihua Cotton Company, a prison enterprise, has boasted of adding 8,000 Uyghur workers annually. Huafu Fashion and Lutai Textile, both suppliers for international brands such as Target, Burberry, Calvin Klein, Hugo Boss, Armani, Gucci, OLYMP, and UNIQLO, have been active participants. As of 2018, 450,000 new Uyghur workers came from impoverished households, were relatives of the convicted and detained, or were re-education camp inmates.

The presence of both judicial and extrajudicial forced labor, at many steps of the cotton supply chain, means that potentially all cotton/textile/apparel products from Xinjiang are produced with forced labor, and some of these products have entered into international commerce, including the U.S., in violation of existing law. To conceal this practice, prison, labor camp, and re-education camp authorities in Xinjiang systematically delete online information regarding these forced labor companies and factories; they change their names and create layers of company ownership to disguise the factories and farms as schools or trading companies.

Because forced labor is used so ubiquitously throughout Xinjiang, it is difficult to separate the province's forced labor economy from its regular economy.[184] All the cotton/textile/apparel products from Xinjiang and China should be banned from importation to the U.S. and other countries. As the trade war with China escalated, former President Trump tried to address the atrocious human rights abuses in China's cotton gulag.

Cotton and textiles produced in this gulag are made possible largely through the abuse of China's Muslim minority. Fundamentally, this situation is occurring because an odious regime created and supports it. The attention of the world's governments, media, and human rights organizations is essential to stop this modern slavery.

3.3.7 Gross Human Rights Abuses in Hong Kong

The crushing of the "one country, two systems" involving Hong Kong, to which China committed itself in the 1984 Sino-UK Agreement, demonstrates the ruthlessness and willpower of the Xi Doctrine, implemented by Hong Kong's chief executive Carrie Lam. Since June 2019, civil resistance, disobedience and clashes with authorities have created a new dynamic that has profoundly impacted the future of Hong Kong and led Xi to smother its independence. To assess the impact of Hong Kong's civil resistance, we must understand its evolution.[185] During China–UK negotiations over Hong Kong's status in the 1980s, civil resistance and the "pro-independence" sentiment were almost nonexistent. The turning point was the Tiananmen Square Massacre, when the PLA crushed student protesters who demanded democracy and a clean government. To this day, we do not know how many hundreds or thousands of innocent people died in Tiananmen Square. The incident had a great impact on Hong Kongers, who wholeheartedly sided with the pro-democracy protesters before and after the massacre. They helped to rescue many student leaders and activists from the mainland through secret means. The city itself was rocked by mass protests condemning the atrocity.

Since Tiananmen, the communist regime has worried that Hong Kong will become the anti-CCP epicenter, threatening regime security. Beijing has all but formally rejected its commitment to the Hong Kong people's self-governance and the "one country, two systems" political framework. One measure Beijing took was to require that the Hong Kong Basic Law Drafting Committee re-draft Article 23, which demands that Hong Kong enact laws prohibiting "treason, secession, sedition, subversion, or theft of state secrets" and "foreign political organizations' activities" in the city.[186] It also prohibits Hong Kongers from having any relations with foreign forces. The alteration of Article 23 is significant because China has used a vague definition of "subversion" to incarcerate many political and human rights activists for criticizing the CCP. New language regarding subversion and foreign forces in Article 23 has caused many Hong Kongers to fear the loss of their freedom to Beijing.

This fear was realized when the Hong Kong government decided to introduce a national security bill to implement Article 23 in 2003, which triggered mass protests. On July 1, 2003, over a half-million Hong Kongers took to the streets to protest this legislation; they stopped traffic and encircled the government headquarters for six hours.[187] When the CCP realized its tactical mistake, it created a Central Coordination Group for Hong Kong and Macao Work, consisting of 18 agencies. Zeng Qinghong, a CCP Standing Committee member, directed the group. He redesigned the CCP's strategy and increased the number of CCP operatives in Hong Kong to tighten controls. This included dispatching a large number of spies and United Front workers, hiring Hong Kong's local "mafia" as Beijing's thugs, and encouraging many pro-CCP mainland businessmen to move to Hong Kong. Since 2003, Beijing has directly interfered in Hong Kong affairs. The unfortunate truth is that the Hong Kong government is merely a puppet of Beijing.

After 2007, Xi replaced Zeng and became the chief of the group. Under his leadership, the group formulated and carried out more sinister policies to Sinicize Hong Kong, as the CCP has done to Tibet and Xinjiang. As the CCP's paramount leader, Xi has abandoned discreet Sinicization in favor of forceful integration and assimilation. The niceties and politeness of China's relationship with Hong Kong have been replaced by threats and broken promises.

In 2014, when Xi refused to honor Beijing's promise to allow Hong Kongers to vote directly for their government chief executives and legislature— which was scheduled to take place in 2017—Hong Kong's civil resistance was resurrected. Pro-democracy demonstrators in the city launched the "Occupy Central" campaign, also known as "Umbrella Movement," which demanded that regime leaders allow genuine universal suffrage.[188] The protesters blocked roads in three downtown districts—Admiralty, Causeway Bay, and Mong Kok. More than a million people participated, essentially paralyzing parts of Hong

Kong for 79 days. The movement failed partly because Hong Kong's majority of elites refused to participate, and also because of Beijing's extensive efforts to sabotage the movement. China's retaliation against leaders of the Occupy Central movement was a stark and severe example of its treatment of those it perceives as subversives.

If Occupy Central was a movement for political rights, then the current Anti-Extradition movement should be considered the last defense of Hong Kong's rule of law. After Occupy Central, the CCP adopted a several-pronged approach to curtail the city's civil resistance. One critical component is the development plan for the Guangdong-Hong Kong-Macao Greater Bay Area announced in early 2021, which will make Hong Kong a permanent political and economic part of the mainland.[189] The CCP even plans to impose its social credit system in Hong Kong to keep people in line with Beijing.[190]

The CCP's increased aggression against the Hong Kong people naturally has caused trepidation. That extraordinary tension was released when the extradition bill was introduced. Even the elite felt that their safety was in danger. Moreover, the CCP's princelings and powerful political families who hide assets in the city became greatly concerned that they may fall victim to the CCP's internal power struggles as the PRC gains greater control over the city.

These factors have made civil resistance partially successful. Among the five demands the protesters put forward, Carrie Lam met only one—the withdrawal of the extradition bill—but refused the rest, including the release of those arrested as "rioters." Her position reflects the pattern of how the CCP handles Hong Kong affairs: one step backward to de-escalate tensions and two steps forward to increase repression. The CCP can do this not only because of the overt pressure it can bring to bear, but also because of its covert ability to ensure its wishes are met. Since 1949, the PRC has had a secret network of agents in Hong Kong.[191] The British transfer of sovereignty in 1997 allowed the CCP to strengthen its network significantly. Of course, Beijing also recruits many Hong Kong elites, with financial and other incentives, to work for the regime and actively participate in overt and covert political actions. The recent violent clashes between Beijing's supporters and pro-democracy activists are evidence of Beijing's muscle and reach into Hong Kong, and the ability to cause substantial unrest.

At the same time, Beijing always blames foreign forces for any civil resistance in Hong Kong—and the most recent resistance is no exception. The CCP launched a smear campaign to blame the U.S. and UK for the ongoing anti-extradition bill protests in Hong Kong to deceive the world. Dusting off the old canard, Chinese Foreign Minister Wang Yi angrily denounced the "Western forces trying to undermine Hong Kong's peace and stability."[192]

However, despite the CCP's disinformation and censorship, more and more mainland Chinese have learned about the protests and are inspired by them. The democratic "spirit of Hong Kong" could jump the firebreak that Beijing has created around Hong Kong and spread to the mainland. Xi's regime is concerned about this, and that explains why the regime was quick to dispatch PLA tanks to crack down on a protest in the city of Wuhan.[193] These protests took place at the same time as those in Hong Kong and ended with a victory, even if temporary, for the protesters when the government withdrew its plan.

But that was only a tactical victory. Hong Kong's civil resistance was a protracted contest between Hong Kongers and Beijing's dictators, which Xi won. The struggle required not only courage and wisdom but also endurance to succeed. Pro-democracy Hong Kongers have proven they will fight for their rights against one of the most formidable and effective dictatorships the world has witnessed. They might have prevailed if the international community had stood in solidarity with them to force Beijing to pay a high price for their repression. Lamentably, what happened in Hong Kong is a window into the future. As China becomes more powerful, it will favor ever-greater control of its agreements and territorial claims, which does not augur well for Taiwan.

The CCP has a perverse Midas touch. At least King Midas turned everything he touched to gold. Everything the CCP touches, it ruins. Control of Hong Kong is more valuable to the CCP than the wealth the city creates. Accordingly, the CCP would rather destroy its wealth than allow Hong Kong to continue with its own political system—which, in fact, Beijing is required to honor according to the 1984 agreement with the UK.[194] The pro-democracy movement in Hong Kong weakens the CCP's power because it reveals its illegitimacy and inspires mainlanders to recognize that a free system is possible, will work, and is far superior to despotism.

This chapter has analyzed Xi as a man, his ideology, and the Xi Doctrine that makes three major arguments. We examined Xi's background as a youth to his rise to power, since both inform his worldview. He truly has "Red DNA"—do as the Party says—and wants to complete the CCP's original mission of achieving communism globally. Second, we presented Xi's ideology and explained how this informs his ruthless domestic and international policies. Third, we presented the Xi Doctrine, the CCP's global expansion strategy based on the doctrine, and its consequences for the United States and the world. The chapter considered the implications of Xi's rule and its negative effects for the Chinese people and for democratic, free societies. As a result of Xi's background, ideology, and the Xi Doctrine, the CCP under his leadership poses the most serious threat to the international liberal order it has faced since the end of the Cold War.

Notes

1 George Soros, "Remarks Delivered at the World Economic Forum," *George Soros*, January 24, 2019. Available at: <https://www.georgesoros.com/2019/01/24/remarks-delivered-at-the-world-economic-forum-2/>. Accessed July 2, 2021.
2 John Simpson, "New Leader Xi Jinping Opens Door to Reform in China," *The Guardian*, August 10, 2013. Available at: <https://www.theguardian.com/world/2013/aug/10/china-xi-jinping-opens-door-reform>. Accessed July 2, 2021.

3 中共河北省委党史研究室，"习仲勋被批批斗后，周恩来发怒：这是给国家发怒,"周恩来纪念网，May 22, 2020. Available at: <http://zhouenlai.people.cn/n1/2020/0522/c409117-31719725.html>. Accessed July 5, 2021.

4 王友群，"先整习仲勋后'叛党自杀'的阎红彦," 大纪元. April 15, 2020. Available at: <https://www.epochtimes.com/gb/20/4/14/n12030496.htm>. Accessed July 5, 2021.

5 深圳卫视，"习仲勋的家人谈习仲勋在文革的被惨遭遇," 中国近代史专题，September 12, 2020. Available at <https://www.youtube.com/watch?v=EMGz_Fa8Fn4>. Accessed July 5, 2021.

6 《习仲勋转》编委会，"习近平：'我坚信我的父亲是一个大英雄'"胡耀邦史料信息网，October 15, 2013. Available at: <http://www.hybsl.cn/zt/xizhongxun1/yong11/2013-10-15/41628.html>. Accessed July 5, 2021.

7 Chris Buckley and Didi Kirsten Tatlow, "Cultural Revolution Shaped Xi Jinping, from Schoolboy to Survivor," *The New York Times*, September 24, 2015. Available at: <https://www.nytimes.com/2015/09/25/world/asia/xi-jinping-china-cultural-revolution.html>. Accessed July 7, 2021.

8 Jean Chesneaux, *China: The People's Republic Since 1949–1979* (Brighton: Harvester Press, 1979), p. 141.

9 Chong Woei Lien, *China's Great Proletarian Cultural Revolution: Master Narratives and Post-Mao Counternarratives* (Lanham, MD: Rowman & Littlefield. 2002).

10 Yongyi Song, "Chronology of Mass Killings during the Chinese Cultural Revolution (1966-1976)," *Online Encyclopedia of Mass Violence* (2011), pp. 311-327. Accessed July 6, 2021.

11 宋永毅，"文革中到底"非正常死亡"了多少人？—读苏扬的《文革中中国农村的集体屠杀》," 华夏文摘，增刊第八一九期，October 11, 2011.

12 张光渝，"话说[联动]," 告别元老，香港北星出版社，August 2, 2007.

13 戴广骞，"文革五十年问文化 –兼谈白卫兵(联动兵)与红卫兵的战斗," 带心看闻网，May 16, 2016. Available at: <http://www.daisoncommon.com/2016/05/28/8425/>. Accessed July 5, 2021.

14 聂卫平, 王端阳; 聂卫平·围棋人生, [北京：文化艺术出版社，January 2011].

15 "习近平和他的老师," 澎湃新闻，September 10, 2020. Available at: <https://m.thepaper.cn/newsDetail_forward_9114796>. Accessed July 5, 2021.

16 Buckley, "Cultural Revolution Shaped Xi Jinping."

17 戴广骞，"文革五十年问文化."

18 Cheng Li, "Xi Jinping's Inner Circle (Part 1: The Shaanxi Gang)." *China Leadership Monitor* 43 (2014): 1–21.

19 王友琴，文革研究掩盖在霧霾中，新世纪，2014年11月23日。Available at: <https://2newcenturynet.blogspot.com/2014/11/blog-post_71.html>. Accessed January 28, 2022.

20 独家专访习近平初中老师陈秋影, 昆仑策，2015-09-10。Available at: <https://www.kunlunce.net/e/wap/show2021.php?bclassid=0&classid=150&id=12608>. Accessed January 28, 2022.

21 《习仲勋传》编委会，习仲勋传, (北京：中央文献出版社，August, 2013).

22 聂卫平，"围棋人生."

23 聂卫平，"围棋人生."

24 "习仲勋两次上书毛主席的往事," 凤凰新闻网，November 13, 2019. Available at: <https://ishare.ifeng.com/c/s/7rYFQ6qPkPG>. Accessed July 6, 2021.

25 杨屏，"习仲勋与近平的父子情,"新浪杨屏博客，March 28, 2013. Available at: <http://m.aisixiang.com/data/61575-2.html>. Accessed July 6, 2021.

26 杨筱怀，"习近平：我是怎样跨入政界的," 中华儿女, no. 7 (2000).

27 习远平，"父亲往事-忆我的父亲习仲勋," 人民网-中国共产党新闻网，October 11, 2013. Available at: <http://dangshi.people.com.cn/n/2013/1011/c85037-23159004-4.html>. Accessed July 6, 2021.

28 习近平, 忆延安插队：它教了我做什么, 2015年02月14日, 人民网-时政频道. Available at: <http://politics.people.com.cn/n/2015/0214/c1001-26566406.html>. Accessed July 5, 2021.

29 习近平, 忆延安插队：它教了我做什么.

30 习近平, "忆延安插队."

31 习近平, "忆延安插队."

32 刘明升, "近平立志办大事, 不搞形式主义", 《习近平的七年知青岁月》中共中央党校出版社, 2017年8月。 Available at: <http://cpc.people.com.cn/n1/2021/0930/c441140-32244087.html>. Accessed October 8, 2021.

33 杨世忠, "近平当村支书就是因为大家都拥护他," 《习近平的七年知青岁月》中共中央党校出版社, 2017年8月。 Available at: <http://cpc.people.com.cn/n1/2021/0930/c441140-32244094.html>. Accessed October 8, 2021.

34 陶海粟, "为群众做实事是习近平始终不渝的信念"——习近平的七年知青岁月," 爱思想网, March 14, 2017. Available at: <http://m.aisixiang.com/data/103568.html>. Accessed July 8, 2021.

35 习近平, "忆延安插队."

36 杨屏, "习仲勋与近平的父子情."

37 田方、范新民、张志功和曹振中, "习仲勋回忆：毛泽东晚来四天 我就会被活埋," 凤凰资讯, January 19, 2009. Available at: <https://news.ifeng.com/history/1/midang/200901/0119_2664_975498.shtml>. Accessed July 8, 2021.

38 高新, "习近平一生只接受过七年时间的正规教育." 自由亚洲电台, December 31, 2018. Available at: <https://www.rfa.org/mandarin/zhuanlan/yehuazhongnan-hai/gx-12312018142054.html>. Accessed July 8, 2021.

39 陶海粟, "为群众做实事是习近平始终不渝的信念."

40 陶海粟, "为群众做实事是习近平始终不渝的信念."

41 习近平, "用好红色资源, 传承好红色基因, 把红色江山世世代代传下去." 求是网, 2021年10月刊.

42 Buckley, "Cultural Revolution Shaped Xi Jinping."

43 齐彪, "'两个不能否定'的重大政治意义," 光明日报, 2013年5月7日01版.

44 高新, "习近平的统治模式脱胎于毛泽东的文革遗产," 自由亚洲电台, October 08, 2018. Available at: <https://www.rfa.org/mandarin/zhuanlan/yehuazhongnan-hai/gx-10082018143140.html>. Accessed July 10, 2021.

45 高文谦, "毛的文革遗产与习近平治国模式," 美国之音, May 18, 2016. Available at: <https://www.voachinese.com/a/gao-wenqian-cultural-revolution-part1-20160505/3317245.html>. Accessed July 10, 2021.

46 高文谦, "毛的文革遗产与习近平治国模式."

47 高新, "习近平的统治模式脱胎于毛泽东的文革遗产." 自由亚洲电台, October 08, 2018. Available at: <https://www.rfa.org/mandarin/zhuanlan/yehuazhongnan-hai/gx-10082018143140.html>. Accessed July 10, 2021.

48 方舟与中国, 客观评价习近平, 2022 年 02 月 07 日. Available at: <https://www.storm.mg/article/4187338?page=1>. Accessed February 5, 2022.

49 Buckley, "Cultural Revolution Shaped Xi Jinping."

50 中共中央, "中国共产党中央委员会关于无产阶级文化大革命的决定," 宋永毅 [Song Yongyi] ed. 美国《 中国文化大革命文库光盘》 编委会 编纂 香港中文大学• 中国研究服务中心 制作及出版 [The Cultural Revolution Database] (1966).

51 倪光辉, "习近平：胸怀大局把握大势着眼大事努力把宣传思想工作做得更好," 人民网-中国共产党新闻网, 2013年8月21日01版.

52 柯大文, "坚守宣传思想主阵地, 学习习总书记在全国宣传思想工作会议上的重要讲话," 解放军报, October 21, 2013.

53 何斌, "在县级领导干部学习贯彻党的十九届五中全会专题研讨班上的发言," 祁连新闻网, February 25, 2021. Available at: <https://web.archive.org/web

/20210226222555/http%3A%2F%2Fwww.qiliannews.com%2Fsystem%2F2021
%2F02%2F25%2F013341147.shtml>. Accessed July 10, 2021.

54 何斌，"在县级领导干部学习贯彻党的十九届五中全会专题研讨班上的发言."

55 "Document 9: A ChinaFile Translation," *ChinaFile*, November 8, 2013. Available
at: <https://www.chinafile.com/document-9-chinafile-translation>. Accessed July
8, 2021.

56 徐光春，"中国共产党百年辉煌与百年未有之大变局," 新华网，April 01, 2021.
Available at: <http://www.xinhuanet.com/politics/2021-04/01/c_1127281691
.htm>. Accessed July 10, 2021.

57 Tanner Greer, "Xi Jinping in Translation: China's Guiding Ideology," *Palladium
Magazine*, May 31, 2019. Available at: <https://palladiummag.com/2019/05/31/xi
-jinping-in-translation-chinas-guiding-ideology/>. Accessed July 10, 2021.

58 XI Jinping, "19th Party Congress: Xi Jinping Outlines New Thought on Socialism
with Chinese Traits," *Straits Times*, October 18, 2017.

59 Xi, "19th Party Congress."

60 Xi Jinping, "Broad, Multilevel, and Institutionalized Consultative Democracy,"
September 21, 2014. Available at: <http://en.qstheory.cn/2021-07/26/c_644488
.htm>. Accessed July 11, 2021.

61 "China," RS. Available at: <https://rsf.org/en/china>. Accessed July 11, 2021.

62 "关于民政、民生、民心，习近平这样说," 新华网，April 03, 2019. Available
at: <http://www.xinhuanet.com/politics/xxjxs/2019-04/03/c_1124323996.htm>.
Accessed July 12, 2021.

63 Xi Jinping, "Report at the 19th CPC National Congress," October 18, 2017. Available
at: <http://www.xinhuanet.com/english/special/2017-11/03/c_136725942.htm>.
Accessed July 5, 2021.

64 "China's Environmental Data: The World's Biggest Polluter in Numbers," *The
Times of India*, April 14, 2021. Available at: <https://timesofindia.indiatimes.com/
world/china/chinas-environmental-data-the-worlds-biggest-polluter-in-numbers/
articleshow/82064532.cms>. Accessed July 12, 2021.

65 Henry Kissinger, *On China* (London: Penguin Press, 2011).

66 Mingfu Liu, *The China Dream: Great Power Thinking & Strategic Posture in the Post-
American Era* (Beijing: CN Times Books, 2015).

67 习近平，"实现中国梦不仅造福中国人民，而且造福世界人民," 人民网-
中国共产党新闻网，July 17, 2015. Available at: <http://cpc.people.com.cn/xuexi/n
/2015/0717/c397563-27322401.html>. Accessed July 12, 2021.

68 仲计水，"祖国统一是实现中华民族伟大复兴的必然要求," 中国日报，May 14,
2020. Available at: <https://cn.chinadaily.com.cn/a/202005/14/WS5ebc9ae3a310e
ec9c72b8c5b.html>. Accessed July 12, 2021.

69 Xi Jinping, "Working Together to Realise Rejuvenation of the Chinese Nation
and Advance China's Peaceful Reunification', Speech at the Meeting Marking the
40th Anniversary of the Issuance of the Message to Compatriots in Taiwan, January
2, 2019." Available at: <http://www.gwytb.gov.cn/wyly/201904/t20190412
_12155687.htm>. Accessed June 25, 2021.

70 方冰，"'为掌权不惜代价' 中共百年后何以成为世界秩序的最大威胁？" 美国
之音，June 16, 2021. Available at: <https://www.voachinese.com/a/how-ccp-
becomes-the-biggest-threat-to-us-and-world-20210615/5929899.html>. Accessed
July 12, 2021.

71 Rodion Ebbighause, "中国眼中21世纪的世界秩序," 德国之声，July 30, 2020.
Available at: <https://www.dw.com/zh/%E4%B8%AD%E5%9B%BD%E7%9C%
BC%E4%B8%AD21%E4%B8%96%E7%BA%AA%E7%9A%84%E4%B8%96%E7
%95%8C%E7%A7%A9%E5%BA%8F/a-54372622>. Accessed July 12, 2021.

72 杨俊峰，"人类命运共同体 国际秩序新选择," 人民网－人民日报海外版，
July 09, 2017. Available at: <http://world.people.com.cn/n1/2017/0709/c1002
-29392215.html>. Accessed July 13, 2021.

73 "习近平在亚洲相互协作与信任措施会议第四次峰会上的讲话　　（全文）", 新华网，May 21, 2014. Available at: <http://www.xinhuanet.com//politics/2014 -05/21/c_1110796357.htm>. Accessed July 13, 2021.

74 "Interview on Current China-U.S. Relations Given by State Councilor and Foreign Minister Wang Yi to Xinhua News Agency," *Ministry of Foreign Affairs of the People's Republic of China,* August 06, 2020. Available at: <https://www.fmprc.gov.cn/mfa _eng/zxxx_662805/t1804328.shtml>. Accessed July 14, 2021.

75 刘立峰，"夯实人类命运共同体，引领国际新秩序," 中青在线，February 21, 2017, Available at: <http://news.cyol.com/content/2017-02/21/content _15632030.htm>. Accessed July 14, 2021.

76 习近平，"努力开创中国特色大国外交新局面," 新华网，June 23, 2018. Available at: <http://www.xinhuanet.com/politics/2018-06/23/c_1123025806.htm>. Accessed July 12, 2021.

77 习近平，"推动全球治理体制更加公正更加合理　为我国发展和世界和平创造有利条件," 人民日报，October 14, 2015. 01 版.

78 Chen Shuisheng, "A Change of China's View of the International Order and Pushing for the Building of a Community of Common Destiny for Mankind," 中国与国际关系学刊，2019 年第 2 期.

79 刘立峰，"夯实人类命运共同体."

80 丁原洪，"深刻变化中的世界形势," 国际网，September 12, 2018. Available at: <http://comment.cfisnet.com/2018/0912/1313736.html>. Accessed July 15, 2021.

81 修丽,李涛，"构建人类命运共同体思想的时代意义," 红旗文稿, 2019/05.

82 "构建人类命运共同体的深远意义," 江苏智库网，March 12, 2018. Available at: <http://www.jsthinktank.com/wap/zhikuyanjiu/201803/t20180312_5185333 .shtml>. Accessed July 15, 2021.

83 "Full Text: Keynote Speech by President Xi at Boao Forum for Asia Annual Conference 2021," *China Daily,* April 20, 2021.

84 "构建人类命运共同体的伟大实践—写在习近平主席提出'一带一路'倡议5周年," 新华网，October 04, 2018. Available at: <http://www.xinhuanet.com/2018-10 /04/c_1123519710.htm>. Accessed July 15, 2021.

85 "一带一路，开创共同发展的光明未来," 人民日报, July 09, 2021.

86 Wenyuan Wu, "How Africa Is Breaking China's Neo-colonial Shackles," *The Interpreter,* October 30, 2019. Available at: <https://www.lowyinstitute.org/the -interpreter/how-africa-breaking-china-s-neo-colonial-shackles>. Accessed July 15, 2021.

87 习近平，论坚持推动构建人类命运共同体（北京：中央文献出版社，2019年）.

88 Cai Xia, *China-US Relations in the Eyes of the Chinese Communist Party: An Insider's Perspective* (Stanford, CA: Hoover Institution, 2021).

89 *Securing the Belt and Road Initiative: China's Evolving Military Engagement Along the Silk Roads, The National Bureau of Asian Research,* Nadège Rolland, ed., September 3, 2019.

90 《人民日报》、《红旗》杂志、《解放军报》编辑部，"列宁主义，还是社会帝国主义？——纪念伟大列宁诞生一百周年," 红旗，no. 05 (1970).

91 《人民日报》、《红旗》杂志、《解放军报》编辑部，"列宁主义."

92 Eyck Freymann, *One Belt One Road: Chinese Power Meets the World* (Cambridge, MA: Harvard University Press, 2020).

93 鄢一龙，"'一带一路'不是地缘政治扩张," 求是网，February 16, 2019. Available at: <http://www.qstheory.cn/llqikan/2019-02/16/c_1124123707.htm>. Accessed July 15, 2021.

94 中央军委政治工作部, "坚定维护核心 坚决听党指挥," 人民网，February 4, 2017. Available at: <http://military.people.com.cn/n1/2017/0204/c1011-29058724-4.html>. Accessed July 15, 2021.

95 江真, "习近平铁腕掌控 军队反腐风暴还在刮," 美国之音, May 19, 2021. Available at: <https://www.voachinese.com/a/Xi-Jinping-consolidates-his-control-of-military-through-anti-corruption-campaign-20210519/5896224.html>. Accessed July 16, 2021.

96 王传宝, "确保二〇二七年实现建军百年奋斗目标," 光明日报, 11版, November 19, 2020.

97 梅世雄, 梅常伟, "国防部介绍如何理解确保二〇二七年实现建军百年奋斗目标," 新华网, November 26, 2020. Available at: <http://www.xinhuanet.com/politics/2020-11/26/c_1126791220.htm>. Accessed July 16, 2021.

98 王若愚, "建军百年奋斗目标——一面令人振奋的精神战旗," 腾讯网, November 02, 2020. Available at: <https://new.qq.com/omn/20201102/20201102A01MRG00.html>. Accessed July 16, 2021.

99 杜尚泽和张晓松, "高远务实的时代擘画 ——党的十九届五中全会侧记," 人民日报, 02 版, October 31, 2020.

100 David Crawshaw and Alicia Chen, "'Heads Bashed Bloody': China's Xi Marks Communist Party Centenary with Strong Words for Adversaries," *Washington Post*, July 1, 2021. Available at: <https://www.washingtonpost.com/world/asia_pacific/china-party-heads-bashed-xi/2021/07/01/277c8f0c-da3f-11eb-8c87-ad6f27918c78_story.html>. Accessed July 16, 2021.

101 Kristin Huang, "Mainland Chinese Magazine Outlines How Surprise Attack on Taiwan Could Occur," *South China Morning Post*, July 2, 2021. Available at: <https://www.scmp.com/news/china/military/article/3139460/mainland-chinese-magazine-outlines-how-surprise-attack-taiwan>. Accessed July 16, 2021.

102 "交付150架歼-20？其中一半用来监视台海和东海？专家：这是警告！" 网易网, June 27, 2021. Available at: <https://www.163.com/dy/article/GDGIO9E80515IDLV.html>.

103 Henri Kenhmann, "DF-17: Ce que l'on sait de cette arme hypersonique chinoise," October 7, 2019. Available at: <http://www.eastpendulum.com/df-17-ce-que-lon-sait-de-cette-arme-hypersonique-chinoise>. Accessed July 16, 2021.

104 唏兮, "歼20、东风17现身威慑"台独"? 国防部：能力始终都在, 意志坚定不移," 腾讯网, October 29, 2020. Available at: <https://new.qq.com/omn/20201029/20201029A0DKY900.html>. Accessed July 16, 2021.

105 Joby Warrick, "China Is Building More than 100 New Missile Silos in Its Western Desert, Analysts Say," *Washington Post*, June 30, 2021. Available at: <https://www.washingtonpost.com/national-security/china-nuclear-missile-silos/2021/06/30/0fa8debc-d9c2-11eb-bb9e-70fda8c37057_story.html>. Accessed July 17, 2021.

106 David Brunnstrom and Daphne Psaledakis, "U.S. Calls Build-Up of China's Nuclear Arsenal 'Concerning'," *Reuters*, July 2, 2021. Available at: <https://www.reuters.com/world/china/us-says-chinas-nuclear-buildup-concerning-2021-07-01/>. Accessed July 17, 2021.

107 胡锡进, 微博 May 27, 2021. Available at: <https://weibo.com/1989660417/KhoTu9pRf>. Accessed July 17, 2021.

108 胡锡进, 微博.

109 Cai Xia, *China-US Relations in the Eyes of the Chinese Communist Party*."

110 自由亚洲电台, "大陆军事评论主张用核弹毁灭日本," *Twitter*, July 12, 2021. Available at: <https://twitter.com/RFA_Chinese/status/1414541296920760320>. Accessed July 17, 2021.

111 Helen Warrell and Michael Peel, "Senior Nato Officer Warns of China's 'Shocking' Military Advances," *Financial Times*, June 25, 2021. Available at: <https://www.ft.com/content/8a0b3975-1938-4815-af3b-22b5d3e6aca4>. Accessed July 18, 2021.

112 王新, "西方虎视眈眈下 解放军透露弹药消耗大的幕后中国," 多维新闻, June 28, 2021.

113 "南海主权事关中国梦," 中国青年网, July 12, 2016. Available at: <https://pinglun.youth.cn/ttst/201607/t20160712_8271615.htm>. Accessed July 18, 2021.

114 Bonnie Glaser and Isaac Kardon, "China Global Podcast: Chinese Investment in Global Ports and the PRC Strategy with Dr Isaac Kardon," *The German Marshall Fund of the United States*, July 20, 2021. Available at: <https://www.gmfus.org/audio/china-global-podcast-chinese-investment-global-ports-and-prc-strategy-dr-isaac-kardon>. Accessed July 17, 2021.

115 Anwei Huang and Yufan Huang, "Col. Liu Mingfu on the U.S. and China as Rivals," *The New York Times*, October 9, 2015. Available at: <https://cn.nytimes.com/china/20151009/c09sino-col-liumingfu/dual/>. Accessed July 18, 2021.

116 斯洋, "以安全的名义--习近平治国"黑科技"有多少?" 美国之音, November 9, 2019. Available at: <https://www.voachinese.com/a/china-techno-governance-20191108/5158612.html>. Accessed July 20, 2021.

117 南方都市报, "中国网民政治立场摸底: 偏左的很少 偏右的多," 中国数字时代, August 19, 2013. Available at: <https://chinadigitaltimes.net/Chinese/309492.html>. Accessed July 20, 2021.

118 "China's Internet Users Hit Almost 1 Billion: Report," *CGTN*, February 03, 2021. Available at: <https://news.cgtn.com/news/2021-02-03/China-s-netizen-population-hits-989-million-report-XzzMZyN71K/index.html>. Accessed July 20, 2021.

119 同学工作室, "学习金句| 重温习近平总书记关于网络安全的那些话," 共产党员网, September 14, 2020. Available at: <http://www.12371.cn/2020/09/12/ARTI1599896298107154.shtml>. Accessed July 20, 2021.

120 Geoffrey Taubman, "A Not-So World Wide Web: The Internet, China, and the Challenges to Nondemocratic Rule," *Political Communication* 15, no. 2 (1998): 263.

121 Edward Cunningham, Tony Saich, and Jessie Turiel, *Understanding CCP Resilience: Surveying Chinese Public Opinion Through Time* (Cambridge, MA: Ash Center for Democratic Governance and Innovation, Kennedy School of Government, Harvard University, 2020).

122 "数字丝绸之路国际合作论坛," 网信办, March 13, 2019. Available at: http://www.cac.gov.cn/2019-03/14/c_1124235401.htm. Accessed July 20, 2021.

123 王义桅, "'数字丝绸之路'面临哪些挑战?" 网络传播, 6月刊, 2020.

124 "华为持续领先全球电信设备市场: 份额逆势增至31%," 新浪科技, March 09, 2021. Available at: <https://finance.sina.com.cn/tech/2021-03-09/doc-ikkntiak6532938.shtml>. Accessed July 21, 2021.

125 Mark Cenite, "Commentary: How to Make Singapore Smile for the Facial Recognition Camera," *CNA*, February 24, 2020. Available at: <https://www.channelnewsasia.com/news/commentary/singapore-facial-recognition-camera-data-privacy-identity-12452916>. Accessed July 21, 2021.

126 Tim McDonald, "Singapore in World First for Facial Verification," *BBC News*, September 25, 2021. Available at: <https://www.bbc.com/news/business-54266602>. Accessed July 22, 2021.

127 Li Tao, "Malaysian Police Wear Chinese Start-Up's AI Camera to Identify Suspected Criminals," *South China Morning Post*, April 20, 2018. Available at: <https://www.scmp.com/tech/social-gadgets/article/2142497/malaysian-police-wear-chinese-start-ups-ai-camera-identify>. Accessed July 20, 2021.

128 "'They Know Everything We Do,' Telecom and Internet Surveillance in Ethiopia," *Human Rights Watch*, March 25, 2014. Available at: <https://www.hrw.org/report/2014/03/25/they-know-everything-we-do/telecom-and-internet-surveillance-ethiopia>. Accessed July 22, 2021.

129 Joe Parkinson, Nicholas Bariyo, and Josh Chin, "Huawei Technicians Helped African Governments Spy on Political Opponents," *Wall Street Journal*, August 15, 2019. Available at: <https://www.wsj.com/articles/huawei-technicians-helped-african-governments-spy-on-political-opponents-11565793017>. Accessed July 22, 2021.

130 Angus Berwick, "How ZTE Helps Venezuela Create China-Style Social Control," *Reuters*, November 14, 2018. Available at: <https://www.reuters.com/investigates/special-report/venezuela-zte/>. Accessed July 22, 2021.

131 Charles Rollet, "Ecuador's All-Seeing Eye Is Made in China," *Foreign Policy*, August 9, 2018. Available at: <https://foreignpolicy.com/2018/08/09/ecuadors-all-seeing-eye-is-made-in-china/>. Accessed July 22, 2021.

132 Cassandra Garrison, "'Safe Like China': In Argentina, ZTE Finds Eager Buyer for Surveillance Tech," *Reuters*, July 05, 2019. Available at: <https://www.reuters.com/article/us-argentina-china-zte-insight/safe-like-china-in-argentina-zte-finds-eager-buyer-for-surveillance-tech-idUSKCN1U00ZG>. Accessed July 22, 2021.

133 Alina Polyakova and Chris Meserole, *Policy Brief: Exporting Digital Authoritarianism: The Russian and Chinese Models* (Washington, DC: Brookings, 2019), pp. 1–22.

134 周远方，"专访四达时代副总裁卢玉亮：在非洲市场，我们是一家'从地里长出来'的公司，" 观察者网，May 12, 2021. Available at: <https://www.sohu.com/a/465980513_115479>. Accessed July 22, 2021.

135 Siegfied Mortkowitz, "Pompeo: Chinese Threat May Be Worse than Cold War Communism," *Politico*, August 12, 2020.

136 "爱国统一战线的提出和确立，" 青岛市统一战线，October 13, 2020. Available at: <http://tyzx.qingdao.gov.cn/n23595625/n32570995/n32571011/201013143336954305.html>. Accessed July 23, 2021.

137 郭松民，"用'国际反霸统一战线'战胜蓬佩奥的'民主国家联盟'，" 腾讯网，July 30, 2020. Available at: <https://new.qq.com/omn/20200730/20200730A0WHSO00.html?pc>. Accessed July 23, 2021.

138 《统一战线知识简明读本》编写组，统一战线知识简明读本，华文出版社, 2018.

139 《统一战线知识简明读本》编写组，"统一战线知识简明读本。"

140 "中共中央印发'中国共产党统一战线工作条例'，" 新华网, Article 37, January 05, 2021. Available at: <http://www.xinhuanet.com/politics/2021-01/05/c_1126949202.htm>. Accessed July 23, 2021.

141 "The World Migration Report 2018, During the 108th IOM Council, in Geneva," *IOM UN Migration*, December 01, 2017. Available at: <https://www.iom.int/news/iom-un-migration-agency-launches-2018-world-migration-report>. Accessed July 24, 2021.

142 "大数据图解美国华人高端人才 (总汇)，" 硅谷中国网，July 09, 2020. Available at: <http://www.guiguzhongguo.com/?module=news&id=2120>. Accessed July 24, 2021.

143 "《2020年中国留学白皮书》图鉴，留学全貌大揭秘！" 搜狐网，February 04, 2021. Available at: <https://www.sohu.com/a/448628702_100291774>. Accessed July 24, 2021.

144 FLG, "Investigative Report on CCPPNR Led United Front Work," *World Organization to Investigate the Persecution of Falun Gong*, May 20, 2011. Available at: <https://www.upholdjustice.org/node/211>. Accessed July 25, 2021.

145 "中央国家安全领导小组，" 百度百科. Available at: <https://baike.baidu.com/item/%E4%B8%AD%E5%A4%AE%E5%9B%BD%E5%AE%B6%E5%AE%89%E5%85%A8%E9%A2%86%E5%AF%BC%E5%B0%8F%E7%BB%84/9739882>. Accessed July 25, 2021.

146 张素，"中联部副部长郭业洲：中国共产党前所未有地走进世界政党舞台中心，" 中国新闻网，June 28, 2021. Available at: <http://www.chinanews.com/gn/2021/06-28/9508751.shtml>. Accessed July 26, 2021.

147 Mark Stokes and Russell Hsiao, "The People's Liberation Army General Political Department—Political Warfare with Chinese Characteristics," *Project 2049 Institute*, October 14, 2013.

148 侯露露，"近三十个对外宣介团在近八十个国家和地区精准传播十九大精神，发展的中国将为世界带来更多机遇，" 人民日报, 03 版，February 02, 2018.

149 孟祥麟,黄发红,刘歌，"服务民族复兴 促进人类进步，" 人民日报, 03 版, December 25, 2019.

150 David Shullman, ed., *Chinese Malign Influence and the Corrosion of Democracy: An Assessment of Chinese Interference in Thirteen Key Countries* (Washington, DC: The International Republican Institute, 2019).

151 Toby Harnden, "MI6 Took Spy Snaps of Nixon and Chinese 'Mistress'," *The Sunday Times*, January 11, 2015. Available at: <https://www.thetimes.co.uk/article/mi6-took-spy-snaps-of-nixon-and-chinese-mistress-bb7dzqj5mft>. Accessed July 26, 2021.

152 Andy Kroll and Russ Choma, "Businesswoman Who Bought Trump Penthouse Is Connected to Chinese Intelligence Front Group," *Mother Jones*, March 15, 2017. Available at: <https://www.motherjones.com/politics/2017/03/exclusive-don-ald-trump-penthouse-buyer-has-ties-group-chinese-military-intelligence/>. Accessed July 27, 2021.

153 Marc A. Thiessen, "Opinion: Explain the Chinese Spy, Sen. Feinstein," *The Washington Post*, August 9, 2018. Available at: <https://www.washingtonpost.com/opinions/explain-the-chinese-spy-sen-feinstein/2018/08/09/0560ca60-9bfd-11e8-b60b-1c897f17e185_story.html>. Accessed July 27, 2021.

154 Bethany Allen-Ebrahimian and Zach Dorfman, "Exclusive: Suspected Chinese Spy Targeted California Politicians," *Axios*, December 08, 2020. Available at: <https://www.axios.com/china-spy-california-politicians-9d2dfb99-f839-4e00-8bd8-59dec0daf589.html>. Accessed July 27, 2021.

155 "中华人民共和国国家情报法," 中国人大网, Article 7, June 12, 2018. Available at: <http://www.npc.gov.cn/npc/c30834/201806/483221713dac4f31bda7f9d951108912.shtm>. Accessed July 27, 2021.

156 Zack Cooper, "Understanding the Chinese Communist Party's Approach to Cyber-Enabled Economic Warfare," *Foundation for Defense of Democracies*, September 2018, p. 21.

157 Josh Fruhlinger, "The OPM Hack Explained: Bad Security Practices Meet China's Captain America," *CSO*, February 12, 2020. Available at: <https://www.csoonline.com/article/3318238/the-opm-hack-explained-bad-security-practices-meet-chi-nas-captain-america.html>. Accessed July 28, 2021.

158 TNI Staff, "China Knows All About the F-35 and F-22 (Thanks to the Data It Stole) Stolen Stealth?" *The National Interest*, June 10, 2019. Available at: <https://national-interest.org/blog/buzz/china-knows-all-about-f-35-and-f-22-thanks-data-it-stole-61912>. Accessed July 28, 2021.

159 谢树华,包含丽, "华人文教疫情冲击下海外华文教育面临的困境与发展趋势——基于组织生态学视角的分析,华侨华人历史研究, 2021年第2期.

160 Luke May, "Cambridge University 'Received "Generous Gift" from Chinese Software Giant with Links to Country's Spy Agency' to Fund Engineering Fellowship," *The Daily Mail*, February 10, 2021. Available at: <https://www.dai-lymail.co.uk/news/article-9245151/Cambridge-University-received-generous-gift-Chinese-software-giant-Tencent.html>. Accessed July 28, 2021.

161 锦官城, "北方网评: 乘船出海 借嘴发声—做好传播能力 '番外篇'," 环球网, June 03, 2021. Available at: <https://china.huanqiu.com/article/43OEgdJ9cWP>. Accessed July 23, 2021.

162 Bradley A. Thayer and Lianchao Han, "'Wolf Warrior' in Sheep's Clothing: Xi Jinping's Latest Ideological War," *The Hill*, June 14, 2021. Available at: <https://thehill.com/opinion/international/557742-wolf-warrior-in-sheeps-clothing-xi-jinpings-latest-ideological#bottom-story-socials>. Accessed July 23, 2021.

163 张焕萍, "中国侨联, 借助华侨华人讲好中国故事," *International Communications*, no. 05 (2020).

164 张焕萍, "中国侨联."

165 Larry Diamond and Orville Schell, "China's Influence & American Interests: Promoting Constructive Vigilance," Hoover Institution, November 29, 2018. Available at: <https://www.hoover.org/research/chinas-influence-american-inter-ests-promoting-constructive-vigilance>. Accessed July 28, 2021.

166 新华社评论员, 不忘初心 继续前进——写在新华通讯社建社85周年之际, 016年11月05日. Available at: <http://www.xinhuanet.com/politics/2016-11-05/c_1119857067.htm>. Accessed July 28, 2021.

167 Sean Mantesso and Christina Zhou, "China's Multi-Billion Dollar Media Campaign 'a Major Threat for Democracies' Around the World," *ABC News*, February 7, 2019. Available at: <https://www.abc.net.au/news/2019-02-08/chinas-foreign-media-push-a-major-threat-to-democracies/10733068>. Accessed July 28, 2021.

168 "IOC Recognizes Xinhua as One of Its International News Agencies," *IOC News*, January 30, 2019. Available at: <https://olympics.com/ioc/news/ioc-recognises-xinhua-as-one-of-its-international-news-agencies>. Accessed July 29, 2021.

169 林澜, "前党媒高官揭：驻外记者当间谍"大纪元， June 25, 2021. Available at: <https://www.epochtimes.com/gb/21/6/11/n13015628.htm>. Accessed July 29, 2021.

170 "故事：费城交响乐团的"中国情'," 中华人民共和国驻纽约总领事馆网， June 13, 2017. Available at: <https://www.fmprc.gov.cn/ce/cgny/chn/whsw/zmwhjl/t1469671.htm>.

171 "互联网思维助力， AI、短视频、直播搭建起'指尖上的党建'," 南方都市报, June 24, 2021. Available at: <https://www.sohu.com/a/473759236_161795>. Accessed July 29, 2021.

172 RFA's Lao Service, "Laos Grants 25-Year Concession to Chinese Company to Manage Power Grid," *Radio Free Asia*, trans. by Max Avary, written in English by Eugene Whong. March 16, 2021. Available at: <https://www.rfa.org/english/news/laos/grid-03162021152622.html>. Accessed July 29, 2021.

173 Anusha Ondaatjie and Asantha Sirimanne, "Sri Lanka Leased Hambantota Port to China for 99 Yrs. Now It Wants It Back," *Business Standard*, November 30, 2019. Available at: <https://www.business-standard.com/article/international/sri-lanka-leased-hambantota-port-to-china-for-99-yrs-now-it-wants-it-back-119112900206_1.html>. Accessed July 29, 2021.

174 李滨彬"持续创新的引领者——香港中资企业新突围," 新华网, December 31, 2018. Available at: <http://www.xinhuanet.com/2018-12/31/c_1123931810.htm>. Accessed July 30, 2021.

175 滕朝, "台摆脱不了对大陆依赖，若大陆动用经济手段，比军事手段更狠," 搜狐网, January 9, 2021. Available at: <https://www.sohu.com/a/443415639_594189>. Accessed July 30, 2021.

176 Weizhen Tan, "China Restricted Imports from Australia. Now Australia is Selling Elsewhere," *CNBC News*, June 2, 2021. Available at: <https://www.cnbc.com/2021/06/03/australia-finds-new-markets-for-coal-barley-amid-china-trade-fight.html>. Accessed July 30, 2021.

177 习近平, "努力成为世界主要科学中心和创新高地," 求是, 2021/06.

178 Helen Davidson, "Beijing Warns China-Linked US Businesses: You Cannot 'Make a Fortune in Silence'," *The Guardian*, December 2, 2021. Available at: <https://www.theguardian.com/world/2021/dec/02/beijing-warns-china-linked-us-businesses-you-cannot-make-a-fortune-in-silence>. Accessed December 4, 2021.

179 Catherine Putz, "Which Countries are for or Against China's Xinjiang Policies?" *The Diplomat*, July 22, 2019. Available at: <https://thediplomat.com/2019/07/which-countries-are-for-or-against-chinas-xinjiang-policies/>. Accessed January 31, 2021.

180 See Jianli Yang and Lianchao Han, "Did a Muslim Slave Make Your Chinese Shirt?" *Wall Street Journal*, October 16, 2019. Available at: <https://www.wsj.com/articles/did-a-muslim-slave-make-your-chinese-shirt-11571264293>. Accessed October 30, 2019.

181 Lianchao Han, Author, David Wong, Amelia Dewell, and Anna Chen, Contributors, *Cotton: The Fabric Full of Lies: A Report on Forced and Prison Labor in Xinjiang, China, and the Nexus to Global Supply Chains* (Washington, DC: The Citizen Power Institute, Citizen Power Initiatives for China, August 2019).

182 James T. Areddy, "Xinjiang Arrests Nearly Doubled in '14, Year of 'Strike-Hard' Campaign," *The Wall Street Journal*, January 23, 2015. Available at: <https://blogs

.wsj.com/chinarealtime/2015/01/23/xinjiang-arrests-nearly-doubled-in-14-year
-of-strike-hard-campaign/>. Accessed June 10, 2021.

183 Rebecca Warren, "Xinjiang and the Belt and Road Initiative," *The Strategy Bridge*,
June 17, 2019. Available at: <https://thestrategybridge.org/the-bridge/2019/6/17/
xinjiang-and-the-belt-and-road-initiative>. Accessed June 10, 2021.

184 Chris Buckley and Austin Ramzy, "China's Detention Camps for Muslims Turn
to Forced Labor," *The New York Times*, December 16, 2018. Available at: <https://
www.nytimes.com/2018/12/16/world/asia/xinjiang-china-forced-labor-camps
-uighurs.html>. Accessed June 10, 2021.

185 These arguments draw upon Bradley A. Thayer and Lianchao Han, "The Importance
of Hong Kong's Resistance to China," *Realcleardefense*, July 26, 2019. Available
at: <https://www.realcleardefense.com/articles/2019/07/26/the_importance_of
_hong_kongs_resistance_to_china_114612.html>. Accessed September 17, 2021.

186 Kang-chung Ng, "Fear and Loathing: Which Way Forward for Article 23 National
Security Law in Face of Stiff Opposition in Hong Kong," *South China Morning Post*,
November 22, 2017. Available at: <https://www.scmp.com/news/hong-kong/poli-
tics/article/2121035/fear-and-loathing-which-way-forward-article-23-national>.
Accessed September 17, 2021.

187 Keith Bradsher, "Security Laws Target of Huge Hong Kong Protest," *The New York
Times*, July 2, 2003. Available at: <https://www.nytimes.com/2003/07/02/world/
security-laws-target-of-huge-hong-kong-protest.html>. Accessed September 21,
2021.

188 Maya Wang, "Three Years after Umbrella Movement, Hong Kongers Soldier On,"
Human Rights Watch, September 27, 2017. Available at: <https://www.hrw.org/
news/2017/09/27/three-years-after-umbrella-movement-hong-kongers-soldier#>.
Accessed September 21, 2021.

189 Eric Cheung, "Greater Bay Area: 10 Facts to Put it in Perspective," *South China
Morning Post*, April 1, 2019. Available at: <https://www.scmp.com/native/economy
/china-economy/topics/great-powerhouse/article/3002844/greater-bay-area-10
-facts-put>. Accessed September 21, 2021.

190 "Today China Extradition Law, Tomorrow a Social Credit Score—Why Hong
Kong Must Stand Up for Its Freedoms," *South China Morning Post*, March 22,
2019. Available at: <https://www.scmp.com/comment/letters/article/3002540/
today-extradition-tomorrow-social-credit-score-why-hong-kong-cant>. Accessed
September 22, 2021.

191 Michael J. Cole, "Nice Democracy You've Got There. Be a Shame If Something
Happened to It," *Foreign Policy*, June 18, 2018. Available at: <https://foreignpolicy
.com/2018/06/18/nice-democracy-youve-got-there-be-a-shame-if-something
-happened-to-it/>. Accessed September 21, 2021.

192 Bradley A. Thayer and Lianchao Han, "The Importance of Hong Kong's Resistance
to China," *RealClearDefense*, July 26, 2019. Available at: <https://www.realclear-
defense.com/articles/2019/07/26/the_importance_of_hong_kongs_resistance_to
_china_114612.html>. Accessed September 21, 2021.

193 "Wuhan Protests: Incinerator Plan Sparks Mass Unrest," *BBC News*, July 8, 2019.
Available at: <https://www.bbc.com/news/blogs-china-blog-48904350>. Accessed
September 23, 2021.

194 Constitutional and Mainland Affairs Bureau, The Government of the HKSAR,
"The Joint Declaration," July 1, 2007. Available at: <https://www.cmab.gov.hk/en
/issues/jd2.htm>. Accessed September 23, 2021.

4

CHINA'S GROWING RELATIVE POWER

Because the US is led by gangsters and is frank-rupt - 10/28/23

This chapter continues our explanation of why China is a threat to the United States and the free world. We examine the relative balance of international power that favors China and emboldens it to challenge the U.S. and force the changes that it seeks in international politics. By "relative balance of power" we mean that, while both superpowers are growing, China is growing at a relatively faster rate; thus, the power differential between them is closing in Beijing's favor. This is not to argue that it always will be so or that the U.S. cannot reverse it, but this is likely to continue for years to come because of the expansion, however diminished, of the Chinese economy. In this chapter, we explore another major factor contributing to the conflict: the tremendous expansion of China's power.

4.1 The Prodigious Growth of Chinese Power

Once in a while, there is something new in the realm of international politics. For the first time in its long history, China is a rising hegemon. That is of historical importance. In the past, it dominated Asia, the world it knew, and even after the British defeated China in the First Opium War (1839–1842), it maintained the pretense that it was dominant until European, Japanese, and American colonization changed that. Now, China is the challenger to the dominant state. China was on top, lost it all, and has returned to greatness—a feat unmatched by any other empire. China's losses in the First Opium War and Second Opium War (1856–1860) were ruinous, shredding sovereignty and conceding to industrialized powers extraordinary territorial, mercantile, and jurisdictional privileges. Arising in parallel, and largely in response, was the worst of all modern rebellions—the Taiping (1850–1864), a societal injury defying full recovery.[1] The next century, although different, was not much better and was followed, from 1966 through 1976, by the Cultural Revolution, a denunciation not only

DOI: 10.4324/9781003283614-4

of the "Four Olds"—customs, culture, habits, and ideas—but of modernity, too. The years from 1839 until Deng Xiaoping's rise in December 1978 indeed were China's Dark Ages.

As Robert Sprinkle and Bradley Thayer have argued, the period since has been a renaissance.[2] China has become a force—in some subsectors, the dominant force—in industry, commerce, science, technology, and finance.

> Its products fill the world's shelves, its graduates and graduate students the world's laboratories, its profits the world's treasuries. Even its main language, Mandarin, has advanced, packing into Western classrooms tonally adventurous students convinced their future will be Sinocentric. These are not Potemkin-village achievements; China's overachievements are real, too.[3]

Its renewable-energy production and consumption lead the world, but much of its productive capacity must stand idle, a threat to overload the national electrical grid. Its quantum science experiment satellite, "Mozi," designed to test data encryption through entangled-photon teleportation, is the first of its kind and has orbited Earth since August 2016. Taikonauts have yet to walk on the moon but are more likely than are astronauts or cosmonauts to recover the golf balls that Alan Shepard hit on the moon's surface during the Apollo 14 mission.[4]

Curiously, though, China is still often called a "rising power" or "emerging power," one challenging "established powers." Connoted by these terms is a ridiculously unhistorical image: that is, China as parvenu.[5] Quite the opposite is China's view of itself and others. The powers plundering China were the newly arrived, the upstarts. China's renaissance means that its determination to cause a profound change in international politics is firm.[6]

We have presented our arguments in various forums for years now. One comment we often receive from U.S. audiences is that China is no threat to the United States because it lacks the power. Since China's power gain happened so quickly, it is not surprising that many in the U.S. have not yet recognized its occurrence. Yet one of the most significant developments in international politics since the rise of Deng has been the growth of Chinese power. It would be difficult to understate its significance. Historical equivalents are the defeat of Napoleon, the French or Bolshevik Revolutions, or the defeat of Germany, Italy, and Japan in World War II. China's rise is a monumental event. It started with its economy.

According to the World Bank and the Congressional Research Service, since Deng initiated free-market reforms and an opening to foreign trade and investment, China has had a real annual gross domestic product (GDP) averaging 9.5 percent through 2018, which the World Bank describes as "the fastest sustained expansion by a major economy in history—and has lifted more than 800 million people out of poverty."[7] On average, as the Congressional Research Service summarized, "China has been able to double the size of its economy in real terms every eight years."[8] The rate of GDP growth has slowed from 10.6 percent in 2010 to 6.7 percent in 2016, 6.8 percent in 2017, and 6.6 percent in 2018, with estimates in 2019 of lower growth, less than 6 percent, in the years to come.[9] According to the World Bank, measuring GDP by purchasing power parity, China's GDP is approximately $25.4 trillion, while the U.S.'s GDP is only about $20.5 trillion.[10] By any metric, China grew so rapidly because of Deng's economic reforms that led to greater efficiency in the economy, increasing output and resources available for investment, augmented by a high rate of savings.[11]

Of course, China has significant economic problems that will retard but not stop its economic growth. These include resource scarcities; economic bubbles, including overcapacity in steel and cement production; environmental destruction; pollution (China leads the world in environmental pollution, including CO_2 emissions); ubiquitous corruption; a collapse of trust in personal and commercial relationships; gross disparities in income and regional development; lack of transparency in banking and the financial sector; and growing debt. These likely will result in a leveling off of China's economic might.[12] Yet, despite these considerable problems, China's impressive economic growth is a wonder of the modern age. That will remain true even if its economic growth diminishes over time.

China's military power has grown in lockstep with its economy. China spent $177.5 billion (1.19 trillion yuan) on defense in 2019, a threefold increase from 2008 and a 7.5 percent increase from 2018, and that total did not capture covert and other programs. Chinese conventional and nuclear forces are being modernized to give Beijing the ability to project power globally and provide extended deterrence to its allies. China's investment in military technologies means that it is competitive with the U.S. military in computer technology, nanotechnology and artificial intelligence, biotechnology, and genetics.

The PRC's conventional and nuclear modernizations have been underway since the First Gulf War, when the military effectiveness of the U.S. and Coalition allies was far superior to the larger, battle-tested but less sophisticated military of Iraq. China knew then that in a future conflict, it would play the role of Iraq; its military would not be effective against the United States in a contemporary conflict. In the wake of Tiananmen, Deng resolved to reverse the imbalance gradually, to avoid alarming the United States and because it would take considerable time to coordinate national- and service-level strategies and modernize China's defense industry as well as military doctrines, force structure and leadership.

In contemporary international politics, the fruits of Deng's and his successors' efforts are evinced. China's military modernization advances its grand strategic objectives, defends and expands its interests, and prevents other countries from challenging those interests by denying access to the maritime domain of the Western Pacific or along its terrestrial periphery through its anti–access/area denial (A2/AD) capabilities. It also means possessing the capability to strike targets in the U.S. homeland. China now has the military

Deng wanted, with significant warfighting, power projection, and nuclear deterrence capabilities.

China's conventional force structure has grown and modernized for each of its services: the People's Liberation Army (PLA), People's Liberation Army Navy (PLAN), People's Liberation Army Air Force (PLAAF), People's Liberation Army Rocket Force (PLARF), and People's Liberation Army Strategic Support Force (PLASSF), as well as its militarized Coast Guard.[13] Of particular note in the conventional realm is the growth of its missile forces devoted to conventional missions—including nascent global strike and anti-satellite (ASAT)—and intelligence, surveillance and reconnaissance (ISR) capabilities, including space-based sensors needed for striking targets at sea, such as U.S. carriers. This includes a growing arsenal of land-based missiles for strategic and conventional missions, and the addition of multiple warheads that are both independently targetable and maneuverable.[14]

China's development of global-strike hypersonic capabilities is advancing rapidly, with 20 percent more hypersonic missile technology tests than the U.S. In January 2018, U.S. Air Force General Paul Selva, vice chairman of the Joint Chiefs of Staff, acknowledged: "We have lost our technological advantage in hypersonics."[15] This was confirmed in 2021 when China conducted two hypersonic missile tests, demonstrating a capability the U.S. does not possess.[16] These tests introduced a potential avenue of attack—Fractional Orbital Bombardment System (FOBS)—that China did not possess and that could circumvent U.S. ballistic missile defenses and at least some ballistic missile warning systems.[17]

Even more impressive than the growth in conventional power have been the advances in China's nuclear arsenal, with respect to improvements in its quality and growing numbers of strategic and non-strategic systems. The PRC's arsenal now fields a modern force of warheads, ballistic and cruise missiles. China also intends to modernize its bomber force, along with the most neglected aspect of China's nuclear forces. Professionally, the development of the PLASSF—founded in 2015 as the fifth branch of China's military to cover cyber, electronic warfare, and space—demonstrates the continued sophistication of China's capabilities.

There has been a shift from China's historical minimal deterrent posture toward a nuclear warfighting capability. Beijing has articulated in its defense strategy the need to use asymmetric and preemptive attacks during future warfare and the need to link geographically dispersed military forces in joint operations.[18] Beijing already has a large and diversified strategic missile force that supports its warfighting military posture. Its strategic calculus in regional conflicts will reflect the capabilities and options it has created in the nuclear and conventional domains to win high-intensity "informatized warfare." China's interest in developing tactical nuclear weapons, theater weapons, and ballistic defense systems has been incorporated into its military posture, increasing its ability to engage in a nuclear conflict—including preemptive strikes—with its likely foes: the United States, India and, in the years to come, perhaps a nuclear Japan. As Vice Admiral David Kriete, deputy commander of United States Strategic Command (Stratcom), stated in 2019, "China is and has been for the last couple of decades on a very clear trajectory where they're increasing the numbers of nuclear weapons that they field [and] they're increasing the number of and diversity of the delivery systems" to support Beijing's objectives, which are now transparent.

> China's leadership has made it clear in recent years that they have goals of becoming a regional power and exerting [power]—economic and military—over the western Pacific at some point in the future ... and then obtaining some level of global influence at some point after that.[19]

The revelation in the summer of 2021 of the expansion of China's intercontinental ballistic missile (ICBM) fields at Hami, Yumen, and Hanggin Banner, near Ordos City in Inner Mongolia, for a total of about 350–400 ICBMs, is more evidence of China's expansion of its arsenal and demonstrates its efforts to match or exceed U.S. capabilities.[20] In August 2021, the Stratcom commander, Admiral Charles Richard, stated that China is engaged in a "strategic breakout" that is "inconsistent with a minimum deterrence posture" because "China has correctly figured out that you can't coerce a peer—in other words, us—from a minimum deterrent posture."[21] Admiral Richard stated that the "explosive growth and modernization of its nuclear and conventional forces can only be what I describe as breathtaking. Frankly, that word—breathtaking—may not be enough."[22] A major consequence of this is that "the breathtaking growth and strategic nuclear capability enables China to change their posture and their strategy" as they desire.[23] Richard identified that "what matters is they are building the capability to execute any plausible nuclear employment strategy—the last brick in the wall of a military capable of coercion."[24] That China seeks a military with conventional and nuclear forces capable of coercing the United States and its allies into defeat is alarming for the future of strategic stability in international politics.

China will continue this trend toward greater and more accurate, maneuverable, longer-ranged, and survivable capabilities with the yields of its nuclear weapons, their delivery systems, and the space, cyber, and intelligence capabilities that support a warfighting strategy. Beijing's 2015 defense white paper clearly delineated that China intends to enhance the PLA's strategic early-warning and command and controls systems "to deter other countries from using or threatening to use nuclear weapons against China."[25] Xi has embraced a warfighting doctrine for China's strategic forces, the PLARF, that permits "full-area war deterrence," including a "counter-strike capability, which is credible and reliable ... and long-range precision strike ability."[26] Because of China's lack of transparency, there are many unknowns about Beijing's nuclear modernization and nuclear doctrine. China's lack of transparency regarding the scope and size of its nuclear modernization weakens strategic stability; they introduce significant doubt about its future intentions and commitment to ensure a stable strategic environment for the 21st century.

The 2019 Beijing defense white paper strongly emphasized the political loyalty of the PLA to the Party, and the defense of China's sovereignty and territorial integrity, with a particular emphasis on Taiwan.[27] Additionally, it stated China's goal of transforming its military into a "world-class" force by the mid-21st century. The document presents China's military power as a "staunch force for world peace, stability and the building of a community with a shared future for mankind."[28] Equally worrying, it emphasizes the protection of China's overseas interests, including in Africa and South and Southeast Asia, which increasingly clash with those of the U.S. and its allies.[29] However, most disconcerting was the white paper's definition of China's defense as being in accord with "Xi Jinping Thought," and thus largely an artifact of his decisions and willingness to take risks.[30] Explicit was the statement of loyalty to the CCP; implicit was the logical conclusion that this means loyalty to Xi and his clique and their dictates.

4.1.1 How the West Aided China's Rise

China did not accomplish this tremendous growth alone; the West greatly helped. Regrettably, it still is. China's rise was made possible because the U.S. allowed it to enter the world's free-trade system. China has flourished precisely because it entered the West's economic ecosystem a generation ago. For decades, China has used this ecosystem to grow like kudzu. And like kudzu, it has come close to killing the indigenous flora in the economic and technological ecosystem.

Over 30 years, China has snatched an astronomical $4.4 trillion from the United States.[31] Additionally, the U.S. has lost $200–$600 billion annually because of China's theft, and the U.S. has lost several million good-paying manufacturing jobs. China achieved economic success in large measure by taking advantage of the working classes in both China and the United States. The Chinese working classes continue to pay a high price for the regime's ambition: wages are artificially low, and labor conditions are Dickensian. Once workers leave factories, they encounter other dangers to their health from chronic air and water pollution in Chinese cities. A consequence of China's entering the West's ecosystem has been to weaken the West's manufacturing power and introduce a dependency on China's products.

The U.S. helped to create its most powerful enemy by giving the PRC access to talent, markets, capital, technologies, and universities. This permitted China to build its economic might, which, in turn, allowed it to create a formidable military with an increasing capability to project its power globally. As Steward Paterson argues, the Chinese leadership was shaken to its core by the Tiananmen Square Massacre and, more significantly, by the collapse of the Soviet Union: "The collapse of the Soviet Union demonstrated the potential political price of economic failure. ... China was keen to learn the lessons of Russian failure."[32] The foremost of these lessons was that

← STAR WARS

isolation from technological progress that Western societies were making almost guaranteed subordination in the world order. ... [China] desperately needed know-how and skills, and this was only likely to come from abroad if it was tied into a rules-based trade system, which meant WTO [World Trade Organization] membership.[33]

Not being a member hindered

technology transfer and foreign direct investment (FDI), which, in turn, was preventing China from taking, as [the Chinese leadership] saw it, its rightful place in the world ... and [the CCP's] ability to deliver better living standards to the population.[34]

Even before China entered the WTO in 2001, it prioritized export-oriented growth and the reform of state-owned enterprises and FDI, which provided a foundation for its economic miracle beginning in the 1990s. FDI flowed into China from multinational companies and, according to Paterson, when combined with the "knock-on effects of this investment, were the major drivers of Chinese productivity improvement and hence economic growth."[35]

The U.S. supported Chinese economic growth and membership in the WTO, facilitating both with the expectation that they would be beneficial for the U.S. economy and that the integration of China into the Western economic ecosystem would compel China to democratize. This was a colossal blunder based on the hubris and ignorance of Western political leaders that existed from the 1990s until Donald Trump's presidency. Predictions that China was on the wrong side of a Hegelian conception of history are painful reminders that Hegelian arguments are far from teleological in reality. Instead of forcing its democratization, China's economic growth fueled its aggressiveness and global ambition. Economic prosperity legitimized China's flawed political system, and made it possible for a dictator such as Xi to rise to power.

The U.S. and European Union (EU) lost any hope of compelling change when both supported investment, trade, and WTO membership for China without linking these "carrots" to the "stick" of political reform and respect for human rights.[36] As James Mann argues, "In 1994, after President Clinton abandoned his attempt to use trade as a lever for improving human rights in China, he and his administration needed to divert attention from this embarrassing reversal." They did not want "to concede that they had just downgraded the cause of human rights," preferring instead to emphasize the integration of China into Western political principles and norms.[37] The consequence, Mann submits, was that "integration became, above all, the justification for unrestricted trade with

China" and compelled the question, which the West no longer can answer with confidence: "Who's integrating whom?"[38]

In truth, the West never insisted upon such measures as capital account convertibility and a floating exchange rate, which would have allowed adjustments, particularly in the financial system, to occur at the expense of the CCP's control of the economy. In sum, China's neo-mercantilist economic model was allowed to survive: The West placed too much faith in China's willingness to play by the rule book and reform its political system, and did too little to compel compliance.[39] As a result, the world confronts the consequences of this choice to not require China to reform.

4.1.2 The Role of 9/11

Lamentably, the 9/11 terrorist attacks against the United States also tremendously aided China.[40] Al Qaeda executed the horrific, unprecedented terrorist attacks, intending for the United States to intervene in Afghanistan and for its military to be defeated there, as the Soviets were in their long war. But al Qaeda made a gross miscalculation. U.S. intervention, however imperfect, never involved the level of commitment the Soviets deployed or that the terrorists sought. However, 9/11 became a windfall victory for China. The attacks distracted the United States from China's expansion by centering its strategic attention on the Middle East. China took full advantage of that preoccupation to rise to great-power status with few impediments, and often the active encouragement of many business partners in the U.S., to its present position as the peer competitor and main threat to the interests and position of the United States.

China's move was premeditated and carefully planned. Within five hours of the 9/11 attacks, Jiang Zemin called President Bush to offer China's support and coop- eration in fighting terrorism. This began the Sino-American cooperation in the war on terror. Later, Jiang was hailed as a wise man who successfully used the 9/11 attacks to reverse the U.S. attempt to contain China, improving China's international envi- ronment and allowing China to seize an invaluable and historically unique strategic opportunity—a period of 20 years to grow its strength while repressing the Uyghur and other Muslim ethnic groups under the guise of the war on terror.[41]

Since 9/11, the U.S. has expended many military and economic resources in its fight in Afghanistan, and later in Iraq and Libya, in the wake of the "Arab Spring," as well as more recently in Syria and Yemen. Washington's focus was devoted to win- ning the wars under U.S. Central Command's rubric. But while it was so occupied, international politics did not stop; the U.S. did not get a "time out." Relative changes in the balance of power continued unabated. The most significant of these was that China grew in power, capabilities, influence, and intentions.

Washington apparently was deaf and blind to peer-competitive threats during its strategic hibernation in the Middle East. A major consequence of 9/11 was that the U.S. did not move to check Beijing's rise when it might have done so at a lower cost. Indeed, effective balancing is only now commencing against China.

Clinton & Bush and both, receiving $ gifts from CCP.

U.S. myopia afforded China a rare gift in international politics: to move from a relatively weak great-power position to that of a peer-competitive rival without effective resistance or counterbalancing. Washington's nearsightedness permitted China to change the status quo against the interests of the U.S. and its allies, such as Japan, in the East and South China Seas. The United States did not seem to notice that the PRC's economic growth allowed it to establish international economic institutions such as the AIIB and BRI, which laid the foundation for a new economic order.[42] It enabled Beijing to spread its influence in Africa, Central and South Asia, the Middle East, Europe, and Latin America. In the military realm, the PRC augmented its conventional and strategic military capabilities, including in cyberspace and space, with the development of hypersonic weapons. Equally important, it professionalized its military and now is preparing it for joint operations against the U.S. and its allies.

Most momentous of all, the period of unchecked expansion allowed the formation of the ruling Xi Jinping clique and the abandonment of the Deng Xiaoping-inspired, more cautious approach to international politics. As we explore in Chapters Two and Three, with Xi's rise, the U.S. faces a leader who has a grand strategy of Chinese dominance. Xi is a bold leader, determined to challenge the U.S., and he is doing so with dispatch. He intends to have achieved victory over the United States by the centenary of the Communist Revolution in 2049.

As a thought experiment, we might imagine a world in which 9/11 did not happen, and incidents such as the April 2001 Hainan Island incident, when a PLAAF aircraft collided with a U.S. Navy EP-3E, provoked measures to preclude China's unalloyed growth and expansion. The U.S. might have been able to ensure that China's economic growth continued, but its territorial expansion in the East and South China Seas might have been denied by a powerful U.S. and allied response. The U.S. and the global community might have impressed upon Beijing that it could not achieve its aims through bullying, and it would have to use diplomacy to resolve territorial claims.

Unambiguously, China is the strategic beneficiary of 9/11 and Washington's decisions in its wake. China acted boldly to solidify its impressive rise while the U.S. directed its prime strategic focus elsewhere. China now is the most formidable peer competitor the U.S. has faced. Whether China defeats the U.S. is the strategically dispositive question of the 21st century—but it is long past time that the U.S. recognizes and responds to the challenge.

4.2 The Consequences of the Change in the Relative Balance of Power

The third level of analysis provides us with two valuable insights. First, through its lens we can compare the Sino-American antagonism with historical cases, such as the Spanish bid for hegemony under Philip II, the French under Louis XIV and

Napoleon, and the German under Wilhelmine Germany and Hitler.[43] This permits us to comprehend that great power conflicts resulting from bids for hegemony are not new and have resulted in some of the most horrific wars the world has witnessed.

Second, this perspective provides us with the recognition that the growth of Chinese power is and will be a major source of conflict in the Sino-American relationship. The relative balance of power between China and the United States is changing in China's favor. China's growth in power matters because increased strength gives China the ability to do what it wants to advance its interests and influence, unfettered by the concerns of the U.S. or its allies. No doubt, this is a welcome development in Beijing. The PRC's interests and influence clash with those of the U.S. We expect this to become much worse because, as we will explain, the interests, values, norms, and visions of the two superpowers are so different and conflicting.

China's rise means that it is willing to confront the United States beyond the East and South China Seas, as it is now doing, and in Africa, at its military base in Djibouti and prospective bases in Cambodia, the Solomon Islands, Equatorial Guinea, and the United Arab Emirates, which will allow the PLAN to sustain operations in the Atlantic Ocean and Indo-Pacific more effectively. In the military realm, China is the principal threat to the U.S. and the reverse. China is able to target the U.S. homeland, the U.S. military abroad, and U.S. allies.

Naturally, as China grows, it will gain more allies because it will have more wealth, power, and influence in international politics. Even steadfast U.S. allies are likely to feel China's pull. No doubt some will abandon the U.S. to join China, but all will feel the strain. As a result, the U.S. will see China as its enemy, as China sees the U.S. as its foe. The interests of China and the United States conflict, and that conflict is becoming sharper and more intense. One nation's defeat is required to resolve the conflict.

Additionally, China's growth matters because with a change in the balance of power comes the ability to replace the United States and the post–World War II international order. China is laboring to replace that world order with one that is amenable to its interests, norms, and values.[44] If China gets its way, the norms and values of international politics will be authoritarian, not democratic.

This has not happened overnight—and not without ups and downs, particularly involving China's economic growth—but measured against historical cases, it has occurred quickly. China will take time to fully convert its economic might into military might, although it has made significant strides in that regard. But like great powers before, it will be, at a minimum, broadly successful—and perhaps spectacularly so, like Germany, Great Britain, Japan, or the United States during their respective rises, each occurring in the span of a generation or two. This greatly impacted the European balance of power with the United States, and negatively affected the relationship between Japan and the United States.

Finally, China's rise is significant because it is a major international event that is happening relatively quickly. Rapid changes in international politics are usually bad for stability, defined as the absence of great-power war in international politics.[45] This is the case whether involving the rise of great powers such as Germany and Japan, or revolutions such as the French (1789), Bolshevik (1917), or Iranian (1979), which generated tremendous unrest because they may threaten neighboring states—likely because of their ideology or religion and instability—and because the revolutionary state is likely to perceive its neighbors as threats since they do not share ideology or religious beliefs.[46]

The rapid rise of Germany, Japan, Russia, and the United States in the 19th century also shifted perceptions of threat. Britain saw the growth of U.S. power as a threat, but was compelled to an entente with Washington because more powerful and immediate threats were greater.[47] Principally, these were France, with whom Britain almost went to war in the Fashoda crisis of 1898; Russia, because of its pressure on British India; and, most importantly, Germany, by the early 20th century.[48] Japan's rapid rise placed it on a collision course first with China in the Sino-Japanese War (1894–1895), later Russia in the Russo-Japanese War (1904–1905), and then with the United States, culminating in World War II.[49]

Unfortunately, rapid changes in international politics usually make the perception of threat worse, as the rapid rise of German power in the 19th century alarmed Great Britain, or the Soviet detonation of an atomic bomb in 1949 and the launch of its Sputnik satellite in 1957 caused alarm in the United States over the growth of Soviet power and technological prowess.[50] The U.S. still does not appear to be at such a point, despite Chairman of the Joint Chiefs of Staff U.S. Army General Mark Milley's comment that the People's Liberation Army Rocket Forces (PLARF) hypersonic missile tests in the summer of 2021 were "very close" to a "Sputnik moment."[51] China's rise seemed to have been an exception until the past few years, but that was a testament to the PRC's ability to convince Western decision-makers that China was not a threat. Equally, Western decision-makers preferred to accept this fiction, rather than coldly recognize the China threat and execute the measures to counter China. China's rapid rise and the concomitant change in the relative balance of power, as well as its precipitous and dangerous actions under Xi's regime, underscore that trouble is overdetermined.

Notes

1 In its long history, China has faced periods of internal conflict and foreign incursions, devastating rebellions, and alien occupations. In the 1850–1864 Taiping Rebellion, the bloodiest civil conflict in history, an estimated 20–70 million people were killed, likely far more than the 27 million killed in World War II or the estimated 15–45 million killed in Mao Zedong's great famine (1958–1962). For a review of the causes of the Taiping Rebellion and its turmoil, see Stephen R. Platt's *Autumn in the Heavenly Kingdom: China, the West, and the Epic Story of the Taiping Civil War* (New York: Vintage, 2012). For an overview of Mao's famine, an event that rivals the Taiping Rebellion in misery, see Frank Dikötter's *Mao's Great Famine: The History of China's Most Devastating Catastrophe, 1958–62* (New York: Bloomsbury, 2010).

2 Robert Sprinkle and Bradley A. Thayer, "China's Strategy in Asia Is Simple: Kick the U.S. Out," *The National Interest*, July 22, 2017. Available at: <http://nationalinterest.org/print/feature/chinas-strategy-asia-simple-kick-america-out-21632>. Accessed September 10, 2020.

3 Sprinkle and Thayer, "China's Strategy in Asia Is Simple: Kick the U.S. Out."

4 Sprinkle and Thayer, "China's Strategy in Asia Is Simple: Kick the U.S. Out."

5 Sprinkle and Thayer, "China's Strategy in Asia Is Simple: Kick the U.S. Out."

6 Sprinkle and Thayer, "China's Strategy in Asia Is Simple: Kick the U.S. Out."

7 World Bank, *China Overview*, March 28, 2017. Available at: <http://worldbank.org/en/country/china/overview>. Accessed September 12, 2020.

8 Congressional Research Service (CRS), *China's Economic Rise: History, Trends, Challenges, and Implications for the United States,* RL33534, Updated June 25, 2019, p. 5. Available at: <https://crsreports.congress.gov>.

9 CRS, *China's Economic Rise*, p. 5.

10 World Bank, *GDP, PPP (Current International $)*, 2018. Available at: <https://data.worldbank.org/indicator/NY.GDP.MKTP.PP.CD?locations=CN-US>. Accessed September 10, 2020.

11 CRS, *China's Economic Rise*, p. 6.

12 Describing these economic difficulties are Ho-fung Hung, *The China Boom: Why China Will Not Rule the World* (New York: Columbia University Press, 2016); James Kynge, *China Shakes the World: A Titan's Rise and Troubled Future—And the Challenge for America* (Boston, MA: Houghton Mifflin, 2006); and Carl E. Walter and Fraser J.T. Howie, *Red Capitalism: The Fragile Financial Foundation of China's Extraordinary Rise* (Hoboken, NJ: Wiley, 2011). An excellent analysis of how environmental problems hinder the Chinese economy is Elizabeth C. Economy, *The River Runs Black: The Environmental Challenge to China's Future*, 2nd ed. (Ithaca, NY: Cornell University Press, 2010); and Economy, *The Third Revolution: Xi Jinping and the New Chinese State* (New York: Oxford University Press, 2018), pp. 152–185. A Rand study estimated that the costs in terms of health and lost productivity from China's air pollution were equal to 6.5 percent of GDP each year from 2000 to 2010. See Rand, *Costs of Selected Policies to Address Air Pollution in China* (Santa Monica, CA: Rand, 2015), p. 3. Available at: <http://www.rand.org/content/dam/rand/pubs/research_reports/RR861/RAND_RR861.pdf>. Accessed September 10, 2020.

13 At the service level, modernization requirements are set by the strategy developed by the PLA, PLAN, PLAAF, and PLARF, in accordance with guidelines required by national-level military strategy.

14 Bill Gertz, "U.S. Tailors Forces to Deter Growing Chinese Nuclear Threat," *Asia Times*, March 5, 2018. Available at: <http://www.atimes.com/article/us-tailors-forces-deter-growing-chinese-nuclear-threat/>. Accessed January 12, 2020.

15 Quoted in Paul McLeary, "China Loves DoD Acquisition Culture, Says R&D Chief Griffin," *Breaking Defense*, March 6, 2018. Available at: <https://breakingdefense.com/2018/03/china-loves-dod-acquisition-culture-says-r/>. Accessed January 12, 2020.

16 At least one test demonstrated a capability in advance of the U.S.'s. See Demetri Sevastopulo's "Chinese Hypersonic Weapon Fired a Missile over the South China Sea," *Financial Times*, November 21, 2021. Available at: <https://www.ft.com/content/a127f6de-f7b1-459e-b7ae-c14ed6a9198c>. Accessed November 22, 2021.

17 Greg Hadley, "Kendall: China Has Potential to Strike Earth from Space," *Air Force Magazine*, September 20, 2021. Available at: <https://www.airforcemag.com/global-strikes-space-china-frank-kendall/>. Accessed September 22, 2021.

18 James Johnson, "China's Evolving Approach to Nuclear War-Fighting," *The Diplomat*, November 22, 2017. Available at: <https://thediplomat.com/2017/11/chinas-evolving-approach-to-nuclear-war-fighting/>. Accessed January 12, 2020.

19 Bill Gertz, "Stratcom: China Rapidly Building Up Nuclear Forces," *Washington Free Beacon*, August 1, 2019. Available at: <https://freebeacon.com/national-security/stratcom-china-rapidly-building-up-nuclear-forces/>. Accessed January 12, 2020.

20 Bill Gertz, "Exclusive: China Building Third Missile Field for Hundreds of New ICBMS," *Washington Times*, August 12, 2021. Available at: <https://www.washingtontimes.com/news/2021/aug/12/china-engaged-breathtaking-nuclear-breakout-us-str/>. Accessed August 13, 2021. An insightful analysis of China's expansion is David J. Trachtenberg, *Back to the Future: A Misguided Understanding of China's Nuclear Intent*, National Institute for Public Policy Information Series, No. 507, November 4, 2021. Available at: <https://nipp.org/information_series/david-j-trachtenberg-back-to-the-future-a-misguided-understanding-of-chinas-nuclear-intent-no-507-november-4-2021/>. Accessed November 5, 2021.

21 Aaron Mehta, "STRATCOM Chief Warns of Chinese 'Strategic Breakout,'" *Breaking Defense*, August 12, 2021. Available at: <https://breakingdefense.com/2021/08/stratcom-chief-warns-of-chinese-strategic-breakout/>. Accessed August 13, 2021.

22 Mehta, "STRATCOM Chief Warns of Chinese 'Strategic Breakout.'"

23 Mehta, "STRATCOM Chief Warns of Chinese 'Strategic Breakout.'"

24 Mehta, "STRATCOM Chief Warns of Chinese 'Strategic Breakout.'"

25 "China's Military Strategy," May 27, 2015. Available at: <http://english.gov.cn/archive/white_paper/2015/05/27/content_281475115610833.htm>. Accessed January 12, 2020.

26 Xinhua, "China Inaugurates PLA Rocket Force as Military Reform Deepens," *Xinhuanet*, January 1, 2016. Available at: <http://news.xinhuanet.com/english/2016-01/01/c_134970564.htm>. Accessed January 13, 2020.

27 The State Council Information Office of the People's Republic of China, *China's National Defense in the New Era* (Beijing: Foreign Languages Press, 2019), pp. 7–14. Available at: <http://en.people.cn/n3/2019/0724/c90000-9600021.html>. Accessed January 23, 2020.

28 *China's National Defense in the New Era*, pp. 12–13.

29 *China's National Defense in the New Era*, pp. 20–21. An excellent study of the rivalry between China and India is Bertil Lintner, *The Costliest Pearl: China's Struggle for India's Ocean* (London: Hurst, 2019).

30 *China's National Defense in the New Era*, pp. 11–13.

31 Bradley A. Thayer and Lianchao Han, "Our Real Problem with China: Xi Jinping," *The Spectator*, May 10, 2019. Available at: <https://spectator.us/problem-china-xi-jinping/>. Accessed May 11, 2019.

32 Steward Paterson, *China, Trade and Power: Why the West's Economic Engagement Has Failed* (Padstow: London Publishing Partnership, 2018), p. 12.

33 Paterson, *China, Trade and Power*, p. 12.

34 Paterson, *China, Trade and Power*, p. 12.

35 Paterson, *China, Trade and Power*, p. 141.

36 This is a major argument of Paterson in *China, Trade and Power*.

37 James Mann, *The China Fantasy: Why Capitalism Will Not Bring Democracy to China* (New York: Penguin, 2007), pp. 103–104.

38 Mann, *The China Fantasy*, pp. 104–105.

39 Paterson, *China, Trade and Power*, p. 148.

40 Bradley A. Thayer, "While the U.S. Wasn't Watching, China Became the Strategic Beneficiary of 9/11," *The Hill*, March 8, 2019. Available at: <https://thehill.com/opinion/international/431620-while-the-us-wasnt-watching-china-became-a-strategic-beneficiary-of-9-11>. Accessed January 30, 2020.

41 新华社，江泽民的大智慧抓住了20年战略机遇期，新华社，2020年07月21日. Available at: <http://cn3.uscnpm.org/model_item.html?action=view&table=article&id=22428>. Accessed December 19, 2021.

42 The development and opportunity provided by the BRI is well captured in Kent E. Calder's *Super Continent: The Logic of Eurasian Integration* (Stanford, CA: Stanford University Press, 2019).

43 On these earlier cases of hegemonic rivalry, see Ludwig Dehio, *The Precarious Balance: Four Centuries of the European Power Struggle* (New York: Knopf, 1962); and William R. Thompson, ed., *Great Power Rivalries* (Columbia, SC: University of South Carolina Press, 1999).

44 These differences are explored in John M. Friend and Bradley A. Thayer, *How China Sees the World: Han-Centrism and the Balance of Power in International Politics* (Lincoln, NE: Potomac Books, 2018).

45 Scholars of international politics in the hegemonic stability theory and power transition theory schools of thought typically have considered rapid changes to be bad because of the value of having a dominant state such as the United States to maintain stability. On hegemonic stability theory, see Charles Kindleberger, *The World in Depression, 1929–1939* (Berkeley, CA: University of California Press, 1973); and Robert Gilpin, *War and Change in World Politics* (Cambridge: Cambridge University Press, 1981). On power transition theory, see A.F.K. Organski and Jacek Kugler, *The War Ledger* (Chicago, IL: University of Chicago Press, 1980); and Ronald L. Tammen, Jacek Kugler, Douglas Lemke, et al., *Power Transitions: Strategies for the 21st Century* (Washington, DC: CQ Press, 2000). A state's time horizon is significant as well—a long-run threat will not be met with the urgency of an immediate one. Exploring this issue in the context of the rise and decline of great powers are David M. Edelstein, *Over the Horizon: Time, Uncertainty, and the Rise of Great Powers* (Ithaca, NY: Cornell University Press, 2017); Paul K. MacDonald and Joseph M. Parent, *Twilight of the Titans: Great Power Decline and Retrenchment* (Ithaca, NY: Cornell University Press, 2018); and Joshua R. Shifrinson, *Rising Titans, Falling Giants: How Great Powers Exploit Power Shifts* (Ithaca, NY: Cornell University Press, 2018).

46 See Stephen M. Walt, *Revolution and War* (Ithaca, NY: Cornell University Press, 1996).

47 On the Anglo-American entente caused by the rise of greater threats to Britain, see Anne Orde, *The Eclipse of Great Britain: The United States and British Imperial Decline, 1895–1956* (New York: Palgrave, 1996). Also see B.J.C. McKercher, *Transition of Power: Britain's Loss of Global Pre-eminence to the United States, 1930–1945* (Cambridge: Cambridge University Press, 1999).

48 On the Fashoda Incident, see Darrell Bates, *The Fashoda Incident of 1898: Encounter on the Nile* (Oxford: Oxford University Press, 1984). Regarding Britain's difficult relations with Russia, see Keith Neilson, *Britain and the Last Tsar: British Policy and Russia, 1894–1917* (Oxford: Clarendon Press, 1996). On the UK's difficult relationship with Germany before World War I, see Correlli Barnett, *The Audit of War: The Illusion and Reality of Britain as a Great Power* (London: Macmillan, 1986); Paul M. Kennedy, *The Rise and Fall of the Great Powers: Economic Change and Military Conflict from 1500 to 2000* (New York: Vintage, 1987); and Robert K. Massie, *Dreadnought: Britain, Germany, and the Coming of the Great War* (New York: Ballantine, 1991). Arguing that the lost possibility of an Anglo-German entente brought about the tragedy that caused World War I is Niall Ferguson, *The Pity of War: Explaining World War I* (London: Allen Lane, 1998).

49 On Japan's decision-making in these cases, see S.C.M. Paine, *The Japanese Empire: Grand Strategy from the Meiji Restoration to the Pacific War* (Cambridge: Cambridge University Press, 2017).

50 On the Anglo-German rivalry, see Paul M. Kennedy, *The Rise of the Anglo-German Antagonism, 1860–1914* (London: Allen and Unwin, 1980) and on the growth of Soviet power, see Robert A. Divine, *The Sputnik Challenge: Eisenhower's Response to the Soviet Satellite* (New York: Oxford University Press, 1993); and Walter A.

McDougall, *Promised Land, Crusader State: American Encounter with the World since 1776* (New York: Houghton Mifflin, 1997).

51 David E. Sanger and William J. Broad, "China's Weapon Tests Close to a 'Sputnik Moment,' U.S. General Says," *The New York Times*, October 27, 2021. Available at: <https://www.nytimes.com/2021/10/27/us/politics/china-hypersonic-missile .html>. Accessed October 28, 2021.

5

MEETING THE CHALLENGE

In this chapter, we consider what the U.S. needs to accomplish to confront China. Our intention is to focus on important topics, but our treatment may be illustrative only of what should be executed in the competition with China. We evaluate eight measures that the U.S. can take to confront China in international politics. While our principal focus is on what the United States should do to meet the challenge, there also are important actions that U.S. allies and the international community can take. Naturally, there are many significant matters and issues absent here that should be addressed in future studies.

First, the United States must see China for what it is: the enemy. China is a hostile, revolutionary state intent on replacing the U.S. as the world's dominant power. Second, ideology matters and U.S. leadership must place greater emphasis on ideology as a central component of why the U.S. should confront the CCP—and why the U.S. must win. China is winning the world's hearts and minds, and so the U.S. must recognize that China's ideological warfare is a U.S. national security threat. The U.S. must elevate its response. Third, as the Trump administration labored to accomplish, the U.S. must use trade as a weapon against China. Fourth, the U.S. should create an international movement to end genocide in Xinjiang, which would include imposing sanctions on the CCP, not just on individual firms, to aid Muslims and other religious minorities. Fifth, the U.S. must call international attention to China's arms race and unwillingness to advance an arms control agenda. This is a strong indication that China is not interested in strategic stability. The world should require that China curb its nuclear and conventional armaments because it is the right policy to prevent an arms race. Sixth, the U.S. must strengthen its deterrence posture in the Indo-Pacific, including by expanding its conventional and nuclear presence in the region, in conjunction with allies, and extend deterrence to Taiwan. Seventh, the U.S. must prevent the

DOI: 10.4324/9781003283614-5

CCP's concerted attempts to control the world's high-technology design and production facilities. The U.S. must prevent the CCP from controlling the commanding heights of technology. Eighth, the U.S. should promote a free and open internet to defeat China's Great Firewall (GFW) designed to police its internet and close the global digital divide to strengthen the liberal world order.

5.1 What the U.S. Can Do to Win the Global Contest between China and the United States

In this section, we address what the U.S., its allies, and other states can accomplish to win the struggle against the Xi Jinping clique's misrule of China. The global contest takes place across all azimuths and in every aspect of the relationship between China and the United States, from the economic to the diplomatic and military, and from technological competition to an ideological struggle. But it also includes aspects of the relationship with their respective allies, as well as the international community. The U.S. must stop China's attempt at domination. To further that objective, we focus on eight areas.

5.1.1 The United States Must View China as the Enemy

Much has been made of the return of great power competition.[1] In truth, it never went away, although the great game was so one-sided for a time that almost everyone in the West tuned it out, assuming the match was over. Attention drifted to other concerns and second- and third-order problems. China's attention did not deviate, and once again it is a great power. Like cholesterol, great powers can be good or bad—good, in that they accept the present international order, or bad, in that they do not. China seeks to overturn the contemporary order the West created. This is the source of what is already the great conflict of the 21st century.

China is not a status quo great power. A partial review of the evidence is its territorial expansion in the Taiwan Strait and the South China Sea; its pressure against India along their common border; its use of "debt trap diplomacy" to exploit less-developed states and to secure its sphere of influence; the loss of Hong Kong's autonomy; and the gross human rights abuses against its Muslim minority in Xinjiang.

But as important as these developments are, there is a greater concern. As described in Chapter 3, this is the intellectual framework that China is creating under the guise of "a community with a shared future for mankind," expressed in the July 2019 defense white paper.[2] What the CCP means by this concept is deliberately vague and nebulous. But it is clear enough from the more tangible comments defining peace, stability, and prosperity in China with the collective good of the world, as is the equation of a strong Chinese military as a force for world peace, stability, and the building of a shared future for mankind.

This shared future is certain to be a communist dystopia. Any community that the CCP creates will be totalitarian and oppressive by nature. Any shared future that it seeks to create will be one in which the rest of the world adapts to serve the interests of Beijing. The future will be shared only because China's power is great enough to trap states in it, either by seduction or coercion. It will be like Foxconn on a global scale. Beijing's conception of global governance is a firm hierarchy with China on top. This shared future will be less free, less diverse, and far more oppressive than the present one.

This phrase should not be dismissed as boilerplate. It matters because China is providing insight into the type of world it seeks to create in place of the liberal international order. In their struggle for power, the Bolsheviks promised "Peace, Land, and Bread," to win supporters, who lugubriously received civil war, the horrors of collectivization, and famine instead.[3]

As we have argued, China's ambition is just as revolutionary as Lenin's. Despite the claims to the contrary, China is truly a revolutionary great power that seeks fundamental and permanent changes to the contemporary order in international politics. The words it chooses are designed to legitimize its position of dominance. However, Beijing's effort to provide a palliative phrase to win the "hearts and minds" of the world cannot mask its form of neo-imperialism. The effort is likely to fail as more states question its ambition and encounter the truth about its behavior.

Washington must recognize that Beijing's new world order of socialism with Chinese characteristics poses an existential threat to the United States and the free world. This strategic competition of great powers is a life-and-death struggle between two opposing ideologies and two political systems. China will not follow any rules that diverge from its interests. The U.S. needs to counter Beijing on all fronts, including in the realm of public diplomacy and global opinion. The U.S. may remind the world of the benefits of a world order based on equanimity and by delineating the reality of Beijing's ideology and the empirical evidence of its actions with its public diplomacy rhetoric. If we want egalitarianism to remain the dominant ideal in international politics, rather than ceding leadership back to totalitarianism, we need to say so more frequently, forcefully, and with greater acuity by describing democidal and genocidal China as a new "evil empire" in U.S. messaging and policymaking, as President Reagan did in the fight against the USSR.

5.1.2 The Importance of Ideology: A Key to U.S. Victory but It Requires an Increased U.S. Response

Ideological warfare is a key component of the U.S. conflict with its peer competitor China. This should play to the strengths of the United States because of its political principles and long history of implementing them—Washington did it well in the Cold War. A clear distinction between the ideologies of East and West was drawn adroitly by U.S. and allied information services. Key developments included founding the Voice of America (VOA) in 1947, and the passage of the Smith-Mundt Act a year later, which authorized the Department of State to launch public diplomacy. The Eisenhower administration created the United States Information Agency to influence the public in other countries to promote the U.S. national interest. Nearer to the end of the 50-year struggle, the Reagan administration reinvigorated public diplomacy in the service of national security with the January 1983 NSDD-77. This included the creation of a Special Planning Group reporting to the National Security Council for planning, coordinating, and monitoring the implementation of public diplomacy, helping to draw clear contrasts between the East and West for new generations.

As they are today, ideological warfare venues were multiple and included CIA-supported organizations such as the Congress for Cultural Freedom led by composer Nicolas Nabokov and *Encounter* magazine. Visits to the USSR by artists such as Van Cliburn were an element. Efforts also included facilitating the publication and distribution of Boris Pasternak's *Doctor Zhivago* and Alexander Solzhenitsyn's writings, including *Gulag Archipelago*. Americans must be of a certain age to appreciate the value of shortwave broadcasts from the BBC, VOA, Deutsche Welle, or Radio Moscow. We should not forget that VOA—and related efforts such as Radio Free Europe—was invaluable in reaching Soviet citizens, many of whom had shortwave radios because of the tremendous distances between settlements in their country. But with the Soviet defeat, U.S. commitment to ideological warfare ebbed, with a faint pulse detected once again after 9/11 and targeted to audiences in the Middle East.

In the competition with China, the U.S. must learn from its past successes to defeat China's global ideological warfare with its own campaign. The United States needs a new focal point, a dramatic and crystalline oration, to define the differences between its ideology and that of the CCP. There were five defining statements in the Cold War: Churchill's 1946 "Iron Curtain" speech in Fulton, Missouri. The 1959 "Kitchen Debate" in Moscow between Vice President Richard Nixon and Soviet leader Nikita Khrushchev. In 1963, in West Berlin, John F. Kennedy drew the indelible differences between Soviet and Western ideology with his masterful "Ich bin ein Berliner" speech. In 1983, Ronald Reagan defined the Soviet Union as the "evil empire," the focus of evil in the modern world, which lifted the spirits of many around the world, including imprisoned Soviet dissident Natan (Anatoly) Sharansky. Finally, in 1987, also in West Berlin, Reagan delivered a rhetorical body blow to the Soviet system with his statement, "Mr. Gorbachev, tear down this wall," in his address.

Today, many years into the struggle, we have nothing similar. We have no defining address that would clearly describe the value of Western ideology in contrast to the CCP's. The U.S. has been slow off the mark with China, which has been targeting the U.S. since the end of the Cold War.

With the Trump administration, this was changing. Trump's National Security Strategy (NSS) of 2017 defined China as America's long-term rival. Although still lacking in specifics years later, the assumptions were sound and closer to the reality the U.S. confronts. We welcome the NSS's recognition of "a strategy of principled realism that is guided by outcomes, not ideology," and we believe that a vigorous implementation of the major components of the Trump NSS by the Biden administration is critical. Given that, at present, the Sino-American clash is fundamentally ideological; it is incumbent on the U.S. to explain with certitude that its ideology, leadership, and security are necessary if egalitarianism is to triumph in the present struggle. Echoing Kennedy and Reagan, American values, freedoms and way of life, and America's respect for human rights are the fundamental principles defining the polities of the free world. This ideology is far superior to the CCP's alternative and must prevail against a rising neo-totalitarian world.

[handwritten margin note: zero chance]

[handwritten margin note: All in a shambles due to the Left.]

To contribute to this objective, we call for three measures. First, we advocate for the publication of a new statement to emphasize the confrontation as it now is—an ideological and economic war. The U.S. must explain, in Kennedy's words, the "great issue" between the free world and the communist world. Such a statement must be clear, distinct, and entice the support of global audiences. The Trump NSS was significant for its attention to the return of great power competition, but America needs a new NSS and it must include a greater focus on the conflict we have with China.

Second, such documents are important but cannot stand on their own; they must be implemented across the government. The U.S. should advance measures akin to Reagan's National Security Study Memorandum 77 (NSSM-77) to organize and implement ideological warfare. As part of this, and as described below, the U.S. must create adaptive, effective, reliable, and safe technological measures to defeat the CCP's GFW and other efforts to control the ability of the Chinese people to have access to information outside of China. The U.S. may need new legislation to adapt government agencies to this task. Equally, it will need to create new technologies and messages crafted for the contemporary world.

Third, the U.S. needs the first political oration defining the present competition with China. Accordingly, President Biden should go to an appropriate Indo-Asia-Pacific venue—perhaps Taiwan—and give his own electrifying speech, as his predecessors did, to make the case for freedom, to confront and condemn the CCP, and draw contrasts between the principles and values of the West and the CCP for the world to witness. Biden must define the "great issue" between the free world and the communist world. He must address the inherent failures of the communist system, call for support from free people around the world, and rally all who favor the West and its international order over the CCP's.

[handwritten margin note: Fat chance]

In the "Kitchen Debate," Nixon explained the benefits of U.S. ideology and society over the Soviets' clearly, forcefully, and directly to the Soviet leader, which was later broadcast to U.S. audiences and, heavily edited and with flawed translation, to a Soviet one. The present issues are as considerable and serious, and to define them for all audiences, Biden should have an exchange with Xi in an international forum with the world watching.

A U.S. response is urgent and should be a top priority. Leading decision-makers must recognize this crisis and engage in strategy formulation and policy implementation to counter China's ideological warfare and turn this crisis into an opportunity. At the least the U.S. government should assign a Cabinet-level member responsible for countering China's efforts. We recognize that the Sino-American confrontation is all azimuths: economic, diplomatic, military, ideological. Each is significant and requires a determined, united response from the United States.[4] While the economic and military elements have received considerable attention, the ideological war waged by the PRC against the United States has not. This must change. China's global propaganda is focused, dynamic, and evolving, and its operations around the world reach billions of people. This is a form of aggression against the United States and should be recognized as such.

The CCP's global propaganda is rooted in an ideology that requires it to control all media to serve as the Party's mouthpiece. Xi and CCP core leadership direct the ideological warfare with a grand strategy to create a "new world media order"; undermine democratic governance in the United States; manipulate public opinion; and attempt to win the hearts and minds of the people to serve the CCP's grand strategy for world hegemony.

The PRC's propaganda has come a long way from disseminating copies of Mao Zedong's sayings known as the *Little Red Book*. It has now deeply infiltrated the Western media by aggressively acquiring media outlets and hiring native English-speaking professionals to advance its propaganda content. Xi recently ordered his propagandists to implement a strategy of media convergence, to integrate communications outlets—print, television, radio, the internet, mobile, and social media—into a single platform to improve the effectiveness of China's propaganda. This will allow the CCP propaganda apparatus such as CGTN New Media—which already reaches 1.2 billion people in English, Russian, Arabic, French, and Chinese, including 30 million U.S. households—to reach even more audiences.[5] The U.S. must revive the communication mechanism it had during the Cold War and allocate more human, technological, and financial resources to systematically counter China's propaganda apparatus in China and across the world under a unified leadership. China's Strategic Support Force (PLASSF) and its antecedents have been waging public opinion, psychological, and legal warfare for more than two decades. The U.S. should add a component of similar force into its military to counter and win this type of warfare.

The U.S. should not underestimate these numbers—or, more significantly, the intent behind them. China is weaponizing its external propaganda to attack Western democracy and Western media and exert political influence globally. China's disinformation—long disguised as benign and neutral media—is gradually changing people's image of China and the CCP. In response, the U.S. should require China's state media organizations, and those funded by it, to register as foreign agencies; the U.S. and its allies should flag these media as China's agents worldwide, as well as identify its internet trolls. In the War on Terror, the U.S. has proclaimed terrorist propaganda as a national security threat and removed accounts from social media and other digital platforms. Such measures are necessary for China, as are steps to contrast its political principles and totalitarian values with those of the democratic West. An ineffective response raises the danger of the U.S. losing the ideological war with China.

5.1.3 Use Trade to Weaken China

When China's military slaughtered hundreds of protesters in Tiananmen Square in 1989, the U.S. trade deficit with the Party-state was a mere $6 billion. But the U.S. government decided to continue engaging China through trade and other exchanges with the hope that economic development would bring China back to the course of reforms. The U.S. granted China most favored nation status, and later permanent trade status, without conditioning it with human rights improvement. It also failed to require significant structure changes before allowing China to join the WTO in 2001, resulting in neither real trade liberalization nor political liberalization. China instead has been taking advantage of the trade system, and it racked up over $5.3 trillion in trade surplus from the U.S. market alone over the past 20 years, becoming the largest supplier for the U.S.[6] This is the main source of China's rapid growth and the drastic increase in its composite strength. China's unfair trade practices have devastated American industries. The U.S. trade deficit with China has led to the loss of over three million American jobs and more than 60,000 factory closures.

The U.S. government must realize that trading with China is like selling the rope to hang itself. To stop China from rising as the world hegemon, the U.S. must cut off China's lifeline by decoupling from China in trade. The Sino-American trade war under the Trump administration unbalanced China and caused fears among many Chinese officials who saw it as a contest to determine the future destiny of the Chinese nation. China needs over $300 billion in annual trade surplus, the largest U.S. market, to maintain performance legitimacy and crackdown on dissent, while pushing for its global expansion agenda. It is foolish for the U.S. to continue to make its ultimate enemy stronger and more powerful.

Before completely decoupling with China, the U.S. must hold China to its trade commitments, remove trade and non-trade barriers, and demand structural changes by breaking the Chinese state monopoly in key sectors such as the internet market, banking, finance, and energy. For years, China has called trade the ballast stone of Sino-American relations. Many American politicians have been sucked into this trap and ignored China's unfair trade practices. For that, America has paid a heavy price. It is time to dump the ballast into the ocean so that China will not have sufficient funds to build advanced space and nuclear weapons, a taller and thicker GFW, mega prisons and concentration camps, and to acquire Hollywood studios and further its interests.

If the U.S. can successfully decouple with China, it not only frees itself from being held hostage by China's control of the global supply chain during emergencies such as the Covid-19 pandemic, but also will disrupt China's plan to reach the CCP's centenary goal of becoming the world-leading superpower. This is because the regime will lose a large portion of its trade revenues from the U.S., and no other market in the world can replace America's.

The U.S. government should pursue a free trade community with democracies in the Indo-Pacific and other regions to counter China's weaponizing its trade to create economic dependence for smaller countries such as Taiwan and bully them into the China-centered new world order. This is critical for eliminating the China threat and defeating China's world order of socialism with Chinese characteristics, considering China today is far more willing to use trade sanctions against U.S. allies such as Australia, Japan, Lithuania, and others.

5.1.4 Create International Movement to End China's Ethnic Genocide

Before leaving office, the Trump administration declared that China was committing genocide against the Uyghur and other Muslim ethnic groups in Xinjiang. The Biden administration continues this characterization. The U.S. government has taken serious actions by banning some forced labor products from Xinjiang and sanctioning individual officials and entities who are responsible for the genocide and other crimes against humanity under the Global Magnitsky Act. U.S. allies have joined in the effort.

Although these actions have helped to improve the conditions of the Uyghur and other Muslim ethnic groups, they have failed to stop China's ongoing genocide and other crimes against humanity. The U.S. must vigorously enforce the new law President Biden signed to ban all products from Xinjiang since the region is the largest gulag in the world and its economy is built by the gulag inmates. All companies in China that have helped to enable the genocide should be placed on the entity list. The U.S. should ban exports to and imports from these companies, and deny the companies access to U.S. capital markets by delisting and deregistering them. Other sanctions such as denying foreign tax credit should be employed to discourage transnational companies from investing in the Uyghur region. Naturally, any U.S. action in this regard must be joined by its allies—indeed, all states concerned with Beijing's oppression of its people in Xinjiang or elsewhere. An insufficient response from the U.S. encourages the CCP's sustained campaign of ethnic, religious, and cultural genocide in Xinjiang.

More importantly, the U.S. and the free world must be aware that the unbearable suffering of the Uyghur and other Muslim ethnic groups could be repeated in Hong Kong and expanded to Taiwan and other Belt and Road countries if China can realize its Chinese Dream. As mentioned in Chapter 2, the regime has committed classicide, democide, or genocide against Tibetans, as well as the Han Chinese. Genocidal violence is in Communist China's DNA. To end the genocide requires a regime change. Short of that, the U.S. should launch an international movement, similar to the anti-apartheid movement opposing

South Africa's regime, by initiating a comprehensive boycott that includes all consumer, sports, academic, and other intercourse.

5.1.5 Maintaining Sufficient U.S. Military Power

When the U.S. cut military spending after the collapse of the USSR, the PRC used its enormous gains from trade with the U.S. and the West to expand its arsenal considerably. It now fields a modern force. China's rapid growth of its nuclear arsenal, doubling it in about the past decade and continuing a trajectory to double it yet again in the next decade, is deeply troubling. China has a large, diversified strategic missile force that supports a warfighting military posture. The world has witnessed significant reorganization through the development of the Strategic Support Force, demonstrating the continued sophistication of China's capabilities.

All signs indicate that China has been preparing for a hot war with the U.S. and its allies. China has changed military strategies to include asymmetric and preemptive attacks during future high-intensity warfare, as well as linking geographically dispersed military forces in joint operations. The scope and magnitude of China's military modernization likely already has gone beyond our assessment. Because of China's lack of transparency, there remain many unknowns about Beijing's centenary goal for its military, which the regime determines to achieve as early as 2027. It is doubtful that the U.S. and the international community can persuade the PRC to avoid an arms race by advancing a new arms control agreement.

To reassure the global community, the U.S. must possess sufficient military power to stop China, as President Reagan did in the 1980s. Facing the Soviets' global aggression, Reagan adopted a series of competitive strategies to defeat the Soviet Union. Perhaps the most famous of these was the Strategic Defense Initiative (SDI). Reagan forced the Soviets to the negotiation table over conventional and nuclear weapons. The panoply of his strategies contributed to the demise of the USSR. Today, the U.S. must respond to China's unilateral frenzied arms race with technological programs such as a new strategic defense initiative that can protect America and its allies from China's nuclear attacks. This will deepen China's existing economic predicament, pushing it to the brink of economic and political collapse.

As a result, China could stop the growth of its nuclear arsenal by exercising a moratorium on the production of weapons and its development of hypersonic missiles. It could unilaterally reduce its strategic nuclear weapons and number of ballistic missiles to signal its interest in strategic stability, and embrace arms control by entering into transparent agreements with India, Russia, and the United States, to demonstrate its support for strategic stability in nuclear arms and acceptance of international norms.

Were China to take these steps, there would be direct costs to China. Its arsenal would be fettered by its own measures and by potential treaty requirements.

Of course, that is precisely the advantage of taking these steps. The value of demonstrating that China supports the status quo is in China's long-term national security interests and promoting stability in international politics. In turn, this would provide China with more security than its military forces could provide. Conveying that it is a status quo power, one that is willing to forsake its immediate advantage in a particular category of weapon systems for longer-term security, would help to dampen the risks of conflict and security competition.

The fact that China does not take these steps is alarming, a stark testament to China's objectives. China is driving an arms race and intensifying security competition because of the ambitions of its leaders. The international community must take heed and should not hesitate to identify the scope of China's ambition and actively counter it. In response, the U.S. and the international community must be clear: The onus is on China. Only through military strength that is superior to China's is there a small hope that China will realize its mistake and change course. However, given the scope and pace of China's expansion of its conventional and nuclear forces, as we presented in Chapter 4, it is unrealistic to expect such an alternation of China's rapid military growth because it is necessary for China to realize dominance.

5.1.6 Deterrence Requires a Robust Military Alliance in the Indo-Pacific

We predict a hot war started by China against the U.S. is likely to occur in the Taiwan Strait and the South China Sea. The best deterrent against China's wolf-warrior aggression in the Indo-Pacific is to form a military alliance like NATO. An Indo-Pacific NATO should be based on the Quad—the United States, Australia, Japan, and India—and expand to other democracies in the region. Without this military alliance, it will be difficult to stop China from annexing Taiwan and the South China Sea.

In Chapter 2, we documented the CCP's history of aggression. Since coming to power in 1949, the People's Republic of China (PRC) has invaded Tibet and South Korea in 1950, aggressed against India in 1962, clashed with the Soviet Union in 1969, seized the Paracel Islands in 1974 from South Vietnam, invaded Vietnam in 1979, and clashed again with Vietnam in the South China Sea in the 1980s.[7]

This aggression did not end with the Cold War. China has confronted Japan over contested territory, the Diaoyu/Senkaku Islands, and declared a new Air Defense Identification Zone (ADIZ) over them; it has clashed with India repeatedly at their disputed border; threatened Taiwan; militarized its facility in Djibouti; created new islands in the South China Sea with the military power to enforce its claims; and has had series of clashes with the Philippines. Additionally, it has rejected the Permanent Court of Arbitration 2016 ruling that found the PRC violated international law in the South China Sea, contravened the 1984 Hong Kong agreement with the UK to crush Hong Kong and, *de facto*, brought Hong Kong completely under its control. The PRC has imprisoned Uyghur, Kazakh, and Kyrgyz Muslims in concentration camps in Xinjiang. It has expanded its influence in Melanesia and Polynesia and is increasingly assertive in opposing U.S. air and sea operations in the South China Sea, East China Sea, and North Pacific.

The PRC's expansion is occurring globally—not just in the Indo-Pacific, but in Africa, Latin America, and even in the Arctic and sub-Arctic. In 2014, Xi announced that the PRC intends to be a polar great power. This ambition was realized in the January 26, 2018, Arctic white paper, which was notable because the PRC had never issued an official foreign policy strategy for an area outside of its geographic region. This action reveals a PRC confident in its growing global interests and expansionist grand strategy. The U.S. intelligence community has warned that the Chinese regime seeks a naval base in Equatorial Guinea for sustained naval presence in the Atlantic. All of these measures are intended to expand the PRC's sovereignty beyond even the ambitions of Mao Zedong.

The ubiquity and pace of the Chinese regime's expansion are a major threat to international stability and U.S. interests. They suggest that Beijing is difficult to deter. To meet this threat requires immediately developing a more robust U.S. deterrent in the Indo-Pacific. The U.S. must take three steps to deter the PRC. First, it needs to expand its conventional military presence in the Indo-Pacific to be able to target Chinese bases, vessels, and military targets within China. The U.S. does not have the conventional capabilities in the Indo-Pacific to halt the PRC's aggression. It must expand the U.S. Seventh Fleet to include more attack submarines (SSNs), cruisers and destroyers, and additional aircraft carriers dedicated to deterring a PRC attack. This deterrence will require the ability to sustain attacks against targets in China. U.S. Air Force, Army, and Marine assets must be expanded within the region to show U.S. presence. They must also possess the capability to attack Chinese military forces within China.

Second, because the PRC is a nuclear state, deterrence requires a robust U.S. nuclear arsenal; Washington must extend deterrence to its allies and friends in the Indo-Pacific. Additionally, U.S. nuclear weapons must be deployed to deter their use at any level of aggression—tactical, theater, or strategic. Tactical nuclear weapons are necessary on the battlefield to deter the PRC from escalating a conventional clash to a nuclear attack against U.S. tactical forces. Theater nuclear weapons serve the same purpose within the region, deterring a tactical exchange from escalating to an intermediate range, the last step before an exchange of strategic weapons between Beijing and Washington. Unfortunately, since the Obama administration's retirement of the submarine-based TLAM-N, the U.S. has insufficient numbers of deployed low-yield weapons—a modified W76 warhead onboard ballistic missile submarines—and no theater nuclear weapons in the Indo-Pacific. Expected deployment of the Long-Range Standoff (LRSO) weapon with its W80-4 warhead will help address this problem.

But the fact is that after decades of neglect, the U.S. only recently has begun to modernize its strategic nuclear forces. In stark contrast, the PRC has exercised no inhibitions about deploying nuclear weapons and developing new capabilities. In early December 2021, U.S. Defense Secretary Lloyd Austin said during a visit to Seoul: "We have concerns about the military capabilities that the PRC continues to pursue, and the pursuit of those capabilities increases tensions in the region."[8] Specifically, he mentioned the PRC's development of new capabilities: "And we know that China conducted a test of a hypersonic weapon on the 27th of July. It just underscores why we consider the PRC to be our pacing challenge."[9] This careful statement means that the PRC is ahead in some military capability, which is adverse for the U.S. extended deterrent, and it must be addressed by increasing the budgets of the departments of Defense and Energy so that U.S. conventional and nuclear capabilities can meet the deterrent challenge of the 21st century. A few days later, at the annual Reagan National Defense Forum, Secretary Austin stated that Chinese incursions into Taiwanese airspace looked like rehearsals for an attack on Taiwan.[10]

Third, the U.S. is fortunate to have exceptional allies who could augment U.S. extended deterrent capabilities. Former Japanese Prime Minister Shinzo Abe stated that a PRC invasion of Taiwan would be an "emergency" for Japan and that Tokyo and Washington could not "stand by" if China attacked Taiwan.[11] This strongly suggests that the formidable conventional capabilities of Japan will be committed to Taiwan's defense if the U.S. is committed. Similar explicit commitments from South Korea would be welcome. Australia's government has suggested it would do the same, after announcing the AUKUS trilateral security pact with the United States and the United Kingdom in mid-September 2021.

The Australian–UK–U.S. submarine cooperative agreement is a good start. The agreement will allow the countries to share, develop, and base in Australia submarines powered by nuclear propulsion (SSNs).[12] Having allied states work together in the military, economic, diplomatic, and ideological realms will be the key to defeating the CCP. During the U.S.'s agony in its war in Vietnam, the Argentine-born Cuban revolutionary leader Ernesto "Che" Guevara said that he sought to create "two, three, many Vietnams" for the United States. Che's spirit should animate the growing cooperation against China. Building on this, we would like to have two, three, or many AUKUSES in the confrontation with China.

The AUKUS agreement is an important milestone on the path. Cooperation between the countries should broaden and deepen beyond AUKUS and the Quad, to develop further in the military domain, as well as diplomatic and ideological domains. In the military arena, cooperation must include collective defense so that an attack against one member state is considered an attack against all. It must accelerate the process of rearming U.S. allies. The United States may not have 20 years for those nuclear submarines to be commissioned, and Washington's allies need a rapid transfer of military technologies and equipment in the interim.

The military cooperation should include new members in areas. India and Japan are obvious candidates as existing members of the Quad. Taiwan could benefit from expanded cooperation in conventionally powered attack submarines, as well as port visits. Canada would profit as well, and the Canadian contribution to security in the Indo-Pacific should be expanded beyond Canada's focus on the Arctic and sub-Arctic regions to other salient areas, including the East and South China Seas.

Beyond the naval sphere, deepening the necessary path of confrontation should include formalized military cooperation among U.S. allies, involving ballistic and cruise missiles, integrated air defense capabilities, defeating anti-access/area-denial systems, cyber, and basing and logistical support. Further cooperation could develop in the military uses of space, professional military education for officers and non-commissioned officers, and out-of-area deployments.

In the economic domain, it is critical that a regional trade agreement on a reciprocal preferential basis must be negotiated and entered among U.S. allies and partners in the Indo-Pacific, which does not violate our commitments under the WTO. China has weaponized trade to punish countries such as Australia, South Korea, Taiwan, the Philippines, and others for their support of the U.S. by banning imports from them. This regional trading bloc not only can help U.S. allies' economic growth, but also can effectively counter China's trade war with its geopolitical rivals in the area.

Deepening cooperation might also usefully include new diplomatic agreements among the Quad members and other states for cooperation in the domains of law enforcement, including counter-narcotics, riverine and other nautical navigation, civilian space exploration, and manned missions to the moon and Mars. Broadening cooperation also will include the realm of ideology. Shared democratic beliefs serve as the basis of a joint ideological campaign directed against the CCP. In fact, the Quad could serve as a clear instrument of ideological cooperation, which might be expanded to include all compatible states.

However, as we have stressed, ideological campaigns must be coordinated and centered around democracy as a superior form of government to CCP totalitarianism. The liberal international order is better than "the common destiny of mankind" that Beijing seeks to create as justification for its dominance. Respect for human rights is a necessary requirement for states. Forcing Muslims into concentration camps is unacceptable and itself demonstrates that Beijing's human rights record is appalling and the world it seeks to create is not one that is acceptable to the world's population. But they need not be uniformly the same—tailored messages can be made by individual states. Thus, the messages in support of democracy and human rights that Japan advances may not be the same as India's. Moreover, a state such as New Zealand could make a contribution by joining its democratic allies in condemning China's human rights abuses, corruption, and predatory economics more than it would in taking on a military role.

The AUKUS agreement shows that progress in balancing against China can be made in single-issue areas. Such measures are necessary and must continue. They show that Australia, the UK, and the U.S. have made a commitment to the security of the Indo-Pacific. Simultaneously, bigger steps are required to combat

China in a unified manner, utilizing military, economic, diplomatic, and ideological aspects.

The Biden administration will manage these efforts because the U.S. is the leader of the free world. Thus, it must build upon the momentum created by the AUKUS agreement and sustain that commitment. AUKUS is tangible progress, but it is a long road. This must be replicated and sustained in all the avenues of confrontation with China. Global democratic cooperation will illuminate the path of freedom for the world, rather than Beijing's intended path, which seeks to fetter the world.

Cooperation with Australia should acknowledge the actions of key leaders, like former Australian prime ministers Scott Morrison and Tony Abbott, who deserve credit for calling attention to the threat from the Chinese regime, for supporting AUKUS, the Quad, and Taiwan, and for working to reduce Australia's economic dependence on China.[13] While these positive steps have been taken, it is not premature to consider additional measures that Australia and the U.S. need to take to combat the Chinese regime.

First, Washington must take a page from its success in the Cold War. During that 50-year struggle, the U.S. persuaded its NATO allies that it was as concerned about British, French, or West German security as the UK, France, or West Germany were about their own. However, the United States has done little in the Indo-Pacific that is as persuasive as what it did in Europe. The U.S. must do more to defeat the tremendous growth of the China threat.

Two major points are salient. First, China can strike Australia with conventional or nuclear weapons. Understandably, this threat occupies the mind of the Australian national security community, but the threat is not new. During the Cold War, the Soviets targeted Australian–U.S. facilities at the Joint Defense Facility Pine Gap (near Alice Springs, Northern Territory), the Defense Support Program satellite downlink facility at Nurrungar, South Australia (which was closed in 1999), and the North West Cape Naval Communication (NWCNC, formally known as the Naval Communication Station Harold E. Holt) Station near Perth. This caused considerable domestic political difficulty for the friends of the U.S. during those years. Similar costs and risks must be expected as security competition with China intensifies. It is up to the U.S. to ensure that its extended deterrent remains credible.

Second, from the Australian perspective, the U.S.–Australian alliance is rather loose and reflects considerable unease with the ANZUS Treaty—precisely how far Australia will go to support the U.S. before being drawn into a conflict with China. This concern has been reflected by senior Australian politicians. Indeed, in the post-Cold War period, the U.S. and Australia have a closer relationship outside of the Indo-Pacific space than within it. This, too, must change.

To tighten the alliance, it must be increasingly institutionalized. Five measures should be taken. First, the two states should use the U.S. relationship with Japan as a model to create a Joint Strategic Concept for ANZUS and beyond. This would have to address key issues such as defining the relationship between

Australian and U.S. long-range strike forces for defense of Australia. Another model is the Radford–Collins Agreement of March 1951, in which the Royal Australian Navy under Vice Admiral John Collins and U.S. Pacific Fleet Admiral Arthur Radford defined what the Australian Navy would do to support the U.S. Navy in war with the Soviet Union. Radford–Collins was a straightforward agreement of seven pages that established a working relationship between the navies and was in place before ANZUS was signed on September 1, 1951. Similar agreements between and among the U.S. and Australian services should be in place today, including ensuring that Australia would serve as a logistical and support facility for the U.S. and other allies, as it did in World War II.

Second, the equivalent of NATO's North Atlantic Cooperation Council (NACC) should be established to cement the alliance and forge its Joint Strategic Concept (or Defense Planning Guidelines, as with Japan) to address directly the hard issues, such as: when there is a crisis, this is how it will be addressed; what the command and control would be, and which bases would be opened to the U.S.; and Australia would protect sea lanes to specific latitudes and longitudes. This would be an important step toward a tighter alliance relationship, along the lines of the NATO model that would include the Quad states, among others.

Third, the U.S. needs to make permanent its deployments, exercises, and use of Australia's ranges to solidify the relationship. The U.S. Marine military presence in Darwin, Northern Territory (Robertson Barracks) is welcome, but additional U.S. forces should be deployed, including on the Cocos Islands in the Indian Ocean. These bases will provide logistical and training support for U.S. and other allied forces in the region. In the spirit of AUKUS, more frequent port calls by U.S. Navy surface and submarine assets will be a component of this expansion, which will be supported by most of Australia's political parties.

The U.S. footprint in Australia must include permanent use of the three main training locations for U.S. forces: the Bradshaw Field Training Area, the Mount Bundey Training Area, and the Delamere Air Weapons Range, about 137 miles southwest of Katherine, Northern Territory. These bases comprise the Australian Defence Force's North Australian Range Complex, which is networked to the United States Indo-Pacific Command in Hawaii. It should be expected that long-range UAVs, other surveillance, and long-range strike capabilities would be stationed in Australia at these or other facilities.

Fourth, the expansion of U.S. and Australian military cooperation must include Australian naval assets attached to the U.S. Navy for joint patrol missions, Freedom of Navigation Operations (FONOPs) in the South China Sea, and joint FONOPs with Japan and India in the East China Sea. Naval cooperation among the U.S., Australia, Japan, and India should become a common feature of global politics and should apply within the Indian Ocean and to Antarctica as well.

Fifth, there should be significant Australian military deployments in the region. These should entail forward-based Australian air and ground forces in Guam and Taiwan, and port visits by the Royal Australian Navy. There has been a significant reluctance in Australia to be tied to the defense of Japanese territory such as the Senkaku Islands in the East China Sea, given a common Australian conception that its security is not directly tied to Japanese security. However, the scope of the threat from the Chinese regime is so great that all of the allies must work together, indivisibly, to defend their interests from a threat that welcomes the chance to play them against each other. Strengthening the alliance relationship with Australia requires focused U.S. leadership to build upon the proud history, prodigious talent, and existing cooperation. Ultimately, capitalizing upon successes will depend upon the Biden administration's decision to do so.

Additionally, the reported doubling of U.S. forces on Taiwan is good news, but its deterrent effect is hobbled by the number released in 2021 by Taiwanese President Tsai Ing-wen—a far-too-modest increase from 21 to 39.[14] These small numbers are orders of magnitude too low. As it did in the Cold War, the U.S. should have thousands of personnel in Taiwan for a credible extended deterrent.

Taiwan's value is strategic and so must be covered under the U.S. extended deterrent because Taiwan is a strategic pivot in the Cold War between the PRC and the United States.[15] Its key role in this struggle stems from three major factors: military, economic, and political. Its military role is informed by its location opposite the PRC and by its sound conventional forces. Its economic role stems from its robust economy and as one of the world's centers of computer chip manufacturing. Taipei's political role is a democratic alternative to the disastrous misrule of the CCP.

These are critical roles, but as security competition between the PRC and U.S. intensifies, there is much more Taipei and Washington must accomplish in the fight against the CCP. The U.S. must allow Taiwan to become a strategic partner the equal of Australia and Japan. To that end, the U.S. must provide Taiwan with the protection necessary to preserve its status as, *de facto*, an independent state and linchpin in the confrontation with the CCP.

This is difficult because the prodigious growth of the PRC's conventional, cyber, space, and nuclear capabilities place Taipei at far greater risk today of an effective attack. Decades of a U.S. policy of "calculated ambiguity"—would Washington come to Taipei's aid in the event of an attack or not—have not strengthened Taiwan's deterrent. Neither has the Biden administration's disastrous withdrawal from Afghanistan, which weakened U.S. credibility, and the administration's warmer approach to the PRC than the Trump administration's.

Strategically, the U.S. needs to preserve Taiwan's independence for four reasons. First, as a barrier to the PRC's navy. Over 100 years ago, British Admiral Jackie Fisher stated that there were five strategic keys that locked up the world and had to be held by the British for naval dominance: the Straits of Dover and Malacca, Gibraltar, Alexandria, and the Cape of Good Hope. To modify Fisher, Taiwan keeps the keys between the East and South China Seas and holds the PLA Navy within the first island chain.

Second, Taiwan's location makes it an important base. However, Taiwan's military deterrent must be augmented by weaponry in sufficient numbers to allow Taiwan to project power against the PRC and to have an arsenal deep enough to fight a sustained conflict. Taiwan, the U.S., and other allies should develop the mechanisms to allow the U.S. and allied military presence in the Republic of China to grow—this might be occasional port visits by U.S. naval vessels leading to a regular presence of U.S. navy ships in Taiwanese ports. Similar steps should be taken for the air force and army. Taiwan had a nascent nuclear weapons program that it terminated in the 1970s under U.S. pressure. To strengthen the Taiwanese deterrent, it is time to revisit the issue of Taiwanese proliferation. A Taiwan that had the ability to inflict unacceptable damage on the PRC even in the face of an attack would go far more toward introducing doubt into the minds of CCP leaders than any other measure. This is the case whether or not Taiwan is explicitly aligned with the U.S.

Third, Taiwan is a key ally to aid with regional problems associated with the PRC's expansionism in the South China Sea, but is, along with Australia, India, and Japan, an important partner for the Indo-Pacific. The United States must acknowledge that Taiwan is a key ally in the fight against the CCP. Taiwan should be weaved into the fabric of the Quad's security cooperation. News that Taiwan has been invited to RIMPAC is positive, as would be exercises with the Japan Maritime Self-Defense Force and in the Malabar exercises hosted by India. Taiwan should become a permanent participant in those exercises and should host similar exercises in its waters.

Fourth, it is in the political realm that Taiwan's role is greatest. Each day, a democratic Taiwan demonstrates what Mainland China could be and what it might be except for the CCP's misrule. Day after day, Taipei shows that China could have a free press, robust civil society, religious liberty, and respect for human rights. The contrast between the two Chinas is stark, even if it has served as a comfortable status quo for decades. Writing about a divided Germany in 1950, the French novelist and poet François Mauriac said: "I love Germany so much I am glad that there are two."[16] For Mauriac, the division of Germany and loss to the Soviet Union and Poland of its eastern territory in the aftermath of World War II advanced French security. After Nixon's trip to the PRC in 1972, a divided China has served Western interests as well, because of the Soviet threat. After the fall of the Soviet Union, the U.S. should have recalculated its strategic interests toward Taiwan.

However, that time is over and the PRC is determined to crush Taiwan's independence. The example of Hong Kong demonstrates that the CCP does not keep its agreements; it would rather have control than the wealth that Hong Kong's alternative economic system produces. This provides ample empirical evidence that the mainland will not allow Taiwan's alternative and superior political system to continue. Xi Jinping has stated that the issue of China's unification will be solved on his watch. Indeed, let it be. With the indomitable support of its allies, Taiwan will meet its security requirements and prosper. The political future of the Chinese people should be decided in Taiwan, not the PRC.

Each of these essential steps for deterrence must be taken because they are reinforcing. The U.S. needs to return to the serious deterrent force posture, training, and culture it possessed during the Cold War to deter Soviet aggression. The Biden administration lacks urgency in advancing any of these measures. Such insouciance, indecision, and lack of a response convey U.S. weakness and lack of credibility. In turn, doubts arise among U.S. allies about whether the U.S. will honor its deterrent commitments. This invites the PRC to continue its path of expansion, confident that the U.S. lacks the capabilities and willpower to arrest it.

5.1.7 Stop China's Bid to Seize the High-Tech Commanding Heights

Whether the U.S. and the free world can win this round of great power competition with China largely depends on whether the West can successfully defend its high-tech commanding heights from China's relentless attacks to control them. Xi has ordered his country's science and technology personnel to carry out this grand strategy—turn China from the world factory into the world center for innovation, once and for all, to solve the vital technologies needed for the rejuvenation of the Chinese nation.

The Chinese often refer to this fight as the new "Battle of Triangle Hill," referring to a forgotten 42-day battle between UN Forces and the PLA to capture a forested ridge called Triangle Hill, in which China claimed victory in defeating its arch enemy. As we mentioned in Chapter 3, Xi requires that China focus on technological innovation as a core component in all of the country's modernization and make technological self-sufficiency a strategic pillar of national development. In other words, China's technological supremacy becomes part of the CCP's second centenary goal—becoming the world's dominant state.

The U.S. and the free world have neglected this competition for technology supremacy for so long that China is catching up fast, largely because there is no China "Sputnik shock wave" sent to the U.S. Washington cannot be cavalier about this threat. The U.S. and other democracies must come up with strategies to counter China's move. The U.S. must reformulate its innovation strategy and reprioritize government research and development spending and programs to focus on the frontier of science and technology—particularly the areas where China has surpassed or is closing in on the U.S., such as artificial intelligence and space exploration. Congress must drastically increase government R&D spending to ensure America's technological leadership. The innovation model of the Defense Advanced Research Projects Agency (DARPA) must continue to improve and be adopted by other agencies for disruptive technologies. Congress and government agencies should formulate new laws and policies to encourage innovation and better protect intellectual property. Increasing prizes for helping the government to solve critical technological problems would help.

The U.S. government must enhance its export control mechanism to ensure key technologies will not fall into China's hands. It should also re-establish the Coordinating Committee for Multilateral Export Controls (CoCom), or establish a new mechanism similar to CoCom, to coordinate with other Western countries to put a technological embargo on totalitarian countries or strengthen the Wassenaar Arrangement by adding China to export control under the arrangement. Meanwhile, the West must intensify the efforts to block Chinese companies such as Huawei, Tencent, ZTE, and others from involvement in 5G and other key infrastructure, in both hardware and software areas.

A key component of China's strategy is to gather the best and brightest in science and technology to take over the commanding heights. This is achieved by taking advantage of the West's openness and academic freedom to lure away Western-trained scientists and researchers. China did this in the 1950s. The talents it got from the West played a key role in building nuclear weapons, missiles for military purposes and for space exploration, and satellites. China will buy talent, labs, and companies from the U.S. to quickly obtain technologies, including chips, mask aligners, and OS systems, which could drain talent from the West. China also plans to set up global science foundations to provide funding for international talent to take on its R&D projects. The U.S. must increase efforts to detect and prosecute those who secretly work for China and help China to steal or recruit American talents. At the same time, the U.S. government must find better ways to develop and retain top talent, by knowing who they are, what they are doing, and whether they have any funding or other problems.

5.1.8 A Free and Open Internet

In our view, the internet is the most critical vulnerability, or Achilles heel, of the CCP, which the U.S. and other democracies must exploit to ensure the free world's victory in the present struggle. Xi repeatedly has warned the Party that failure to control the internet or cyberspace domain will spell disaster for the Party's perpetual rule over China. The CCP recently wrote this warning into its third historical resolution. It is understood that because China relies largely on deception, lies, and indoctrination to rule its peoples, the absolute control of information is key to the regime's survival.

As China's strength increases, Xi's digital dictatorial ambition expands. He has intensified China's global public opinion and psychological warfare campaigns against democracies. The CCP is concentrating its forces in both of these forms of warfare to what the Party terms "Gong Xin," meaning literally "to storm the hearts." The CCP believes that whoever rules information, rules people's minds and hearts. Whoever rules people's minds and hearts dominates global opinion and narratives. In this war, psychological supremacy is key. Therefore, to gain dominance, the CCP deploys a large internet army to patrol and propagandize within cyberspace. It also employs the ever-increasing heights of the GFW to protect the regime, and advanced AI to facilitate its defenses and permit its offensive campaigns to be more effective. The present cognitive war against Taiwan is a good example, and the world should not underestimate these weapons.

On the other hand, there are over one billion internet users in China, and truth and knowledge can empower the population and revive civil society organizations, if they can safely defend their rights and expose the CCP's atrocities and corruption through a free and open internet. We believe that tearing down the GFW is perhaps the best way to advance human rights, civil society, and democracy in China. In doing so, we could change our reactive and defensive response to China's ideological aggression into a proactive, offensive one. We should bring information warfare into the enemy's territory and allow the Chinese people to fight their own fight and hold the CCP accountable. Effectively, the GFW has sealed the country and fostered ignorance among its citizens. Therefore, penetration of the GFW should be a key U.S. response to defeat China in the ideological struggle. Were the wall defeated, Chinese netizens, intellectuals, dissidents, and activists could gather in a virtual public square to express their views and compare and debate ideologies. They know how evil the CCP is because they have witnessed horrific crimes committed against the Chinese people. They are America's strongest allies and advocates in the ideological war. But this volunteer army can be raised only when the GFW is smashed.

However, the challenge is that the Party-state has been using the country's huge resources to build a stronger, more sophisticated GFW, which results in few netizens being able to have full access to the internet. Even though many circumvention tools have been developed by nongovernmental organizations in the free world and in China, it seems they are largely ineffective. According to a team of university researchers, China's GFW currently blocks 311,000 domains, with 41,000 domains blocked by accident.[17] China's vast censorship apparatus also uses a new technique for rooting out banned contents, phrases, and words. At the same time, its potent propaganda machine uses fake news and spreads lies to incite ultra-nationalism and hatred toward the U.S.

Our research shows that most netizens jump the GFW by using a virtual private network (VPN). But in 2017, the CCP's Ministry of Industry and Information Technology started a large-scale crackdown on VPNs and forced Apple to remove 674 VPN apps from its app store in China. Through big data, machine learning and AI, the GFW can detect and block VPN services, and authorities began to target VPN developers and providers. The CCP has drafted detailed rules to ban developing, providing, and using circumvention tools to access censored overseas websites, which indicates that China wants to patch any holes in the GFW and achieve absolute control of the internet.

Another challenge is that democratic countries cannot overtly or covertly attack the GFW, which China would consider an act of war. Additionally, the game between the GFW and counter-GFW is a cat-and-mouse one. No single tool or solution is completely effective. Everything is relative. Therefore, it must be a multidimensional approach to circumvent the GFW.

One of the recommendations we advocate is to strengthen the liberal world order to counter totalitarianism and digital dictatorship by closing the global digital divide. This can be accomplished by providing a free and open internet for the world, through spaced-based direct, free internet access. During the Cold War, the Soviet Union launched the first communications satellite—Sputnik— which resulted in a fierce space race. Behind the race, there was potential information warfare in the hope of using satellites at some point to broadcast signals directly to foreign countries. In the end, the U.S. spent more than $30 billion to stay ahead of the Soviets. In the following three decades, two camps fought in the United Nations about how to regulate or not regulate satellite direct TV broadcasts. Although some international agreements were concluded, no consensus was reached. In the cold war 2.0, control of the internet gives us an odd sense of déjà vu. Unfortunately, this time there is no "Sputnik shock wave" and most Americans still do not realize the grave danger of China's digital dictatorship.

However, unlike the international direct broadcast satellite controversy, a free and open spaced-based internet is just a platform, a tool to bypass big or small firewalls. The peoples of receiving countries decide what content they would surf and read. More importantly, this approach would level the playing field for disadvantaged peoples in the Indo-Pacific and other regions by empowering them through democratization of education, knowledge, information, healthcare, and commerce. The liberal world order's great advantage over China's repressive system lies in the free flow of information—free speech, free press, free-market ideas. A free and open internet can augment these advantages, which, in turn, will strengthen the liberal world order and undermine the CCP. New-generation technology such as spaced-based direct internet access is commercially available. For example, Elon Musk's Starlink, which consists of 42,000 satellites, Amazon's Project Kuiper, Branson's OneWeb, Google's Project Loon, and others all work to deliver internet service. The U.S. government should form partnerships with private companies to find a solution for closing the global digital divide. Certainly this technology can be improved and made less expensive, but the U.S. (and its allies) will get there if it has a clear goal and the determination to do so.

We believe that the inherent contradictions of Xi's ideology and the regime's rule by terror and deception ensure that China's political system is vulnerable and unsustainable. To defeat its new world order of socialism with Chinese characteristics, we must strengthen our liberal world order globally. The free flow of information—the key advantage of the liberal order—is both sword and shield for the West, and must be employed to defend the free world and defeat the CCP.

Democracies must take concerted actions to address the CCP's ideological threat and the illegitimacy of the regime. The West has passed the point of managing China's rise. Regime change to remove the threat should be the way to move forward, but it risks conflict escalation, or requires other drastic measures such as deep decoupling, which the West is not ready to do. Therefore, the best strategic option at this moment lies in asymmetrically strengthening the existing liberal world order to counter China's new order and undermine the regime. Were the West to create the positive externality of a free global internet, the world would benefit not only from the elimination of the CCP threat but through the improvement of the education and health of the world's population.

To aid this, we suggest four measures. First, the U.S. government should use its leverage to force China to destroy the GFW. For example, it must confront Xi's claim that the internet must be cyber sovereign. Washington must confront this oppressive idea by supporting the value of a free, open internet. Additionally, the U.S. should use its muscle in trade negotiations to open up the Chinese internet market and advance online freedom, and at the same time require U.S. tech companies to stop aiding China's development of its digital dictatorship.

Second, the U.S. government should have DARPA and the National Security Agency partner with the private sector to develop technologies to defeat the GFW.[18] This might include creating a free web, based on blockchain technology, so that it cannot be censored; developing the next generation of VPNs; building globally accessible internet access from space; and developing other tools of cyber circumvention.

Third, the U.S. government should set up an office within the National Security Council to lead the effort to counter China's digital dictatorship. It should formulate strategy and policy, and oversee its implementation, while coordinating with inter-agencies' messaging and actions to defeat China's GFW. At the same time, it should work with other democracies to take concerted actions in this regard.

Fourth, extant federal agencies, such as the U.S. Agency for Global Media (USAGM), must be reformed to generate innovative content advocating America's ideology, and contract third parties to produce honest assessments of the Chinese regime's deleterious actions against its own people.[19] The USAGM might illuminate the dangerous audacity of Xi's ambition, including the use of the BRI to mask China's desire for control and determined intent to undermine the liberal international order.[20]

China has spent tens of billions of dollars on building the GFW and digital dictatorship, and the U.S. and other democracies must be ready to allocate sufficient funds to carry out this fight. If the free world is determined to win this competition, it will find the resources to do so. In the December 2021 Global Summit for Democracy, the U.S. government proposed to target the assets of corrupt officials from China. The CCP's corrupt officials and their families hide trillions of dollars in the West. All these assets should be forfeited and used for tearing down the GFW and aiding other human rights projects; the money should not return to China to strengthen the totalitarian regime.

The United States is engaged in an ideological war with China. This is a war the United States must win, given the strength and attractiveness of its ideology. But victory is possible only if the U.S. chooses to fight war with the determination and the focus it possessed in its previous great power conflicts—World Wars I and II and the Cold War.

Notes

1 See our argument in Bradley A. Thayer and Lianchao Han, "America Should View China as a Hostile Revolutionary Great Power," *The Spectator USA*, August 9, 2019. Available at: <https://spectator.us/america-china-hostile-revolutionary-power/>. Accessed January 14, 2021.

2 2019 Defense White Paper, *China's National Defense in the New Era.* Available at: <http://www.andrewerickson.com/2019/07/full-text-of-defense-white-paper-chinas-national-defense-in-the-new-era-english-chinese-versions>. Accessed January 14, 2021.

3 For the Bolshevik propaganda see Jeffrey Brooks, *Thank You, Comrade Stalin! Soviet Public Culture from the Revolution to the Cold War* (Princeton, NJ: Princeton University Press, 1999); Sean McMeekin, *The Russian Revolution: A New History* (New York: Basic Books, 2017); and Robert Service, *Comrades! A History of World Communism* (Cambridge, MA: Harvard University Press, 2007).

4 We first advanced this argument in Bradley A. Thayer and Lianchao Han, "China's Global Propaganda Is a U.S. National Security Threat," *The Hill*, July 10, 2019. Available at: <https://thehill.com/opinion/national-security/451850-chinas-global-propaganda-is-a-us-national-security-threat>. Accessed January 14, 2021.

5 Sean Mantesso and Christina Zhou, "China's Multi-Billion Dollar Media Campaign 'A Major Threat for Democracies' Around the World," *ABC News*, February 7, 2019. Available at: <https://www.abc.net.au/news/2019-02-08/chinas-foreign-media-push-a-major-threat-to-democracies/10733068>. Accessed January 14, 2021.

6 United States Census Bureau, *Trade in Goods with China.* Available at: <https://www.census.gov/foreign-trade/balance/c5700.html>. Accessed December 17, 2021.

7 See Bradley A. Thayer, "Right Here, Right Now: Necessary Measures to Deter China," *Epoch Times*, December 8, 2021. Available at: <https://www.theepochtimes.com/right-here-right-now-necessary-measures-to-deter-china_4142261.html?slsuccess=1>. Accessed December 9, 2021.

8 Demetri Sevastopulo and Christian Davies, "China's Test of Hypersonic Weapon Raised Regional Tensions, Says U.S. Defence Chief," *Financial Times,* December 2, 2021. Available at: <https://www.ft.com/content/9156f354-973c-44e5-ac63-efeb-3f802eea>. Accessed December 2, 2021.

9 Sevastopulo and Davies, "China's Test of Hypersonic Weapon Raised Regional Tensions, Says U.S. Defence Chief."

10 Demetri Sevastopulo, "U.S. Defence Chief Warns China on 'Rehearsals' for Attack on Taiwan," *Financial Times,* December 4, 2021. Available at: <https://www.ft.com/content/21711040-5123-4077-a5ec-b76731fcba1e>. Accessed December 4, 2021.

11 Kathrin Hille, Robin Harding, Eri Sugiura, and Demetri Sevastopulo, *Financial Times,* December 1, 2021. Available at: <https://www.ft.com/content/f4140801-a688-4703-825d-236fab4818e1>. Accessed December 1, 2021.

12 We advanced these arguments in Lianchao Han and Bradley A. Thayer, "After AUKUS: The Next Steps Towards a Confrontation with China," *The National Interest*, October 11, 2021. Available at: <https://nationalinterest.org/feature/after-aukus-next-steps-toward-confrontation-china-194988>. Accessed October 11, 2021.

13 Thayer advanced these arguments in Bradley A. Thayer, "Building upon Success: Strengthening the U.S.-Australian Alliance to Counter China Threat," *Epoch Times*, November 11, 2021. Available at: <https://www.theepochtimes.com/building-upon-success-strengthening-the-australian-us-alliance-to-counter-china-threat_4099516.html>.
Accessed November 12, 2021.

14 Erin Hale, "U.S. Nearly Doubled Military Personnel on Taiwan this Year," *VOA News*, December 3, 2021. Available at: https://www.voanews.com/amp/pentagon

-us-nearly-doubled-military-personnel-stationed-in-taiwan-this-year-/6337695 .html>. Accessed December 3, 2021.

15 See Bradley A. Thayer, "Taiwan's Strategic Value for the U.S.," *Epoch Times*, October 1, 2021. Available at: <https://www.theepochtimes.com/taiwans-strategic-value-for -the-us_4027011.html>. Accessed October 1, 2021.

16 *"J'aime tellement l'Allemagne que je suis heureux qu'il y en ait deux."*

17 Nguyen Phong Hoang, Arian Akhavan Niaki, Jakub Dalek, Jeffrey Knockel, Pellaeon Lin, Bill Marczak, Masashi Crete-Nishihata, Phillipa Gill, and Michalis Polychronakis, "How Great is the Great Firewall? Measuring China's DNS Censorship," *arXiv preprint arXiv:2106.02167* (2021).

18 See Defense Advanced Research Projects Agency. Available at: <https://www.darpa .mil/>. Accessed January 28, 2021.

19 United States Agency for Global Media. Available at: <https://www.usa.gov/federal -agencies/u-s-agency-for-global-media>. Accessed January 31, 2021.

20 "China Wants More Countries to Join Its Belt and Road Program," *ABC News*, April 27, 2019. Available at: <https://www.abc.net.au/news/2019-04-28/china-wants -more-countries-to-join-its-belt-and-roads-program/11051956>. Accessed January 29, 2021.

6
CONCLUSIONS

This book has explained why China is a threat to the United States, why the U.S. and China are fighting a cold war that might turn hot, and why the U.S. must win the confrontation. From both the Chinese and American perspectives, we argued that two fundamental factors explain the source of the conflict: the change in the relative balance of power thus far in China's favor and China's ideology—in the past and as now interpreted by Xi Jinping. Using our analogy of a car crash, in this case the car, the CCP's driver, and the road conditions are such that China and the United States will collide.

6.1 The U.S. Can and Must Win the Sino-American Conflict

As an envoi, we present four major conclusions of the study which should inform U.S. policy in the years ahead. The American people and government must recognize that the China threat is real and growing. Communist China will not be a benign superpower. The ascendancy of Chinese power in the 21st century is similar to the rise of the Third Reich and Japanese militarism before World War II. The U.S. faces a cold war initiated by China, one that the United States can and must win.

The war with China, either cold or hot, provides the United States with the ability to explain the ultimate reason for the struggle: freedom is legitimate and superior to repressive rule, but freedom must be defended. We have argued that the U.S. is essentially engaged in an ideological war. It must acknowledge this and develop a strategy for victory. U.S. national security decision-makers must draw upon the ideology of the U.S. This ideology unifies the American people and like-minded people around the world and explains why China should be resisted—ideology once again explains "why we fight." The United States must contrast its dynamic, innovative, free, and open society, one that is welcoming of immigrants and able to correct its flaws, with the increasingly wealthy

DOI: 10.4324/9781003283614-6

but ethnocentric, racist, and closed society of China. An illustrative and poign-
ant example is found in the wake of the 2021 U.S. evacuation of Afghanistan.
Afghan refugees sought to come to the U.S. and the West, which received them
by the hundreds of thousands. They did not flee to China. That stark recognition essentially captures the profound differences between the two societies.
Additionally, U.S. ideology may serve to undermine the legitimacy of the CCP's
rule in the minds of the Chinese population—if an understanding of that ideology can penetrate the CCP's efforts to prevent it.

In this book, we have focused on ideology not only because China has been
using it to win the minds and hearts of the world's peoples, but also because
it provides the U.S. with key advantages in the Sino-American conflict. As a
free and open society, the U.S. is a better ally for states in Africa, Asia, and
Latin America than is China, whose alliances and partnerships are most often
characterized by the abuse of its erstwhile allies' people and resources. In contrast
to China, U.S. decision-making is transparent to allies. It is a dynamic, inclusive
society and has a history of protecting the interests of its allies and treating them
as equal partners. Its free and open political principles make the U.S. a more
valuable and dependable ally than China.

While the interests of its allies are varied, U.S. ideology serves as the cement for
alignment against China, particularly for states in Africa, Asia, and even Europe,
where economic interest might cause an alliance with China, or neutrality in
the face of an intensifying Sino-American conflict. The U.S. cannot fight this
struggle alone—and the good news is that it need not. The ideology of the
United States allows it to maintain relations with Asia-Pacific and European
states based on common interests and political principles. But the struggle does
require U.S. leadership. Additionally, the U.S. must use its potential, resources,
and ingenuity to defeat China. However, to accomplish this, there must be a
whole-of-society response.

In contrast to the vision of victory advanced by the U.S., the CCP's conception
of victory is deeply disturbing, disagreeable, and dangerous for stability: China
ruling the world, the CCP ruling China, and Xi Jinping ruling the CCP, with
all other states in a subordinate position. "Why China fights" is for the Party's
position and benefit, which is the rule of China and possibly much of the world
by the Xi clique. "Why the U.S. fights" is to preserve a future free and open,
and to prevent the hegemony of a great power governed by a nation-based
supremacist ideology. The Sino-American conflict will determine whether the
security and position of the U.S. is maintained, and freedom and open societies
remain the dominant ideal in international politics—or whether the U.S. will
lose, and freedom is supplanted by totalitarianism.

6.2 The Critical Role of Ideology

The U.S. and its allies must recognize that Communist China has always placed
ideology at the forefront in all of its work during wartime or peacetime. It has

an industrial-scale ideological workforce numbering in the millions and an enormous global network to research, design, and implement it. China's ideology is highly deceptive because it deliberately covers up its communist revolutionary components by amalgamating it with Chinese traditional political and cultural elements and other measures to desensitize the targeted audience. It has gained a huge following in the developing countries, and even accords with young Americans' increasing interest in socialism. It continues to morph into a benign and benevolent ideology of the post-revolution era, which is peaceful, fair, and good for the world. China's soft power capabilities should not be underestimated.

As U.S. power declines relative to China's, Washington is likely to depend more on ideology than economic and military power. Consequently, the United States will have to depend more on its allies and other cooperative states in Europe, Asia, and Africa. This situation plays to the United States' ideological strength and is a great advantage for Washington. China seeks resources globally, offering infrastructure development and foreign direct investment to the many states willing to partner, if not yet align, with it. Thus far, the United States has chosen not to match China's ability in these categories, but it does—hands down—far exceed China's ability to inspire the people of the world.

The United States, as a free and open society, provides a better alliance partnership with states around the world than does China. China's presence, particularly in Africa, is all too often defined by the exploitation of the local populations and the environment. As Guy Scott, former agricultural minister, member of the Zambian parliament, and former head of the Patriotic Front party, said to *The Guardian* in 2007: "People are saying, 'We've had bad people before. The whites were bad, the Indians were worse, but the Chinese are the worst of all.'"[1] The U.S. provides the rest of the world with a better alliance relationship and future through the preservation of the liberal international order than China's repressive vision.

U.S. ideology is a coherent, unifying force for alignment against China, particularly for states in Africa and Asia, where the liberal U.S. serves as a far better ally and partner than the CCP. In Europe, U.S. ideology allows it to maintain relations with states based on common interests and political principles. As the West stood together against the Soviets, so, too, a common ideology allows it to stand united against the challenge from China.

However, if the United States continues to neglect the ideological component in its statecraft it will be increasingly hard-pressed to maintain its position as the dominant state in international politics. Should the United States lose its dominant position, China will fill the vacuum. China's rise means that it is supremely important to understand what Xi and his clique believe and how they conceive of the world and the CCP's and China's place in it. The key strategic question is: "How does Xi see the world?" The answer is deeply unsettling and unpalatable—and dangerous for stability. China sees the world with China as its core and all others in a subordinate position. According to the CCP, it is impossible to stop both the U.S.'s rapid relative decline and China's rapid and inexorable rise. Again according to the CCP's narrative, the rule of China and the CCP's ideology are superior to democratic governance and American values. Therefore, China's victory of dominating the world will be historically inevitable.

Given the odious nature of the CCP, we have argued that the U.S. must define and execute a strategy that defeats the CCP. The U.S. must win this struggle; it must defeat China. This is the mission of the United States for the remainder of the 21st century. It has many arrows in its quiver to defeat the CCP, but its ideology is essential and its greatest weapon.

6.3 Possess the Confidence That the U.S. Can Win

The U.S. leadership and population must have confidence that the United States can win these anticipated peer competitive struggles. The great Ohio State football coach Woody Hayes argued that when you throw the ball only three things can happen, and two of them are bad. U.S. choices with respect to China are multifaceted but ultimately are: cooperation, containment, or China's defeat—and the first two are bad.[2] Cooperation with China was folly and has been since the 1990s. The Covid-19 virus was less a *deus ex machina* for the world's relationship with China than the latest negative epiphenomenon of the CCP. Containment possesses many advantages but is too passive because it cedes strategic initiative to China. Victory over China is the best choice for the U.S. and should be the goal. At the root, victory is the preservation of the U.S.'s global position, which requires defeating the grand strategic objectives of CCP.

To achieve victory, U.S. senior national security decision-makers must be convinced that the United States can win—that is, maintain its position as the dominant state in international politics with no hostile peer competitor challenging its position. This might appear self-evident but is not. When we examine the history of America's grand strategy, there have been many times when the United States seemed weak or in decline and unable to cope with the British threat in the 18th and 19th centuries, the Soviet threat, or the rise of Japan in the 20th century, or China today. Equally, at these times, there were senior U.S. officials and experts in accord with this declinist sentiment. U.S. leaders and other policymakers may not have such confidence because of their overestimation of the opponent's strength or an exaggeration of the U.S.'s own weakness. U.S. national security decision-makers must have confidence that they will be victorious in a long-term competition with a peer rival.

During World War II, President Franklin Roosevelt and the Joint Chiefs of Staff were confident that the United States would win the long war against the Germans, Japanese, and Italians, for sound reasons. The foundation of the Allied victory was the relative balance of power in its favor, in part because of superiority in manufacturing the material—and through training, the men—necessary for victory. What this meant was profoundly complicated in the course of the war, but it often meant that "good enough" military equipment, such as the M4 Sherman tank, was produced, distributed, and deployed utilizing a doctrine that was not perfect but adequate.

Naturally, confidence cannot be misplaced, and, indeed, will not be if it is anchored on a clear understanding of strengths and advantages in the possession of the United States, and knowledge of U.S. weaknesses. On the other side of the coin, U.S. decision-makers must have an awareness of the rival's strengths and weaknesses and a strategy to move competition—ideally—to an arena of U.S. strength versus its opponent's weakness.

The great manufacturing strength of the United States heavily favored the Allies against their German, Japanese, and Italian enemies who may have had specific advantages in doctrine, combat effectiveness, or categories of weaponry, but never could match Allied production that was key to victory in that attritional struggle. Roosevelt did have confidence and a valid assessment of Allied and Axis strengths and weaknesses, and these facts heavily inform the explanation of why the United States and its allies fought, sustained the fight, and ultimately won.

The Cold War was similar. Soviet military strength, intelligence collection, and ideological prowess served Moscow well. However, the totalitarian system that Stalin created could never adapt to competition with the advantages of the capitalist West at the dawn of the information age. Additionally, despite Soviet attempts, key U.S. allies such as West Germany and Japan were steadfast and loyal and would not abandon Washington for Moscow's promises of unification or return of occupied territories.

Today, if the U.S. is to maintain its position as the dominant state, its decision-makers must understand that they can defeat the challenge posed by China. This comprehension is not misplaced. The United States has many advantages over China, including its political principles, open society, adaptive and innovative economy, rule of law and low levels of corruption, its universities and financial sector, military might, robust intelligence community, diplomatic acumen, and worldwide network of alliances. China has notable advantages, to be sure, and they need to be checked, equaled, or exceeded. The United States can compete with China as, indeed, it now is. The United States can also win that struggle.

Unfortunately, the U.S. is not yet positioned for victory. There is considerable work to accomplish in every area. Americans have drawn on the capital accumulated during the Cold War and assumed that the American order would last. For a generation, the assumption that the U.S. never again would face a peer competitor was taken as the geostrategic Eleventh Commandment. The most benevolent explanation for this supreme folly was that it was a grave misapprehension of the CCP and our power to influence China's growth and domestic politics.

Fundamentally, U.S. decision-makers must believe that engaging in the competition is the correct path of action and that a U.S. victory is possible. The United States must squarely face a threat from China, including by publicly acknowledging that it is in order to raise awareness of the threat, mobilize resistance to it, and plot the course to victory. Not terming China a foe of the U.S.—or clearly identifying intensifying Sino-American security competition as such because of a fear of worsening it—does not dissuade China from its challenge. Nor does it reassure U.S. allies and others in the Indo-Asia-Pacific that the United States possesses the willpower to resist China and will be a steadfast ally. In the past, U.S. grand strategic victories were anchored on a clear understanding of why Americans were in the conflict and why the U.S. would win it. This is needed today.

In the history of America's grand strategy, there have been many times when the United States seemed weak or in decline and unable to cope with the British threat, the Soviet threat, or the rise of Japan, or China today. Equally, at these times, there were senior United States officials and experts in accord with this declinist sentiment. U.S. senior decision-makers may not have such confidence because of their overestimation of the opponent's strength or an exaggeration of its own weakness. Strategists may correct this so that U.S. national security decision-makers have a clear understanding of U.S. weaknesses and strengths. They must have confidence that they will be victorious in a long-term competition with a peer rival. If the U.S. is to maintain its position as the dominant state, its decision-makers must believe that engaging in the competition is the correct choice for the United States and that they can defeat the challenge posed by the CCP. Thankfully for U.S. security and the preservation of international stability, the U.S. can defeat the CCP.

6.4 Target the CCP's Major Weaknesses

To win, the U.S. not only must have the confidence that it can do so, but also must target the CCP's major weaknesses. In the war against the CCP, the Chinese people are the greatest ally of the U.S.; they will join the U.S. in the fight if Washington can capitalize upon the three weaknesses. First, the CCP is an illegitimate regime.[3] Political legitimacy requires explicit or implicit consent from the population. The CCP's ideology rejects explicit consent from the Chinese people. In actuality, China's ideology is dangerously incoherent, and the neo-Maoism of Xi Jinping is believed only by diehard Party members. Indeed, it is not clear that Xi is even seen as legitimate by many members of the CCP. Thus, implicit consent anchored on the performance of China's economy has been the pillar of the CCP's support to the Chinese people. The tacit agreement was that the Party's control, corruption, and misrule would not be questioned in return for increasing wealth among the population. However, even before China's—and the world's—economy slowed because of the consequences of Covid-19, there was ample reason to question the validity of the bargain.

With declining rates of economic growth, the CCP cannot keep its side of the bargain, and tension will increase. The Chinese people cannot resist the CCP's misrule; the Party has a headlock on Chinese politics. The Chinese people are in a political labyrinth from which escape is impossible. Protest cannot be funneled into a movement for political reform or democracy because the omnipresent modern surveillance state prevents protest movements from being successful, except in rare and local circumstances. There is no hope of a reform movement within the CCP similar to Gorbachev's *glasnost* and *perestroika*. In fact, the Soviet experience is framed by the Party as an example of what it must never do. Equally, there is no possibility of the Party moderating as long as Xi is in control.

The Party has lost legitimacy, and so it rules through its monopoly of power and intense and efficient control of the Chinese people. But power and control cannot be the source of political legitimacy. There are two major implications of this. First, the regime knows it is not legitimate; thus, the desire to ever tighten its grip on Hong Kong, religious freedom, and its Tibetan and Muslim minorities. This suppression will continue and is likely to worsen because the source of these crackdowns is rooted not in other actors, but in the Party itself. The Party is hollow. From its illegitimacy comes insecurity, and so repression flows. But the world should not expect that this repression will cause significant unrest that could lead to political change. This is because of the power of the surveillance state and ruthlessness in suppressing individuals and movements that might blossom into viable political alternatives. The world should lament the suffering of the Chinese people, and lamentation should be followed by action to aid China's population.

The CCP's China should not be treated as a legitimate regime. It is not a normal state operating within the bounds of accepted convention. Undeniably, the CCP is in control of China now and in the foreseeable future. But the United States and the rest of the international community should not allow the CCP to bolster its claims to be the legitimate government of China. The Chinese people must determine their political legitimacy. If given a choice, they likely would prefer the government of the Republic of China or another form of representative democracy.

Because the CCP rejects popular consent, the international community must treat it as beyond the bounds of acceptable international political conduct and outside international society. The world should view the CCP as akin to the apartheid regime in South Africa. Many measures were taken to isolate the South African regime; for example, entertainers boycotted South Africa. With China, a multifaceted approach is required and will include boycotts but also minimizing diplomatic contacts, removing Beijing from international and nongovernment organizations, and decoupling the world's economy from China. This will require significant changes for many states for whom China is the leading investor and provider of infrastructure and development. In response, those opposed to the CCP should ensure that alternative forms of infrastructure and development, through the World Bank or bilateral approaches such as Japan's Asian Development Bank, are preferred. No state should participate in the BRI and those who are, including European states and other U.S. allies, should recognize that they are complicit in aiding an illegitimate polity.

Additionally, this illegitimate regime produces systemic corruption far worse than any of China's dynasties because the CCP monopolizes all power in China.

The Party rejects checks and balances, an independent judicial system, its dual track economic system encourages rampant rent seeking, and so the Party has created a hierarchical system that offers unprecedented privileges to the Party leaders at all levels. All of this runs contrary to the self-proclaimed people's government—that the people are the masters of the country, and all the CCP wants is to serve the people. Trillions of CCP officials' money has been moved to the West. Exposing this hypocrisy will help the U.S. to win the ideological warfare.

It is time for the world to hold the CCP to account. The CCP keeps power through its security apparatus, advanced information systems, and fear. The world may not be able to change the CCP, but it can identify the regime as illegitimate and increase the cost of its rule. It should be united in supporting the liberation of the Chinese people from the CCP and fostering its replacement by a legitimate regime.

The second major weakness is China's enforced digital isolation, which permits the CCP to sustain its grip on power and prevent the protection and strengthening of civil society that could serve as an existential threat to the CCP.[4] In our view, the internet is the most critical vulnerability of the CCP that could ensure America's victory in the present struggle. The CCP's recognition of its weakness is evident. As we have argued, it attaches great importance to the internet as the main arena, battleground, and front line of the ideological struggle. Like all tyrannical regimes, the CCP relies on deception, lies, and misinformation to firmly control the free flow of information. This permits the CCP to conceal and obfuscate its atrocities and gross human rights abuses and thus maintain its grip on power. For years, the internet made it more difficult for the regime to hide the truth.

When Xi came to power, he identified the CCP's ideological loss of control because of the internet as the Party's most critical vulnerability. Therefore, at the outset of his rule, Xi ruthlessly cracked down on the internet by launching a series of aggressive ideological campaigns seeking to suppress any ideas that deviated from the CCP's ideology. Online opinion leaders, vloggers, public intellectuals, human rights lawyers, and other civil society organizations fell victim to these campaigns, and the CCP effectively silenced all dissenting voices in today's China. Xi then pivoted to weaponize the internet, allowing the regime to surveil, detect, and remove security risks and control information to facilitate the indoctrination of people.

Third, the West must close the digital divide and promote the free flow of information. As China's strength increases, Xi's digital dictatorial ambition expands. He has intensified China's global public opinion and psychological warfare campaigns against democracies. As we have argued, the CCP is concentrating its forces in both of these forms of warfare in its "Gong Xin," or "to storm the hearts," strategy. The CCP believes that whoever rules information rules peoples' minds and hearts. Whoever rules people's minds and hearts will dominate global opinion and narratives. In this war, psychological supremacy is the key. Therefore, to gain dominance, the CCP deploys a large internet army to patrol and propagandize within cyberspace. It also employs the ever-increasing heights of the Great Firewall to protect the regime, and advanced artificial intelligence to facilitate its defenses and permit its offensive campaigns to be more effective. The present cognitive war against Taiwan is a good example, and the world should not underestimate these weapons.

However, the inherent contradictions of Xi's ideology and the regime's rule by terror and deception ensure that the political system is vulnerable and unsustainable. To defeat China's new world order of socialism with Chinese characteristics, we must strengthen our liberal world order globally. The free flow of information, the key advantage of the liberal order, is both a sword and shield for the West, and must be employed to defend the free world and defeat the CCP.

We believe the best approach to strengthen the liberal world order, and to counter totalitarianism and digital dictatorship, is precisely to close the global digital divide. This should be accomplished by providing a free and open internet to the world by way of satellite-based direct access. In doing so, we can change our reactive and defensive response to China's ideological aggression into a proactive and offensive one. Such an open internet architecture brings the fight into our strategic rival's territory and allows the Chinese people to fight their own fight and hold the CCP accountable.

More importantly, this approach levels the playing field for those disadvantaged peoples in the Indo-Pacific and other regions by empowering them through democratization of education, knowledge, information, healthcare, and commerce. The liberal world order's great advantage over China's repressive system lies in the free flow of information, free speech, free press, and free market. A free and open internet can augment these advantages, which in turn will strengthen the liberal world order and undermine the CCP. New-generation technology, such as satellite direct internet access, is commercially available and surely can be financed to make it free for all.

Democracies must take concerted actions to address the CCP's ideological threat and the illegitimacy of the regime. The West has passed the point of managing China's imperial rise. Regime change will remove the threat and should be the way to move forward, but it risks conflict escalation, or requires other drastic measures such as deep decoupling, which the West is not ready to do. Therefore, the best strategic option at this moment lies in asymmetrically strengthening the existing liberal world order to counter China's new order and undermine the regime. Were the West to create the positive externality of a free, global internet, the world would benefit not only from the elimination of the CCP threat but through the improvement of the education and health of the world's population.

Finally, in the consideration of the CCP's weaknesses, as the Chinese people are the greatest ally of the U.S. in the fight against the CCP, we recognize that their support in the struggle is more effective the greater the voice they possess. The U.S. and other democracies should work to advance democracy in China. They should not be afraid of advocating democracy transition or regime change in China. The CCP is cognizant of their vulnerability. To shield themselves, Chinese government propagandists use Harvard scholar Graham Allison's proposition of the "Thucydides's Trap"—which is defined as "the natural, inevitable discombobulation that occurs when a rising power threatens to displace a ruling power … the resulting structural stress makes a violent clash the rule, not the exception"—to justify China's aggressive rise, and demand that the U.S. accommodate China, the emerging superpower, if it wants to avoid a war.[5] In this vein, Allison himself also offers several options to appease China.

As we have argued, we believe that China sees itself today not as a regional power but a contender for global hegemony. It sees itself as the creator of a superior political-socioeconomic system, and so is fully justified in setting the rules, laws, and norms for its global order. It is convinced that it can take on and defeat the U.S., the declining superpower, by 2049, and likely far sooner. Although we agree the coming war between the U.S. and China is very likely, it is not inevitable. We argue there may be room for compromise if China moves toward democracy. We appreciate that this is a significant and hitherto unlikely condition.

In his 1795 essay, *Perpetual Peace*, Immanuel Kant first advocated that republican forms of government would not fight one another. Employing Kant's logic, modern international relations scholars call this the democratic peace theory, and argue that democracies will not go to war against other democracies. Therefore, when China becomes a democracy, the U.S. and China can compete peacefully under the liberal international world order to avoid a violent clash. Historically, this is akin to the U.S. surpassing the UK in the late 19th and early 20th centuries.

As we described in the book, the CCP falsely promised democracy to gain support and seize power. Xi continues this rhetoric and claims China's dictatorship as a people's democracy. When China opened up in the late 1970s, there was a genuine effort for democratization in China, but the CCP's paramount leader Deng Xiaoping stopped it to ensure the one-party rule. However, the Chinese civil society is still alive, even though it has gone underground, and many people support democracy. The West must make the Xi clique realize that American ingenuity, power, and determination, when threatened by imminent danger, will deal fatal blows to its enemies, as it did to the Nazi and Japanese militants in World War II. The only chance that the CCP has to avoid conflict with the U.S. and its allies is to transition to democracy. Were it to do so, it would be a legitimate and responsible power. Even if the chance for China's democratic transition is small, democracies must openly and unequivocally promote democracy in China as a critical component of ideological warfare—but more importantly to provide the Chinese people with an understanding of a better political system and superior future than will be provided or can be promised by the CCP. A Sino-American conflict is not the Eleventh Commandment. It is not inexorable. Democracy in China will allow an infinitely safer driver and car, and that very likely will be sufficient to avoid the Sino-American car crash. But until this outcome can be achieved, if it ever can be, the U.S. should expect that the present Sino-American conflict will only broaden and intensify.

Notes

1 Guy Scott is quoted in Chris McGreal, "Thanks China, Now Go Home: Buy-Up of Zambia Revives Old Colonial Fears," *The Guardian*, February 5, 2007. Available at: <http://www.guardian.co.uk/world/2007/feb/05/china.chrismcgreal>. Accessed January 2, 2021.
2 Bradley A. Thayer, "Confidence and Conviction Will Lead to U.S. Victory over China," *The Hill*, May 15, 2020. Available at: <http://www.thehill.com/opinion /international497285-confidence-and-conviction-will-lead-to-us-victory-over -china>. Accessed March 12, 2021.
3 These arguments were also made in Bradley A. Thayer, "The Chinese Regime Is Not Legitimate," *RealClearDefense*, June 4, 2020. Available at: <https://www .realcleardefense.com/articles/2020/06/04/the_chinese_regime_is_not_legitimate _115348.html>. Accessed June 5, 2020.
4 We advanced this argument in Lianchao Han and Bradley A. Thayer, "The Fight against China's Ideology Requires a Free and Open Internet," *The Hill*, December 2, 2021. Available at: <https://thehill.com/opinion/technology/583489-the-fight -against-chinas-ideology-requires-a-free-and-open-internet>. Accessed December 3, 2021.
5 Graham Allison, "The Thucydides Trap," *Foreign Policy*, June 9, 2017. Available at: <https://foreignpolicy.com/2017/06/09/the-thucydides-trap/>. Accessed December 31, 2021.

INDEX

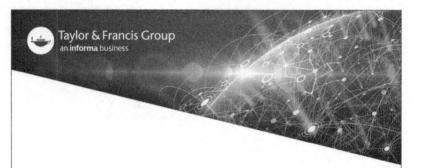

23 CCP = violence
56 "... not afraid of nuclear war"
88 Xi is a threat to the
    human race.
100 New World Order Doctrine
110 Xi - Nuclear war.
&111 unresticted warfare.
124 U.S. politicians on the take $
125 Every Chinese citizen &
    company is a spy. My Lenovo
    laptop too?
127,128 Infiltration of media
130 CCP use of AI in media
132 World domination via tech.dom.

Made in United States
Orlando, FL
13 December 2022

26403346R00122